*"Better is a dinner of herbs
where love is, than a stalled ox and
hatred therewith."*

PROVERBS 15:17

Illustration from a brass in St. Margaret's Church, King's Lynn, near Sandringham. The church dates from 1091. The complete plate, of which this is the center portion, appears under the title "A Peacock Feast" in Richard Warner: *Antiquitates Culinariae,* 1791.

Herbs and Savory Seeds

Culinaries, Simples, Sachets, Decoratives

[formerly titled: *Magic Gardens*]

by
ROSETTA E. CLARKSON

With a new Foreword by GERTRUDE B. FOSTER
Editor, *The Herb Grower Magazine*

DOVER PUBLICATIONS, INC.
NEW YORK

"Time tries the troth in everything,
Herewith let men content their mind,
Of works which best may profit bring,
Most rash to judge, most often blind.
As therefore troth in time shall crave,
So let this book just favor have."

—THOMAS TUSSER (1573)

Published in Canada by General Publishing Company, Ltd., 30 Lesmill Road, Don Mills, Toronto, Ontario.
Published in the United Kingdom by Constable and Company, Ltd., 10 Orange Street, London WC 2.

This Dover edition, first published in 1972, is an unabridged republication of the work originally published by The Macmillan Company in 1939 under the title *Magic Gardens: A Modern Chronicle of Herbs and Savory Seeds*. This edition contains a new Foreword by Gertrude B. Foster.

International Standard Book Number: 0-486-22728-6
Library of Congress Catalog Card Number: 72-77995

Manufactured in the United States of America
Dover Publications, Inc.
180 Varick Street
New York, N.Y. 10014

FOREWORD
TO THE DOVER EDITION

It is not often that people can pick out one book that changed their whole lives for the better but it is true that this book led my husband and me to a way of life in a series of gardens which has never ceased to be satisfying and exciting. Rosetta E. Clarkson was a great teacher for many years before she became an author. Yet through her writing she has influenced more people to discover the history, happiness and practical benefits found in herb gardens than ever could have met in a classroom in one individual's lifetime.

It has been my privilege to learn the personal stories of hundreds of other readers of this, her first book. They, like myself, were caught up in the romance of plants she describes as serving man for centuries as flavorings, medicines and sources of perfumes and pleasure. Through her word pictures of gardens from earliest written records until the present day, many of us have been inspired to take to herbs as a means of adding new flavors to cooking and bringing the scented garden's rewards into the house. Herbs give a sense of permanence to one's garden and housekeeping. They have not changed in thousands of years and are bits of living history available to all.

Much of this book first appeared as *The Herb Journal* which Mrs. Clarkson wrote and published as a monthly booklet, and which her husband mailed to thousands of gardeners without charge. Through the influence of the little leaflets, my husband and I have shared the fun of growing hundreds of herbs, such as those described in Chapter XVII, "A List of Noteworthy Herbs," for over thirty years. We turned our experience into the basis for a quarterly magazine, printed, published and mailed from a garden of herbs by subscription only.

The Herb Grower Magazine began with a nucleus of subscribers who were first of all readers of this book. Mrs. Clarkson wrote the lead article for the first issue of our magazine twenty-five years ago. When she retired from writing and publishing, her work continued through our interest.

As herbs speak to the needs of people today through their fragrance and beauty, we often reflect on how we came upon them as an obligation and opportunity to live in a small New England community where we could have room enough for a series of herb gardens. It may have been just a matter of "magic" that Mrs. Clarkson describes so well in Chapter VIII:

Odors grasp and hold our imagination and memory. Above all others, the fragrances of green growing herbs, not gaudy or showy, but comfortable and homey, have the power to cast a spell over us so that we recall only the pleasant past, with all the sharp hard corners of grief and sadness softened.

Living a life of herbs has had few sad corners for us and for many others who were inspired to share herbs with integrity and humor.

GERTRUDE B. FOSTER

Falls Village, Connecticut
February, 1972

CONTENTS

The magic gardens of man that have
brought him food, industry, science,
health and happiness

PREFACE

This is not merely an "herb book" but is meant to be
rather a foundation book for any gardener and still of
interest to the general reader who likes the thought of a
garden or who loves to dream of the gardens of long ago.

The only ancient plants we have are the herbs. For the
most part all our garden plants have come from them but
herbs are not important just because they are now being
restored to the garden in their old-time unassuming form.
They are of importance because the study of herbs has
given rise to three great sciences—botany, medicine, and
household chemistry. The study of herbs, too, has created
great industries—perfumes, cosmetics, soaps, drugs, con-
diments, fumigation, tobacco.

From undated times herbs of the field have played an
almost unbelievably prominent part, not only in the life
of the individual in his own home, but in the existence of
civilized nations. From herbs man obtained food and
health, first from the plants he found growing wild; then
from the varieties he transplanted to his garden and
domesticated. Today, any fragrant flower or leaf is
almost certainly a descendant of an old-time herb.

Fragrance played a large part in days gone by. An
attempt was early made for sanitation in home and community by the protective measures of strewing, burning
and inhaling aromatic herbs. Pleasing odors had beneficial effects and vile odors would ward off evil. Fragrance

masked the odors of the burning sacrifice and the custom
of incense burning, the belief in the lure of perfume,—
these have not yet disappeared.

All through the centuries there was a gradual change
in the scheme of gardens cultivated to grow these necessary herbs, and finally one group of plants was set apart
for what we now call vegetables, a second group for
medicinal plants, another group for fragrance and the
beauty of blossoms. So then we had besides the herb
garden, the kitchen garden, the physic garden, the flower
garden. The physic garden all but disappeared with the
advent of the drug industry. The home vegetable garden
dwindled as large commercial farms appeared and truck
gardens grew up around our cities. In English speaking
countries the herbs for culinary flavor gave way to imported spices now available in every corner grocery. As
each section of the utilitarian garden gave way to some
industrial development, many plants of historic interest
fell by the wayside. Those with startling, flamboyant
blossoms were placed about to decorate the land. The
sale of flowers began in the cities and men slaved night
and day to make the flowers brighter, larger, more
attractive to the eye, more outstanding. The lowly herbs
with all their friendliness and fragrance were neglected
by the florist but treasured by the people.

Now, with modern transportation, the great urban
population has gone about and discovered in the country
gardens, in old neglected spots, in woods and fields, that
there are really plants like those their grandmothers told
about, the great plants of history, of literature, of commerce. Herbs are here again. Through the centuries their
soul-satisfying fragrance has drifted down to us. From
Egypt of four thousand years ago, the sweet-smelling

herbs for fumigating; from Greece of classic times, the baths redolent with a mingling of perfumes as each part of the body was anointed with the oils of a different kind of herb; from the Monastery gardens of the Middle Ages where skilled monks carefully tended the fragrant simples to cure their brothers and the people. From the formal Tudor gardens where we can catch a faint whiff of the herbal tobacco which the Elizabethan gentleman smoked as he trod on the fragrant path of thymes after a colossal dinner flavored with savory herbs, little dreaming of our great cigarette industry. From the still-rooms of the 18th century where the mistress of the house busily distilled the oils of herbs to be later used in cosmetics, medicines and household preparations; from the lovely Colonial gardens where the culinary herbs gave promise of many a memorable dinner-to-be, and the aromatic plants told of fragrant linen chests and potpourri.

Peppermint, horehound, and tarragon; sesame, caraway, anise; lavender, rosemary, rue; peony, sweet marjoram, and thyme—their flavor and fragrance again carry romance, mystery, legends, and magic, lifting us out of the hurrying present, even for just a little while.

ROSETTA E. CLARKSON

Salt Acres
Milford, Conn.

APPRECIATION

My thanks to E. J. Alexander, Assistant Curator of the New York Botanical Garden, who has so painstakingly gone over the whole manuscript.

ILLUSTRATIONS

CHAPTER I

MAGIC FRAGRANCE

John, almost four score in years, was on his knees in the sunny earth, working the soil gently around a plant of sage. He broke off a fragrant gray sprig and, with a smile crinkling around his kindly old eyes, said, as he offered it to me,

> "He that would live for aye,
> Must eat sage in May.

"That means *she,* too, you know," and standing up slowly but sturdily, gazed affectionately over the garden.

"Is that how you keep so well, John?"

"Sure, 'mum. Never missed a day since I began working for your father. That was—how long—thirty-five years ago."

"It must have been hard work all these years, till your Danny grew up big enough to help do the heavy digging."

"Yes, 'mum. Digging do be hard work, but I keep my

Note. The decorative headpiece is from Estienne and Liebault: *Maison Rustique,* translated by Richard Surflet in 1600; revised by Gervase Markham in 1616. Taken from copy owned by Lord Battersea, now in the possession of the author.

health. These yarbs is what does it. Nothing like smelling 'em and eating 'em to make a man fit."

And there he was, full of years, yet hale and hearty, working at the very source of health—the old "yarb" garden, still perfuming the air with fragrance, as it had when my grandmother was a little girl. Its squarish dimensions are defined by a hedge of lavender, the lower stalkish part hidden by a soft inner hedge of grayish-green bushy santolina, sometimes called lavender cotton. In the center of the garden, a sundial, toward which the stone-flagged paths lead, "counts none but sunny hours," as John counts only the fragrant ones spent among the herbs.

If you have ever walked through an herb garden, treading on sweet-smelling thyme growing out between the stones, brushed against the spicy basils, the stimulating bergamot and mints, the dill and anise with scents so familiar to everyone, how could you have resisted rushing straight home to start such a sweet garden yourself? Down on your knees, working among these fragrant growing things, you feel an exhilaration, an exaltation of your soul, a complete contentment enveloping you—a wholesomeness of mind and body never achieved through other means. This is really living. Miss Howitt has said about *The Poor Man's Garden,*

> Yes, in the poor man's garden grow
> Far more than herbs and flowers—
> Kind thoughts, contentment, peace of mind
> And joy for weary hours.

My thoughts travel backward from John to another gardener, the seventeenth century Yorkshireman, William Lawson, who was still so enthusiastic after forty-eight years of loving devotion to his herbs and flowers that he wrote *The Country House-wife's Garden,* the first book definitely for women horticulturists. I always feel that he was looking forward, beyond the centuries, to years when depressions, bridge clubs, movies, speed mania, night clubs, would be too much with us—and gardens could be a haven for our jangling nerves.

As the old herbalists constantly preached the great curative effects from continually smelling herbs, so also have modern scientists come more and more to believe that health-giving oxygen and even ozone is produced by the sun's rays acting on certain aromatic trees and plants. Instead of tonics, diets, and rest cures, why not try fragrant hours in sunny gardens? In the olden days black magic was warded off by the use of herbs and weird incantations. In these days, who can predict how many evils may be exorcised quite simply by working among our sweet-smelling lavenders and rosemaries?

My tiger cat, taught only by nature, is a great believer in the efficacy of fragrant breathing and nibbling. For long intervals Orphie will sit in his favorite spot surrounded by catnip, thyme, burnet, and rue, swaying and rocking gently back and forth singing to himself—his eyes slowly closing—his nose high, sniffing, sniffing—this side, now that side—the collected fragrances of the garden. Orphie knows the virtues of my herbs. Occasionally he picks his way delicately among the plots nipping off a leaf here and a flower there, then stretches out on his favorite flagstone, the fragrant thyme all about him, and goes to sleep feeling that all's right in his world, at any rate.

Through the centuries fragrant herbs have been generally praised and accepted as health-giving. In ancient days in Italy during a plague people were advised to go to the town that is now San Lorenzo where sweet bay flourished.

Breathing the air into which that fragrant odor was released was believed by doctors to be a preventive against plague contagion.

John Evelyn, almost as famous a diarist as Samuel Pepys, after the Great Plague of 1665 in London had a splendid vision of surrounding the city with hedges of sweet-smelling bushes and herbs for their wholesome qualities.

Two hundred years later Charles Dickens wrote in *Bleak House:* ". . . the smell of sweet herbs . . . made the whole air a great nosegay."

What matter if it be the ancients, the students of sociology, famous authors, a gardener, or one's own tiger cat? We can learn the same lesson of sweet healing from one or all.

Let us have flowers in our gardens, but we shall have herbs, too. Flowers are so transitory; they must call our attention to their loveliness for fear we won't be aware of them before it is too late. So they impress themselves on us by flamboyant colors, penetrating odors. They insist on our noticing them, whether we choose or not. Many gardeners are satisfied with the vast masses of color they can produce for display and for effect—blue borders, white gardens, red plots. We admire an especially large flower or a new variety. It is a wonderful exhibition of man's ability to mold nature to what he desires. Yet, we don't love these marvels. They bring no train of memories, no centuries-old traditions and associations that have floated fragrantly down through the ages. These are things of the spirit.

Our Puritan grandmothers—how many times great by now—homesick for the England they had left, bravely, hopefully planted their gardens in the New World. The first entry in the Plymouth records was of the assignment of meresteads *and* garden plots. Can't you imagine the herb garden near the kitchen window? As our grandmother was making an Indian pudding, or perhaps pumpkin pies, she would pause—a mist in her eyes shutting out the crude room—as the fragrance of basil and marjoram drifted through the open casements. For a moment, three thousand miles of angry ocean were gone and she was standing in her English garden left so many months ago. No insistent heavy odors wrought that miracle, but a delicate fragrance that would forever bring to her the most loving memories. Our grandmother would sigh, smile, and then with a brisk movement carry on with her pudding and pies.

If you will but repeat the very names of these sweet herbs you will sense the poetry of them:

> Balm, basil, borage,
> Chamomile, chervil and chives,
> Catmint, clary, costmary,
> Lavender, dill and fennel,
> Marjoram, rue, rosemary,
> Tarragon, tansy and thyme.

But what about our herb garden, which will be, oh, so fragrant? What shall we grow and how shall we grow it? First of all a hedge or fence, high or low, we *must* have, so that when we open our garden gate all the herb fragrances will be there on tiptoe to greet us. They won't hurl themselves at us but will be waiting, eager. Let us have flagstoned paths with thymes of many varieties growing in the cracks, or maybe walks thickly carpeted with the white flowered creeping thymes. Francis Bacon says, in his *Essays on Gardens:* "Those ⌊herbs⌋ which perfume the air most delightfully, not passed by as the rest, but, being trodden upon and crushed, are three; that is, burnet, wild thyme and watermints. Therefore, you are to set whole alleys of them, to have the pleasure when you walk or tread."

In the beds near the path have those herbs which more readily release their scents as we brush by: by all means the refreshing bergamot, the clove-like basils, the nutmeg-like marjoram and rosemary, the spicily aromatic yarrow and minty lemonish costmary, the lemon-spiced southern-wood, lemon balm, clean-smelling lavender, the spicy sweet-scented geraniums. The mints and so many kinds, too, are lovely to have about a sundial. So confident of our approach are they that the minty odor greets us almost before we touch them.

Other fragrant herbs will also be enjoyed: the dill, fennel and lovage—tall, graceful, delicate plants with umbels of yellow flowers; sweet cicely, the downy-leaved gray-green horehound, the spicy summer and winter savories and sweet woodruff—a compact little plant with the fragrance of new mown hay.

No bought perfumes can give us such particular exhilaration and delight as these odors, especially as we linger among our herbs in the heat of a summer day that wilts even the hardiest of us. Then these herbs stand out in contrast to our more exotic blooms by their cheerful freshness. They vie with each other in seeking to refresh the drooping spirits of us weak mortals.

For the most part, the fragrance of the herbs comes from the tiny glandular hairs spreading over stem and leaves. These can be seen only under a magnifying glass, yet on an entire plant there are innumerable hairs which contain the fragrant oils released only by pressure or by the force of the sun's rays. Since these herbs are not so prodigal of their fragrance we derive a more lasting satisfaction from them than from the heavier, sometimes overpoweringly insistent flower odors.

We must be sure to have chamomile with its trim daisy-like flowers. If we plan to brew soothing teas from it we should have, not the true chamomile—*Anthemis nobilis*—but rather the German chamomile—*Matricaria Chamomilla*—which makes a more soothing tisane. Not only for our own health but for that of our garden must we have chamomile—the true chamomile—sometimes called the "Plants' Physician." Set about the garden it will keep its neighbors healthy, and there is the belief that a dying or drooping plant will recover if chamomile is planted near it. Chamomile is lovely planted in the cracks of a flagstone path or forming a thick, bright green carpet for an entire walk.

Besides the invigoration we derive from the herb odors we find a soothing balm to our eyes by looking upon an herb garden in a blazing summer day. A wonderful focus for sun-tired eyes is this study in cool greens—the dark green of rosemary, hyssop and the savories, the blue-green of rue, the yellow-green of coriander, woodruff and chamomile, the light green of sweet basil, chervil and feverfew, all tempered by the lovely gray-green of santolina, sage, southernwood and horehound. The eyes linger lovingly and gratefully on these cool shades and tints when summer heat engulfs us in waves of exhaustion.

One of the great satisfactions in our herb garden comes late in fall and winter, long after the gay summer flowers have gone. Our herb doctors stay with us all year round. They are the first to spring to renewed life, even before the snow has quite gone—the first bits of green I see in the garden as the winter retreats are the new shoots of hyssop, burnet, horehound, thyme, perennial marjoram, bright green feverfew, the yellow-green fuzzy pads of chamomile and the sturdy mounds of lemon thyme. At the end of autumn some herbs are still green when we have put our more tender plants to bed for the winter, or until the hardier ones have been completely covered with a blanket of snow. At Christmas time what a sweet delight still to linger in the fragrant garden among the thymes, burnet, balm, rosemary, winter savory and southernwood. What lovely winter bouquets we can make. What unusual holiday wreaths we can have by mingling our evergreen herbs with the usual background of ground pine, hemlock, balsam or holly. We may add to these sprigs of thyme, several of the artemisias like Silver King or ghost plant, southernwood, beach wormwood, mugwort. Or we may fancy rosemary, santolina, sage, hyssop or a bit of the lacy rue. How delighted our friends would be to receive such an offering.

So our herb garden may well become a great joy and a lasting one since the source of the pleasure it offers is not artificial. I long ago learned from John and from my tiger cat to prize the sunny fragrant hours among my herbs. But I also carry the thoughts of those hours into the house and through the rainy snowy hours of winter months when I plan and make more plans for new herb friends whose acquaintance I am eager to make.

CHAPTER II

HERBS IN THE FLOWER GARDEN

He who offers violets must in love be held to offer roses. Of all the fragrant herbs I send, none can compare in nobleness with the purple violet.

Thus the sixth century bishop-poet Fortunatus, to the abbess-queen Radegonde who had laid out a garden in the nunnery she had founded at Poitiers. Violets surprisingly enough were always grown in the physic gardens from ancient and medieval times to Colonial and Victorian days. Even now we find them in lists of crude drugs. In the Middle Ages these lovely flowers were bruised and bound on the foreheads of those suffering from insomnia. It always astonishes me, in reading the lists of herbs for the old kitchen gardens, to come upon many names that we find now only in catalogues for the flower gardens. Violets again—grown in abundance to be cooked with fennel and savory for a broth or to be mixed with onions and lettuce for a "sallet."

John Evelyn, the seventeenth century diarist, recommended for "spring fever" a favorite violet dish which might be a shadowy ancestor of the modern candied violets. He says in his *Acetaria* (1699) that tansy, *qualified* with violets, at the entrance of spring fried brownish and eaten with Orange or Lemon Juice and Sugar is one of the most agreeable of all the herbaceous dishes. Perhaps he liked to precede that concoction with a soup of rose-mary—the one herb, above all, that I like to set apart as an herb of sentiment and romance; but it *is* good in biscuits!

In *De Proprietatibus Rerum* (1280) by Bartholo-maeus Anglicus, we find described a particularly beautiful flower which was used as it is today for healing wounds. "The lily is an herb with a white flower. And though the leaves of the flower be white, yet within shineth the like-ness of gold." In the tenth century books on medicine we find Madonna lilies, but listed simply as white lilies. We find peonies in both Greek and Roman physic gardens and later in Anglo-Saxon kitchen gardens: the flowers used for flavoring and the seeds carried as a charm against evil spirits. Many of us grow in our flower borders *Lunaria annua* for winter bouquets with the ubiquitous Chinese Lantern. *Lunaria* has been given the pet names of honesty, poor man's shilling, silver dollar, and many another term because of the parchment disk remaining when the outer coverings of the seed pod have been slipped from each side. The seventeenth century herbalist John Parkinson, calling it "Penny-flower," said the roots were eaten in salads.

So we ask in amazement, "Are flowers herbs?" The usual conception of herbs is the dusty bunches of dry stalks hanging from rafters, picturesque but too unsanitary for practical use, or the grayish powdered herbs found in the containers of certain commercially packaged products. We think of herbs as the culinary basil, savory, marjoram or dill and the old-fashioned medicinal pennyroyal, hore-hound, senna or peppermint.

So often people who have not seen my garden have said to me, "How can you grow so many herbs—so much

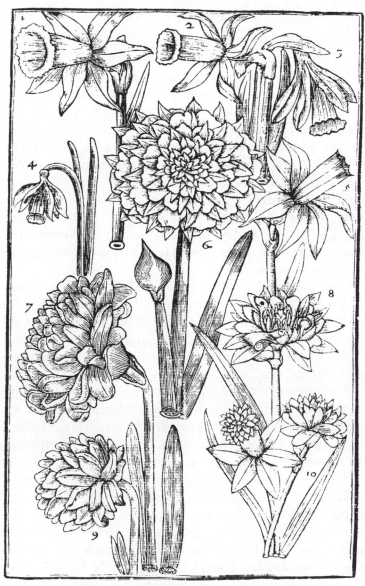

Daffodils—Parkinson's "Outlandish" flowers
from *Paradisi in Sole*, 1629.

green and so little color?" The "uninitiated" are always taken aback when I tell them they really have a good many herbs in their own flower gardens. To convince one particularly stubborn supporter of flowers versus herbs, I went through a recent book on perennials. I myself became much interested in learning how many "Perennials for the Flower Border" are today used to some extent in medical practice. I found some eighty plants in this book listed in a commercial catalogue of drugs now used in medical formulas. You might be interested in a few of these plants—hollyhock, English daisy, bachelor's button, lily of the valley, bleeding heart, sunflower, iris, peony, primrose, violet, feverfew, crocus, squill, geum, pyrethrum, and scabiosa.

In reading old gardening books and herbals I discovered again and again in lists for the physic garden the lovely colorful flowers—marshmallow, hollyhock, valerian, peony, and honeysuckle. In Richard Surflet's *Countrie Farme* (1600) we find among the list of pot herbs, marigold, borage, bugloss (*Anchusa*), and poppies.

But if we have asked, "Are flowers herbs?" after studying these old books, we may well ask, "Are herbs flowers?" Leonard Meager in his *New Art of Gardening* (1697) suggests for a flower garden Madonna lilies, hollyhocks, elecampane, lovage, chicory, clary, wallflower, gilliflower (probably our clove pink), heart's ease (pansies), sweet rocket, thyme, lavender, rue, tansy, angelica, bugloss, and marigold. William Lawson in his *Country House-wife's Garden* (1617) divides a garden into two parts. One, the summer garden for which he recommends roses, rosemary, lavender, bee-flowers (quite possibly borage), isop (hyssop), sage, time (thyme), cowslip, piony (peony), daisies, clove gilliflowers, pinks, southernwood and lilies.

Many another list for flower garden or "summer garden" suggests beautiful patterns of color and bouquets of fragrance in a happy mingling of the showy flowers and the more modest appearing herbs, but laden with the aromatic oils they so generously yield. Could we moderns do better than follow the example of our ancestors in making our gardens which will take on more of real charm because of introducing the old-time herbs?

For every part of the garden—in the paths, on each side of them, around the pool, in the rock garden, in the beds or in the borders—you will find herbs that will grow there happily. These cool, green-growing things are especially fresh in the heat of summer that brings out their volatile oils, the same heat that wilts human beings. As the fragrances laden with ancient lore and legend float up to us they bring with them not only a magic healing for the senses, but mystery and forgotten romance.

If your garden is extensive enough for paths through it you can plant herbs in and along the edge so that walking on and brushing past them will be a fragrant progress on a midsummer day. In the early seventeenth century Gervase Markham in *English Husbandman* suggested a new kind of path just imported from France, tiles with a covering of powdered marble. He admitted the costliness of this and recommended gravel or sand for the tile covering. "Grass walks," said Markham, "are only for those hours of the day when there is no dew, otherwise you must provide shoes or boots of extraordinary goodnesse." Besides this, the green of the grass was not sufficient contrast for the foliage of the plants. We might add that unless just the right kind of grass be used, it will bristle up like a hog's back. A lovely green, soft as chenille to walk upon, is a path sown with German chamomile, not

really a chamomile at all, but "matricaria chamomilla."
Do not enrich the soil, because the plants will be more
fragrant if grown in poor ground, and be sure to keep
them trimmed and to roll the path after each mowing.
But if you are not accustomed to putting on "boots of ex-

Garden Form and Garden Apparel
from Tabernaemontanus, *Neuw Kreuterbuch,* 1588.

traordinary goodnesse" for a stroll along the garden path
after the dew has fallen, I would recommend paths of
flagstones irregularly laid, or of brick in as simple or
elaborate patterns as you choose. These will be firm under
foot in wet weather, while in the torrid heat of summer
they will be most fragrant if the crevices are planted with
creeping thymes. The most delightful ones for this purpose which are to be had from most nurseries are the

crimson thyme (*Thymus Serpyllum coccineus*) with dark green leaves which become almost hidden under masses of small red flowers practically all summer, and the white thyme (*Thymus Serpyllum albus*) with tiny light green leaves covered with a powder of white flowers. Both varieties of thyme spread out into fragrant mats within a few weeks. Other lovely carpeting thymes are the Azores thyme with a dark green foliage and purplish flowers in summer, woolly thyme with soft silvery blue-green leaves and purplish flowers; but these are not as fragrant as the crimson and white thymes and are more slow growing. They grow best on steep slopes or over stones.

Along each side of the path you will enjoy the fragrantly aromatic herbs, clumps of the same kind on opposite sides to emphasize a particular odor, color of flower or height. The path itself will no doubt be lined by low border boards, upright bricks or stones. On the path side of the supports, plant perhaps herba barona—a thyme with a distinct odor of caraway. It has purplish flowers, dark green leaves, and such spreading habits that it will soon climb over the hard boundary and give a softening effect like a tiny leaved ivy. It would be fascinating to collect varieties of thyme: some twenty obtainable from nurseries in the United States, seeds of others from foreign firms and still others found by long search through friends of your friends who have ways of getting in touch with unusual plants. All this adds zest to your search, and when a variety of thyme previously unknown to you comes into your hands you will look at it as upon a famous jewel now yours, to have and to grow with great pride of possession. This may be a very wrong and wicked feeling, but that's the way it will affect you when you have once begun to collect varieties of a certain plant.

Groups of thymes of sprawling yet not prostrate habits would be just the thing to set on the inner edge of the boundary at intervals down the entire length of the path. There are so very many that we can but suggest a few varying in odors, sweetly fragrant, pungent, and others so unusual that a true description is impossible. But do have the lemon thyme (*Thymus citriodorus*), silver lemon (*Thymus citriodorus argenteus*), golden (*Thymus Serpyllum aureus*), thymus jankae with a whiff of fresh varnish, and *Thymus lanicaulis,* something like a mint in odor. A layer of crushed charcoal spread under the foliage of these thymes not only will keep the soil sweet but will set off beautifully the various shades of green. Back of the thymes other fragrant herbs could be set, ranging from those one-foot high to shrubbery plants stretching up to three feet. Directly behind the half-erect thymes might be the spicy dwarf basils (both purple and green), clove pinks, dwarf lavender, and some of the low growing sweet-leaved geraniums, such as nutmeg, coconut-scented, lemon, apple-scented and Schottesham pet (filbert-scented). Farther back you would like lemon balm, camphor plant, costmary (mint-geranium), pineapple sage, and santolina (lavender cotton). Finally would come the lemony southernwood and lemon verbena. The geraniums and lemon verbena are not hardy, so the medieval custom of setting pots of growing plants on the beds of flowers might well be adopted so that the tender growth may be easily transferred to the house for the winter.

The paths through the garden should lead to a focal point, a vine or rose covered arbor or, if the space is too small, a sundial or a clump of sweet or bitter fennel which is a high perennial herb not cut down in the harvesting of the seeds. You might like an old-fashioned straw bee

skep, sure to be admired by your friends and to be taken
as a fine house-to-rent by the bees. The skep may be closed
up if your cheeks blanch every time a bee comes in your
direction.

Perhaps you have a shady cool spot, just waiting for a
pool, surrounded by the moisture-loving mints, with lovage like a giant celery and the tropical-looking angelica
as a background. Walafrid Strabo wrote in his *Little Garden* in the ninth century: "Mint I grow in abundance
and in all its varieties. How many there are, I might as
well try to count the sparks from Vulcan's furnace beneath Etna." Arrayed against the light greens of the
angelica and lovage, and curving from the back around
to the sides of the pool, the taller mints would look well:
the black and white varieties of peppermint, spearmint,
the lemon-scented and the anise-flavored spearmint, water-
mint, woolly mint and curly mint. In front of the pool
and curving to meet these would be what I think are the
sweetest, loveliest varieties, orange mint, golden applemint, the silver or striped applemint and the Southern
Oregon mint (*Monardella villosa*). To carpet the ground
for many feet around the pool, nothing could be more delightful than the Corsican mint (*Mentha Requieni*) with
its tiny round, bright green leaves intensely fragrant of
crème de menthe. It lies absolutely prostrate and makes
a thick soft mat that is unbelievably beautiful for a summer, but unfortunately not inclined to be hardy.

For a less compact ground cover, pennyroyal also a
great spreader would be delightfully pungent and reminiscent of the pennyr'yal teas your grandmother probably
gave you for many ills. Costmary (mint-geranium) and
bergamot, near relations certainly in odor, rightly belong
at the side of the taller mints. Near the lower growing

mints, a shade-loving herb is the sweet woodruff with the unmistakable odor, when dry, of new mown hay. It will spread over the little stones at the edge of the pool and its star-like leaves will soften the sharp lines there. Dead nettle (*Lamium maculatum*) with white and purple flowers and its spotted dark and light green leaves would grow happily with the mints. Also the varieties of bugleweed, blossoming in May, would be delightful. This herb has a square stem like a mint with leaves about an inch long and sends out runners which makes it a good carpeter. There are several kinds: *Ajuga reptans rubra* with purplish flowers and leaves; *Ajuga genevensis,* more upright, with flowers varying from red to white and blue; and the *Ajuga reptans variegata* with leaves having a yellow mottled effect.

In connection with ground covers we must speak of calamint, nepeta mussini, and the semi-prostrate varieties of thyme. If you plant bulbs among them, you will be pleased to see how well these herbs take away the bareness of the lower part of the flower stalks, as of the tulips, crocuses, hyacinths, daffodils, and jonquils. These ground covers also help support the taller stems and during hard rains keep the flowers of lower stalks from being mud-spattered. Thymes, if used, should be kept somewhat thinned out so the bulbs can come up.

If you go in for rock gardens, herbs will offer you a variety in addition to the customary plants. A pleasing background would be the artemisias, like beach wormwood, Silver King and hawthorn-scented mugwort. Through the little garden itself could be planted varieties of the feathery-leaved yarrow, the white silky furry leaves of the old-fashioned medicinal woolly betony, clumps of the lacy blue-green leaved rue, dwarf lavender, the short shrubby sweet-leaved lemon geraniums set in pots in hollows artfully made by grouping the rocks. Then there are clove pinks, the glossy dark green-leaved germander, violets and violas, the smaller artemisias like the fringed wormwood (*Artemisia frigida*) with delicate silvery leaves, and the Roman wormwood (*Artemisia pontica*) with soft feathery foliage. Fragrant carpeting plants will be the pungent pennyroyal and the red and white creeping thymes so especially colorful for a long time during the hottest summer. The nepetas planted in masses will be a cloud of soft bluish lavender when in flower.

In planning the flower beds and borders let us begin at the edge, which will need a low supporting boundary as simple or elaborate as you choose. In later medieval days these boundaries were of complicated trellis work which in Tudor times was simplified to a low fence of painted railings. In the Holbein pictures done for Henry VIII, the backgrounds are frequently garden plots where the railings were green and white—the Tudor colors. If the plots were raised, the necessary supports were of oak boards, tiles, lead, or shank bones of sheep. The seventeenth century John Parkinson recommended "oaken inch boords foure or five inches broad." He liked tiles but admitted they were not practical because they were easily broken. Lead made into crenelated form at the top looked pretty but took too much of the summer's heat and the winter's cold. If shank bones were used they were set close enough together so that the broader ends came upward and met across the top. As the bones whitened they "prettily graced out the ground." He thinks the foreign custom of using jaw-bones "too grosse and base." The very newest fashion, Parkinson said, were "whitish and blewish pebbles, stones of some reasonable proportion

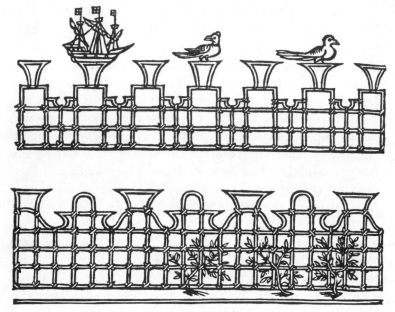

Fancy trellis boundaries in 1600
from Markham, *Countrie Farm.*

and bignesse"; these for beds on a level with the ground. Such stones he believes to be durable and handsome and "of all other dead material the chiefest."

Just inside the boundary we sometimes have a difficult problem—hard lines, a little bare and a little ragged. If you have "boords foure or five inches broad"— which should be impregnated, if new, with creosote—that will be low enough for a sort of "piping" on the inside of the boards. If it is in a shady spot, parsley or sweet woodruff would fill in and give a softening effect. If the location is sunny, erect varieties of thyme are just the herbs to fill up ugly gaps—*Thymus nitidus* like a gray-green Irish yew with sweet scent and pinkish flowers, *Thymus erectus* like

a dwarf juniper with pale pink flowers, the upright green-
leaved English thyme or gray French thyme, both forms
of *Thymus vulgaris,* the common garden thyme which is
not so prim and erect. A favorite edging in the Middle
Ages was thrift (*Armeria maritima*) growing in soft
green mounds but inclined to die out in spots in summer
droughts. *Nepeta mussini* with its lavender haze of flowers will droop gently over the hard boundary, while winter
savory will make a fragrant softening edge. One of the
loveliest sights in late spring is an edging of chives with
its flower heads like mauve-colored globes, which will last
three or four weeks when the flower stalks must then be
cut down to the ground. Other attractive edges will be
found in gray tones; if you like, the gray santolina (but
only for wide edgings), the nepetas, French thyme, dwarf
lavenders, Roman wormwood, and the fringed wormwood. For a beautiful light green edging, though not
hardy, are the sweet-leaved geranium *Pelargonium crispum* like a prim miniature tree, and the green dwarf basil.
Or you may prefer the dwarf purple basil with a backing
of gray-green foliage as that of the artemisias, a beautifully striking effect. A good hardy edging is one of germander with its shiny dark green leaves and purplish rose
flowers, or the duller green hyssop blossoming out into
blue, white or pink flowers.

Plan carefully your groupings of flowers keeping in
mind color combinations and height of plants. In *The
Country House-wife's Garden* William Lawson had, for
the second part, the "Herb Garden" and listed the herbs
according to height. Part of the list I set down here so
you may see how an old-time gardener arranged his
plants. He recommends having "your herbs of great
growth by walls or in borders."

Herbs of great growth: fennel, angelica, tansy, holly-hock, elecampane, French mallows, lilies, French poppy, succory (chicory), clary.

Herbs of middle growth: borage, bugloss (anchusa), sweet cicely, stock gilliflower, wallflowers, aniseed, cori-ander, fether-few (feverfew), marigolds.

Herbs of smaller growth: pansies, marjoram, savory, strawberries, saffron, daffodils, leeks, chives, skirrets, on-ions, bachelor's buttons (our double buttercup), daisies, pennyroyal.

Lawson did not go in for color combinations but we can arrange, by careful forethought, beautiful color effects in brilliant contrasts or "close harmonies." A group of catnip, sage, lavender, lavender cotton, the nepetas with rosemary, flax, chicory, blue-flowered hyssop and a few plants of Silver King or any other of the gray artemisias, offers a delicate symphony of blue, lavender and gray. A blush-rose combination is a grouping of anise, coriander, summer savory, dwarf basil, pink-flowered hyssop—all blooming in July. For showy contrasts have blue flowers against those of yellow or orange, as the blue larkspur, chicory, flax, blue-flowered hyssop, speedwell, bachelor's buttons (*Centaurea cyanus*), delphinium, Canterbury bell and borage against the old-fashioned single pot marigold (*Calendula*), the fringed daisy-like heads of elecampane, delicate yellow flower heads of fennel, the bright yellow tansy buttons and compact orange balls of the safflower. Any blue or orange tones against the red bee balm, red yarrow, Jupiter's Beard, hollyhock or the rosy flower heads of burnet are striking in appearance. Before some of these stop blooming in summer others will take their place for color.

For early spring use the prim yellow daisy rays of the

coltsfoot and the yellow crocus against grape hyacinth or blue squills (*Scilla sibirica*). In the fall aconite is a lovely blue against the hardy yellow chrysanthemums. One of the most striking combinations is an edging of rue (yellow flowers and blue-green foliage), with an inner row of dwarf French marigolds.

If any of the beds or part of the border is in a shady spot you will find several herbs that will thrive especially well there: cohosh bugbane (*Cimicifuga racemosa*), hawthorne-scented mugwort, thoroughwort, hyssop, sweet woodruff, angelica, lovage, sweet cicely and bergamot. Sun-loving herbs are lavender, sage, chicory, elecampane, fennel, bugloss, woad, rue, the satureias, the wormwoods, horehound and tansy.

Careful planning will repay you for that forethought during the hot weeks of summer when drought, continuous broiling days and oppressive nights plunge us into a midsummer spiritual depression. At that time you will be glad there are lovely grays and green herbs which need but a good hot sun for them to yield their aromatic fragrance and revive your drooping spirits. Not only will the herbs refresh you but they will keep the whole garden from having that dried-up look of midsummer and of early fall when the stems of so many flowers have turned brown and the leaves hang down dispiritedly from the dull stalks. This is the time when the gray artemisias work overtime in their endeavor to fulfill their purpose in being. The gray foliage does not show dust, and the bushy plants fill in successfully and pleasingly those depressing bare spots; Silver King among the taller flowers, Old Woman (*Artemisia Stelleriana*) and artemisia frigida toward the front. We also have the gray santolina, woolly speedwell (*Veronica incana*), and the nepetas. For a year-round filler, you will like green santolina with foliage resembling coral strands.

You must grow certain herbs simply because of their odors, fragrant, aromatic or pungent, and the association of those odors with early days. It is really great fun to take visitors around the garden and to pick a leaf here and there for them to sniff. To get the odor they must bruise the leaf in their warm hands to release the volatile oils, the source of the fragrance. The camphor plants are always a surprise, the leaves so redolent of camphor that you feel as though you might eventually make a great harvest of camphor balls. It is an especially good plant to start with in your stroll around the garden with visitors uninitiated in herbs. At first they may be a bit skeptical about herbs having much odor. They may sniff politely but apathetically as they obediently bruise the camphor leaf, but as the odor comes to them they will be sure to exclaim delightedly over it as more than one of my visitors has. After that they will seek odors and want to smell all the varieties you have. However, don't let them take up a coriander spray! It is quite awful and seems to cling to your hands.

Many a visitor has departed from my garden with a handful of sweet smelling leaves carefully treasured in handkerchief or pocket. One enthusiastic newspaper reporter stuffed one after another of the leaves into his pocket after a lusty sniff and carried away a pocketful of sweet fragrances. The last thing that went into that pocket was a paper. I've often wondered what happened afterwards when he removed that paper, perhaps in a group of colleagues, and showered the sweet-scented leaves about him.

Another fragrant joy is the group of "geraniums"

named because of their distinctive odors : citronella, lemon, nutmeg, apple-scented, coconut-scented, rose, peppermint, filbert-scented. Then, too, borage and burnet taste and smell of cucumber; jimson weed of Irish potato. Sweet cicely, lemon balm and sweet marjoram yield such pleasantly aromatic oils that in early days handfuls of the leaves were rubbed over the heavy oak furniture and floors of baronial halls to give a fragrant polish. Corsican mint is used in crème de menthe; wormwood (*Artemisia Absinthium*) gives the flavor to absinthe. Caraway thyme used to be rubbed into a baron of beef before cooking, and from that customary use came to be called herba barona.

Not only will you grow the flowering herbs in your garden for their beauty, color contrasts and odor, but also because they will lend a charm to the garden from old associations, symbolism, and superstitions. There used to be, and in some rural sections there still are, many quaint ideas about the uses of herbs. Chamomile is often called the "Plants' Physician" because of a belief that it will revive drooping plants when placed near them. Ancient Egyptians worshiped chamomile above all other herbs because of its healing properties. In later times, the dried herb was smoked in a pipe to relieve asthma. Good King Henry was spinach to medieval folk in search of their vitamins and is still eaten in Normandy and some rural sections of England. Leaves of costmary were used as fragrant markers in hymnals and Bibles, so commonly that the plant came to be known as "Bible leaf." The seed heads of dill and fennel were usually carried in handkerchiefs to church by women and children who nibbled at the seeds during the long service to prevent sleep overtaking them. This was so generally the custom that the seeds were called "Meetin' seeds." Tansy used to be steeped in white wine and used as a face wash to whiten the skin. Gerard recommends strawberries "to quench thirst and take away, if they be often used, the redness and heate of the face." There is the story that a spray of sweet woodruff presented to a subject by Queen Elizabeth was a mark, temporarily at least, of that capricious lady's fancy.

Dishes of caraway seeds were served with apples to top off those heavy English feasts in the London Guild Hall, from medieval to comparatively recent times. Both seeds and apples would tend to be effective in "keeping the doctor away." In olden days woad, because of the dye obtained by steeping its green-blue leaves, was grown in large quantities. Julius Caesar found that the natives of Britain before they went into battle painted themselves blue with this dye. The inhabitants in the north of the island (Scotland) were called Picts because of this custom, *pictus* being a part of the Latin verb meaning to paint.

There used to be absolute faith in the "Doctrine of Signatures." Certain qualities attributed to herbs were connected with their appearance—Nature's way, so it was thought, of indicating to mortals what herbs would cure a particular disease. Lungwort with mottled leaves and distinctive shape was used for diseased lungs; the willow growing near wet places was for rheumatism and colds. Strangely enough, salacin obtained from the bark of the white willow which grows in damp places conducive to the development of rheumatism is used to cure that very ailment. Buttercups, saffron and dandelion cured jaundice, while rupture wort with its knot-like flowers healed rupture. Garlic with its hollow stalks was good for troubles in the windpipe, and Canterbury bells with throat-like corolla cured a swollen throat.

Be sure to include, also, in your garden herbs that for centuries have so claimed the affection of the people that certain qualities or attributes have become attached to them. Alkanet came to be synonymous with falsehood and insincerity because from the root was obtained a red dye furnishing the color for lip salve used by court ladies. Sympathy was associated with lemon balm; sincerity, with digitalis which affects the heart; resignation, with clove pinks; flattery, with fennel. Mignonette represented hope for the lover who rolled in a bed of it three times. Thyme was a symbol of bravery because the herbal bath infused a tired soldier with strength which made him brave. Cumin, which in later times was a symbol of fidelity and remembrance, in ancient Greece meant avarice and was the nickname given to Marcus Aurelius, notorious for that quality. Another herb with different attributes is basil, according to geography. In Greece it stood for hatred; in Italy, for love and was colloquially called "Kiss me, Nicholas"; in India it stood for sanctity, and a bush of the holy basil stands in every courtyard.

Finally, we must grow some of those herbs laden with superstition, romance and ancient lore. Practically every herb is enveloped in stories that are fascinating. Wormwood, for example, is supposed to have grown up along the path through which the serpent wound its way out of the Garden of Eden, this no doubt explaining the bitter taste. There was the belief that where sage flourished in a garden the master of the house was sure to be a success in business. Mugwort hung over the door warded off lightning, and put into a traveler's shoe prevented fatigue. Rue bestowed second sight; our unlearned gardener tells us that the old Italians put it on their eyes for certain diseases. Strabo in his *Little Garden* advised the herb to be so placed "that the sun and air can reach all its parts, great as its power over evil odours." He also claims: "southernwood of the hairlike leaves cures fever and wounds; it has well-nigh as many virtues as leaves." Angelica (*Angelica archangelica*) received its name because an archangel told a monk in his dream that the herb wards off the plague. In Esthonia angelica was rubbed on the body of a person touched by magic. European peasants hang the fresh branches of St. John's Wort over doors and windows to protect the inhabitants of the house from the evil eye. Hyssop and anise also warded off the evil eye. If a person gathered flowers of thyme where the fairies lived, and put the herb on his eyelids, he would be able to see the "little folk." Rosemary sprays were a part of a bride's bouquet to insure her happiness and the fidelity of the bridegroom, while a concoction of periwinkle (myrtle) leaves given to a husband or lover would renew a fading devotion.

Irish women dyed their bed linen with saffron that their limbs might gain strength as they lay between the yellow sheets. Sicilian children placed pennyroyal among the evergreens in their *crèches* at Christmas time and believed that exactly at midnight its flowers opened to the glory of Christmas day.

Many were the beliefs about the medicinal virtues of herbs for troubles of the mind and spirit as well as for the body. Feverfew was supposed to be "good for such as be melancholike, sad, pensive and without speech." Gerard claimed that eating flowers of borage would drive away sorrow and increase the joys of the mind. If mint were smelled of, it quickened the brain. In the old herbals, the description of symptoms accompanying the use of herbs are often naive and of a simplicity that is refreshing. A tea of the leafy tips of lemon balm was "good for those that cannot take breath unless they hold their neckes upright."

We find from old books on medicine that much of the virtue of the herb depended upon the position in the heavens of the sun and the moon at the time the herb was harvested. In a fourteenth century medical poem, twenty-four herbs for healing are described. It begins with betony, "powerful against wicked spirits," and discusses among other herbs marigold, pimpernel, periwinkle, rose, lily, sage, rue, fennel and violet. He says of marigold that "only to look at it strengthens the eyesight, picked only when the Moon is in the sign of the Virgin and not when Jupiter is in the ascendant." And whoever gathers it must "be out of deadly sin and must say 3 Pater Nosters and 3 Aves. . . . Lilies must be plucked when the sun is in the sign of Leo, from myddle July to myddle August."

This spring do plan your garden and borders to include some of these herbs which mingle so appropriately with your flowers, most of which are really herbs anyway. You will enjoy studying them as they grow, and having made their acquaintance by working among them you will enjoy studying more about them from old and modern books, reading their history and the legends that have grown up about them. This will give you a busy, happy winter when you are not in the garden. John Lawrence in a book on gardening called *A New System of Agriculture* (1726) said, "I flatter myself the Ladies would soon think that their vacant Hours in the Culture of the Flower-Garden would be more innocently spent and with greater Satisfaction than the common Talk over a Tea Table where Envy and Distraction so commonly preside."

CHAPTER III

WALLS AND WATTLES

I saugh a Gardin right anoon
Ful long and brood and everydel
Enclos it was and walled wel
With hye walles embatailled . . .
—CHAUCER, "The Romaunt of the Rose," *e*.1372.

Such a garden as this "enclos . . . and walled" im-
agined by the French Guillaume de Lorris about 1230
would have been a familiar sight to anyone living in
the Middle Ages. It might have been dotted with several varieties of plants and trees, or graced with merely a
single tree and a fountain; but an inclosure made it a
garden. In Dr. Frank Crisp's *Mediaeval Gardens,* containing over five hundred illustrations, we find the determining factor in the exclusion of some of the pictures
from the huge collection the author had amassed.

Many have also been excluded for the reason that while showing
interesting arrangements of flowers growing on the ground or in
the grass, as if in a garden, they were not enclosed, and therefore
could not be said to represent a true garden, though they only
wanted an enclosing fence of some kind to give them a legitimate
place here.

In other words, No wall—no garden.
If you are etymologically inclined, you will be inter-

30

ested in tracing the genealogy of the word "garden"
through various branches—of yard, geard, to its northern European forbears; Garthr and garda, all meaning
"yard" and implying a sheltered or protected place for

A Wattle Fence
from *Speculum Humanae Salvationis,* Augsburg, 1471.

some special purpose, to inclose vines, and so "vineyard,"
or to protect an area of grass, or plums, or beets. To our
Teutonic ancestors the word "plants" was "worts," derived indirectly from the basic form of the Latin *"hor-
tus,"* the name the Romans gave to the area where the

plants were grown. A wortyard or ortgeard, nowadays
written "orchard," was then in Anglo-Saxon times what
we now call a garden, and not an area for growing fruit.
Our ancestors, instead, had appleyards, peachyards, pear-
yards. The true descendants of their orchards are our
parks with pleasant avenues or walks and flower beds.

A series of geards or yards, producing the necessary
food for a family, had to be jealously guarded from thiev-
ing neighbors, wild animals, or even domesticated Bossy
or Chanticleer and family. So the man of the hut pounded
saplings or posts into the ground around the already inclosed gardens, and wove osier or willow branches around
and between the stakes. This was the beginning of the
wattle fence to be so universally used for centuries. Sometimes, instead, a hedge of some thorny bush was set.
Often a ditch was dug all around the outer boundary.
Having this doubly strong barricade was in good Biblical
tradition, as may be interpreted from Isaiah v: 5:

And now I will tell you what I will do to my vineyard: I will
take away the hedge thereof, and it shall be eaten up; I will break
down the wall thereof, and it shall be trodden down.

The double inclosure was a feature of all gardens until
well into Elizabethan times when life had become more secure with the accession of that queen who knew what she
wanted and brooked no nonsense from either foreign or
domestic sources.

In ancient Eastern countries with a high degree of culture centuries before Western civilization existed, pleasure gardens were being enjoyed within high walls which
shut out the unpleasant sight of poverty and nature in the
raw. Egyptians, Babylonians, Assyrians, all had their
magnificent pleasure domes with elaborate, secluded gar-

dens. The jewel-like little retreats of the Persians were well protected from devastating sand storms, while the huge garden acreages in India were inclosed by castellated walls with entrances at four large gates. The Japa-

A Double Inclosure Symbolizing a Protected Garden. An illustration of "Vines that bearc so great grapes that a strong man shall have enough to beare a cluster of Grapes."

from *The Voyages and Trauailes of Sir John Mandeuile, Knight,* 1633. (An unrecorded edition from the Library of the Marquis of Lothian, now in the Sterling Library at Yale University.)

nese really went in for fences with intent to be symbolic or to have architectural significance. Bamboo was the favorite material, the pole lengths put together in various ways with wistaria or cords of hemp. The outer fence was the real secluding screen while the inner ones, of slats erected in various ways, were more ornamental and carefully placed to hide an unpleasant view or to make a dramatic approach to some choice spot in the garden. In Spain we find the Mohammedan influence with lovely gardens shielded from public view by high walls. Within were the customary fruit trees and stream of running water. We have a record of Pliny's Roman villa of the first century A.D., with a garden inclosed by a box hedge —a type not commonly used in England until Elizabethan times.

Bringing to England many seeds and plants from the home country, the Roman legions laid out their gardens like those they had left. But from the fifth century, with the recall of the army for that last futile defense against Attila and his Huns, there were few elaborate gardens for centuries in England, although Roman models again appeared later with terraces, lawns, fountains, topiary work.

During the long period of the Middle Ages (from the sixth to sixteenth centuries), the business of life was fighting, what with the oncoming of Picts, Anglo-Saxons, Danes and Normans. Still later, when not attracted by Crusades to the Holy Land or engaged in the Hundred Years' War in France, the English were busy with the Peasants' Revolt and War of the Roses at home. With the arrival of the missionary monks from Europe, gardens had been again established, and it was by these agricultural and horticultural minded men that many varieties of plants were introduced into England and native species did not entirely die out during these centuries. The early crudely-built monasteries were located in low-lying fertile country where other people dared not build for fear of attack, or would not build—as in the eastern section called

The monks were the horticulturists of the Middle Ages.
from Matthioli, 1565.

the Fens, generously donated for monasteries by the
Crown because it was practically a swamp. But the ingenious monks filled in the marshland and built near the
banks of streams that whole section which is today dotted
with beautiful cathedrals—Ely, Peterborough, Norwich,
Lincoln.

Many gardens grew within monastery walls, but most
important were the physic garden near the infirmary and
the kitchen garden near the gardener's cottage, both
areas laid out in space-saving, rectangular-shaped beds.
Fruit was grown both in a special area and along the
walls of the cemetery. In the cloister garden, flowers and
aromatic herbs were raised for decoration of the church.
The fifteenth century Henry VI in his will endowed such

a garden for the church of Eton College. This garden was to be surrounded "by a good high wall with towers convenient thereto."

In the twelfth and thirteenth centuries, while life was a continual warfare, the area within the castle walls was very restricted, housing not only the family, servants, livestock, but often the Knight's retainers for months at a time. Little space was left for gardening, but small as it was, a walled area was set aside near the kitchen door of the castle for the necessary medicinal and culinary herbs, tended thriftily by the Lady who was physician and surgeon to her fighting knight and vassals.

In early days, protection was the first essential to be considered in making gardens, from those of royalty down to the lowest rank of subject. Inclosures varied from crenelated walls to crude paling fences and ditch; but always there were barricades. Besides the herb garden closely connected with the castle, an orchard or pleasaunce was built somewhere within the outer moat. In the twelfth century it was built between the two moats and entered by a door nearest the castle, while another door usually opened upon a meadow or mede. Sometimes even when located in the courtyard and surrounded by a crenelated wall, a moat was dug about the walls, and entrance was achieved only over a drawbridge from a rear door of the castle. These early pleasaunces were circular in shape.

The medieval orchard, not an area for fruit trees, was a shady retreat with grass plots and trees, somewhat like our parks. Rarely the area might be huge like Charlemagne's orchard, easily accommodating fifteen thousand people, sometimes to witness tournaments there, or it might be so small as to permit only one tree. Generally, however, the orchard was of moderate dimensions, built

Crenelated Wall Boundary. A symbolic print of the early 15th century, showing the Church (spiritual) in a garden guarded, and indicating the Church (temporal) by an unarmed angel unlocking the gate.

from *Cantica Canticorum*, a Flemish block book, c. 1430.

as a place of relaxation, of enjoyment for the family. The grass plots were made gay, not with cultivated ornamental blossoms but with wild flowers springing up at random in the grassy mede. As we look at the pictured representations of medieval orchards we can imagine the gay appearance of Chaucer's "yong squyer":

> Embrouded was he, as it were a mede,
> Al ful of fresshe floures, whyte and rede.

Along the wall on the south side would be fruit trees and opposite to this, near the grass plots, would be beds of aromatic herbs and a few varieties of flowers, all really crude drugs for medicinal preparations, lilies, roses, violets, iris. Flowers were not then grown in a separate garden as now-a-days just for their beauty of form, color or fragrance. Not until the seventeenth century did the Garden of Pleasure or flower garden rate attention as a distinct type.

Town life was congested and unpleasant in the Middle Ages because of the huddling together of buildings inside the walls, as limited in circumference as possible not only for the sake of expense but also for protection. There was simply no space or light available for gardens, which consequently were made beyond the town ramparts in areas heavily protected by a wall of stone, brick or earth, or a fence of wattles or of palings, or a thorny hedge. Finally a ditch was dug around the entire barricade. Of the several types of boundary the wattle fence was one of the earliest and most popularly used. In description, to make an impression vivid, we do not clutter up the picture with details but select only the telling points. So, in early days, when an artist wanted simply to indicate a garden he selected its prime essential—the boundary—and ordinarily the wattle fence was chosen. We find it even on coats of arms and coins. Long after other types of fences were introduced people still had a fondness for wattle fences, perhaps because of simplicity of structure and slight expense for material.

A type of paling stockade began to make its appearance at the beginning of the seventeenth century. Thick boards

Along the Castle Moat

about four inches wide and four feet high were set up and nailed to horizontal rails or held together by osier branches. In the south of England we find more stone or brick walls. The walls had two gates: one the entrance from the house, another opening upon the orchard or vineyard. One is reminded of Shakespeare's *Measure for Measure*, iv, 1 : 26–29 :

> He hath a garden circummured with brick,
> Whose western side is with a vineyard back'd;
> And to that vineyard is a planched gate,
> That makes his opening with this bigger key:
> This other doth command a little door,
> Which from the vineyard to the garden leads;

Sometimes flowers were grown between the bricks on the top of the walls. Thomas Hyll in the sixteenth century wrote: "If you will have them grow upon a wall, dig little holes between the bricks or stones with an old Knif, and put in the seeds and they will grow there."

In the northern sections of England, gardeners constructed walls of earth mixed with straw and usually had flowers growing along the top. Against the south wall and sometimes along the other sides as well, fruit trees were grown; while the garden proper was laid out in beds in front of the trees and in the center of the inclosure. This "earthen wall" is unusual to us but was much used even to the eighteenth century. In John Lawrence's *The Clergyman's Recreation* (1726), we find that they are the best for ripening fruit and protect ripening fruit from rain. William Lawson, in his *New Orchard and Garden* (1618), approves of the earthen walls for keeping bees warm, "but these fences are both unseemly, evil to repair and only for need, where stone or wood cannot be had." He also says,

They waste the soonest unless they be well copt with Glooe and Morter.

Lawson thought little of rail or paling fences, but considered stone walls are the "best of this sort both for fencing, lasting, and shrowding of your young trees; but about this, you must bestow much pains and more cost, to have them handsome, high and durable." However, since the cost of walling a garden was much more than the establishing of it, many an Elizabethan and Stuart simply had to have mud walls or palings.

At the end of the fifteenth century, life and living conditions began to expand. When Henry Tudor last of the

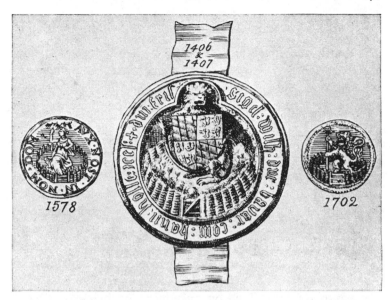

Symbolic Use of Wattle Fence. Seals and coins of Holland, 1406 to 1702, from the Sotheby Collection. Facsimiles from a plate made in 1827.

Lancastrians defeated Richard III in the battle of Bosworth Field, the War of the Roses was at an end. Henry married the daughter of the Yorkist Edward IV, and the great House of Tudor was inaugurated. The new king determined to keep his kingdom in order, and among the first steps forbade the fortifying of private castles. A new interest was taken in gardening, because horticultural ideas were permitted expansion along with space for gardens which now were made across moats and town walls. Homes of former retainers were built beyond the castle, often whole towns springing up at the foot of a hill. With these new homes there were gardens, which always develop in times of peace. Massive barricades were no longer needed but there still were thieves and mischievous small boys.

Usually the fence was a tightly woven lattice with decorative gateway. Inside the inclosure were the beds themselves. Now, as previously in the Middle Ages, was a period of "sparse planting," only a few pots of very special or rare plants set on top of the beds which had been turfed. Sometimes there were simply wild flowers scattered informally through the beds. The kitchen and physic gardens, however, were filled with aromatic herbs. In other beds were vegetables. The shape of the beds, which in early Middle Ages was rectangular, later became square in a chessboard arrangement; curves were not introduced until much later. The beds were almost always raised but with no uniformity. Even in the same garden they varied from a few inches to over two feet, the earth held in place by an edging of brick or board. We find the later Elizabethan and Stuart gardeners having definite opinions on beds and borders.

William Lawson says that because soil for plants should be somewhat dryer than for trees, is the cause (if they knew it) that gardeners "raise their squares." Thomas Hyll says, "In a moist and watry Garden plot" the bed should be "reared two feet high for the better prospering of the seeds committed to the earth, and the plants come up. But in a dry ground the edges of the beds, raised a foot high shall well suffice."

In addition to the construction work necessary to support the raised beds, a wire or wooden lattice work was often erected on top of them. Sometimes we find iron or wooden railings with flowers trained to grow over them. As an added decoration, oftentimes the lattice and railings were gilded or painted, as in the Holbein picture of

The wattle fence indicates the presence of a garden
from *The Passion of Christ*, 1460.

Raised Beds and Tree Seat Between the Moats
from Gerard, 1597.

Henry VIII with his family in his garden at Whitehall,
mentioned before. Here we see the Tudor colors of green,
symbolizing eternity, and white for purity. Thomas Hyll,
author of *The Gardeners Labyrinth* had something to say
about garden inclosures to discourage "Thieves or Rob-
bers, fowls and beast." We are told to stew up, with
honey, a mixture of the ripe seeds of eglantine, briar
berries, brambles, white thorn, gooseberries and bar-
berries.

The same mixture lay diligently into old and untwisted Ship or
Welropes, or other long worne ropes, that the seeds bestowed or
couched within the soft haires of them may be preserved and de-
fended from the cold unto the beginning of spring.

The seed-filled rope was planted in two furrows about
three feet apart and eighteen inches deep, no doubt the
first seed tape. Within a few years the bushes resulting
from this planting would "grow to a most strong defense

of the Garden . . . that, with diligence cut, waxeth so thick and strong that hardly any person can enter into the ground, saving by the Garden doore." This hedge, says Hyll, is preferable to "dead and rough inclosures" such as brick or mud walls or paling fences, but even he realized a satisfactory hedge takes time to grow.

Thomas Tusser, who wrote of his farm in Suffolk, was particular about the care of boundaries. For September, we read:

> Keep safely and warily thine uttermost fence,
> With ope-gap and break hedge do seldom dispense:
> Such run about prowlers, by night and by day,
> See punished justly for prowling away.

And for January, he advises:

> In making or mending, as needeth thy ditch,
> Get set to quickset it, learn cunningly which—
> In hedging, where clay is, get stake as ye know,
> Of poplar and willow, for fuel to grow.

Inner fences took a fantastic turn in the seventeenth century, and Gervase Markham, in his 1616 edition of Surflet's *Countrie Farme,* suggests that the idea of bordering with herbs was not good because the plants were liable to be trampled. Instead, he recommends a boundary of "fine curious Hedges, made battlement wise, in sundrie formes, according to invention," as shapes of flowers, birds, ships, trees, etc. In making such a hedge of "dead lattice work" you stake out the area with laths of the desired length, then make a lattice of "Wyar or Oziers" about two feet above the earth. "Then with shorter poles and wands made plyant for your purpose, fashion your battlements of what shape so ever you please to have them." Plant at the base white thorn or eglantine and as they grow "you shall wind and plash them within the Lattice work." Then your only care is to keep the vines trimmed to "that shape and proportion to which you first framed your Lattice worke." Strangely enough, this elaborate trellis had been popular in ancient Rome, was not found at all in Medieval England, but in the seventeenth century sprang full grown from the past.

With the defeat of the Spanish Armada in 1588 began an era of national expansion and of an individual exuberance. Wealthy people went in for gardening in a big way, often to the extent of Francis Bacon's thirty acres which he considered but adequate. John Rea in his *Flores, Ceres and Pomona* (1676) claimed that a nobleman would need 80 yards square for growing fruit and 30 yards square for flowers but average people could get along with half this. A brick wall 9 feet high would be a suitable outer boundary, with a 5 foot wall for an inner division. Rea also suggests a bed border of boards showing 4 inches above the ground, held by wooden stakes painted stone color and driven on the inside of the boards instead of the outside, as in the sixteenth century.

As the seventeenth century advanced, we find for inner divisions of the garden (instead of trellis or railings) hedges of privet, box, rosemary or thorn. The beds themselves were bordered in many ways by living herbs or by dead material. Parkinson in his *Paradisus* (1629) sets down what is proper for the "knots alone of a garden," but his suggestions may be weighed when deciding on borders for our own beds. Living herbs he likes because they can be sheared and the clippings used for strewing or for decoration in the house. His recital of the "commodities and discommodities" of each edging herb is most amusing. Thrift grows bushy and bears pretty flowers but it will

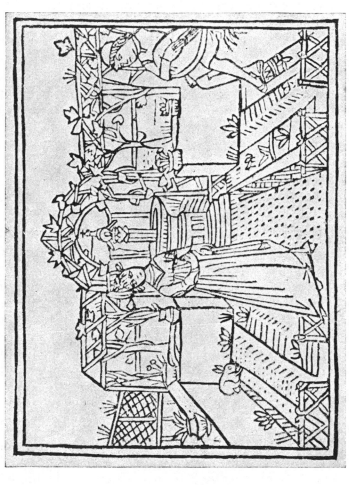

A Walled Garden. Showing raised beds, walled garden, spaced pots, sparse planting, center fountain, latticed arbor, turfed seats.

from a rare Portuguese work before 1500, *Opera Del Thebaldeo.*

spread, may winter kill, and shelters "snayles and noysome wormes." Germander, although pretty and sweet, often dies out, the roots spread underground and the stalks grow woody so that it must be renewed every four years. Hyssop grows rapidly above ground and the roots do not spread, but often die after a first year's setting. (I have never found this so.) Marjoram, savory and thyme are good only for a year, he says. (Sweet marjoram and summer savory, to be sure, but the erect thyme with frequent clipping can be kept several years.)

Lavender cotton was "much liked of late daies both for beauty and forme of the herbe, being of a whitish greene mealy colour, for his sent smelling somewhat strong and heavy." But, he says, it will grow unmanageable, will have to be renewed every third year and will die out in spots if you "doe not strike or put off the snow, before the Sunne lying upon it dissolve it." Parkinson approved of juniper, especially since "it hath not that ill sent that Boxe hath, but grows too great and has to be renewed sooner than Box"; he does commend box "chiefly and above all other herbs" especially the dwarf box, but its discommodities are the "unpleasant sent" and spreading roots.

Of the dead material Parkinson suggests lead four inches wide, the lower edge "bowed outward" to lie on the ground and the upper edge cut like battlements. This was inexpensive and not easily damaged, but "over-hot for Summer and over-cold for Winter." He gives both sides of the argument for "oaken boardes," for "shank bones of sheep, boiled to remove the fat," for "half-tiles," "Pebbles, of some reasonable proportion and bignesse."

By the time of the Restoration of Charles II, Elizabethan gardens were considered archaic, and the wealthy were still more feverishly and expensively enlarging their

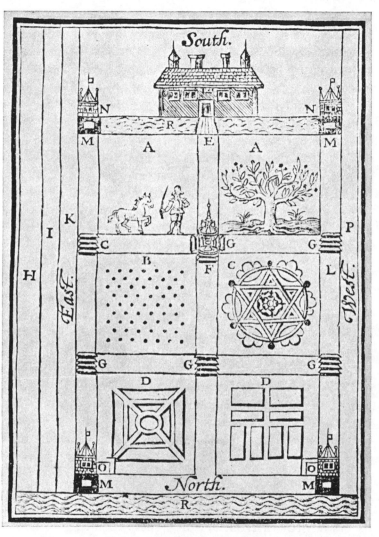

Lawson's Ideal Garden
from Lawson: *A New Orchard and Garden*, 1618.

already spacious gardens in the grand manner of the French style, so favored by the Merry Monarch. Clipped hedges were coming into vogue, gardeners working topiary atrocities on beautiful living bushes. John Evelyn was inordinately proud of his holly hedge at Says Court, 160 feet long, 7 feet high and 5 feet broad, "which I can shew in my poor garden at any time of the year, glistening with its armed and varnish'd leaves. It mocks at the rudest assaults of the Weather, Beasts and Hedge-breakers." Evelyn's dream for London, the visionary project often referred to, is described in his *Fumifugium: or the Smoake of London Dissipated* (1661). He proposed that all "low grounds circumjacent to the City especially East and Southwest" be divided into square fields separated by fences to serve as a backing for "shrubs as yield the most odoriferous Flowers," as sweet brier, jessamin, syringas and all roses, lavender, "But above all, Rosemary, the Flowers whereof are credibly reported to give their scent above thirty Leagues off at Sea." Evelyn suggested that when the shrubs are pruned, the waste "be burnt to visit the City with a more benign Smoake."

Leonard Meager in his *English Gardner* (1670) writes of garden and of bed boundaries. He praises the box hedge which doesn't grow so fast "and so by consequence not draw so much vertue from the place where it grows," but he advises cutting the root once in two years close to the shrub on the inside and adding a little fresh mold. His idea on hedges is that they should be made of "one entire sort of stuff . . . for being mixed, one sort differs in growth from another, some requiring to be cut twice to others once." For borders of beds, he likes the dwarf box. He also suggests hyssop, thyme, germander, rosemary, lavender, marjoram, pinks, lavender cotton,

rue. He likes primroses and double daises for a semi-shady
spot. Lawson also approves of daisies for a border:
"Daisies be good to keep up and strengthen the edge of
your borders, as Pinks [do], they be red, white, mixt."

In the early eighteenth century, English gardening tradition had a great fall, and "all the King's men" couldn't
have put it together again if it had not been for the lovely
cottage gardens, preserving their irregular regularity of
form and filled with the descendants of herbs and flowers
that their ancestors had planted. The wealthy went ber-
serk, and before anyone realized it landscape gardening
was raging in all its fury with its avowed purpose of imi-
tating Nature who, they "major-premised," abhorred a
wall. Down came the inclosures and in came grottoes,
ruins, waterfalls, statues, zigzag walls going nowhere and
inclosing nothing. One feature then introduced has always
amused me—the "Ha-Ha's."

When inclosing walls were abandoned, "sunk fences"
were the vogue—just plain ditches dug about the garden
area which was rapidly becoming a wooded park through
which wound innumerable paths. Instead of being able to
see the end of the walk ahead of him, the visitor would
suddenly be brought up short with a ditch in front of him.
The "common people" called this innovation a "Ha-Ha"
from the expression automatically uttered as the stroller
almost pitched into the "fence" below him. Imagine the
hazard to fond lovers looking only into each other's eyes,
as they wandered about such a wooded garden of an evening! But contemporary correspondence avows their true
worth: "The walks are terminated by Ha-Hah's, over
which you see a fine country and variety of prospects every
time you come to the extremity of the close winding walks
that shut out the sun." From another letter, "What adds

to the bewty of this garden is, that it is not bounded by walls, but by a Ha-hah, which leaves you the sight of a bewtifull woody country."

But what about our own American traditions to guide us in making our gardens? In the first place, we were a brand new, unformed country when Elizabethans were enjoying their espaliers, pleached alleys, orchards, pleasure gardens, kitchen gardens. New Englanders struggling through the first precarious years had remembered visions of those lovely spots as they were trying out new soil and new kinds of plants, or coaxing their carefully cherished seeds and cuttings to grow far away from English climate. For many years longer the hardy settlers were much too busy obtaining simple necessary food, shelter, and clothing to give even passing attention to the refinements of garden construction. When gardens finally were established, quite naturally they were modeled on the ones the New Englanders had left in Old England. Boundaries were gathered from fields or woods, and our early gardeners builded, perhaps, better than they knew. What could have been a better background for green plants and colorful flowers than the gray stones they lugged from fields to be plowed or the soft tan saplings cut that all would not continue a vast wilderness. Eventually appeared rail fences and hedges of roses, or privet; but the stone walls of New England are so distinctly American; stones such as Robert Frost describes:

> And some are loaves and some so nearly balls
> We have to use a spell to make them balance;

In Virginia, gardens developed in true English style with box planted in patterns on lawns of velvety green with "sparse planting" of flowers or often none at all. Box

The Inclosure for the Garden
from Evelyn: *French Gardiner*, 1675.

hedges have been much grown from Elizabethan times, and for very practical uses, too. Laundry was spread to dry upon it, often for days, and homespun material was often bleached on a hedge for weeks, much to the advantage of thieves. For a garden boundary, the shiny green leaves all compact make a beautiful background for color. As Meager and Parkinson instruct us, if we find the roots

New England stone wall

too spreading we can cut deep down through them, next to the hedge.

Do have some inclosure for your herb garden. Preserve the old tradition and let this fragrant garden be a lovely retreat for relaxation, like the castle Pleasaunce. Instead of just a place for plants the garden can be a peaceful spot where inclosing wall, hedge or rose-covered paling or picket fence holds the aromatic herb scents for a fragrant welcome as you open the gate. The inclosure will also help protect the plants from drying winds and driving rains. Reading Thomas Hyll's *Gardeners Labyrinth* by the light of a cluster of candles just after the 1938 hurricane I came upon a passage that was reassuring, although much too late to be of any help:

The famous learned man Archibius, which wrote unto Antiochus King of Syria, affirmeth that tempests shall not be harmful to plants, or fruits, if the speckled toade inclosed in a new earthen pot, be buried in the middle of the Garden or Field. Others there are, which hang the feathers of the Eagle or Seales skin, in the middle of the Garden, or at the four corners of the same.

I would be in favor of placing a toad and eagle's feathers and seal's skin in each of the four corners and in the middle, too, if they would do any good.

Besides the main garden inclosure you should have protection for the beds themselves to keep the herbs from being trampled on, except the creeping thymes which like to be pressed to release their oils and odors. Have paths sufficiently wide for walking among the plants. Then, after the beds have been made border them with perhaps inchboards, 6 inches wide, or strip steel, 6 inches wide and ⅛ inch thick, set 2 inches into the ground and the beds filled up inside to the top. These edgings may be painted a green or soft gray to accent the color of the plants. You may prefer borders of living herbs. Evelyn says that "Chervill is handsom and proper for the edging of kitchen garden beds and Lavender cotton kept clip'd makes a pretty hedge or bordure for a Flower garden and may be maintained a foot high."

Whatever boundary you choose, it will give you great satisfaction, practical as well as spiritual, as we learn from the great seventeenth century French gardener, De la Quintinye:

Walls are so necessary for Gardens, that even to multiply them, I make as many little gardens as I can in the Neighborhood of the Great one, whereby I have not only Wall-fruits or Espaliers and shelter, which is very considerable; but am also thereby enabled to correct some defects and irregularities which would render the Garden disagreeable.

CHAPTER IV

KNOTS AND PARTERRES

Than in we wente to the garden gloryous,
Lyke to a place of pleasure most solacyous:
Wyth Flora paynted and wrought curyously,
In divers knottes of marvaylous gretenes;
Rampande lyons stode up wondersly,
Made all of herbs with dulcet swetenes,
With many dragons of marvaylous likenes,
Of dyvers floures made ful craftely,
By Flora couloured wyth coulours sundry.
—Stephen Hawes, "Pastime of Pleasure," 1506.

"A place of pleasure most solacyous, . . . the garden gloryous," always the center of an Englishman's life from the time the first Anglo-Saxon made garths—in which to grow his onions, radishes, beets; his cherries, peaches, pears; his lilies, roses, peonies—down to the present day when the commuter rushes from his office in London out to his home in the country where he can do a spot of gardening in the long twilight of English summer.

How joyously the early medieval castle dwellers must have welcomed the first signs of new green-growing herbs in spring which meant freedom, for a long season, from the confines of glowering castles, massive damp walls, cold floors, drafty rooms, narrow slits of windows just wide enough for range of arrows. So in they "wente to the garden gloryous," and there they stayed during daylight hours in sun or shower, for there were covered arbors to provide protection from the variable elements. There the children romped while the grown-ups danced or sang or listened to the music of the minstrels. There the lady worked at her tapestry or rested after an exhausting expedition with her maids in pursuit of moths. There the knight looked over his gardener's accounts, or perhaps recuperated from a hard fought tournament. The great game of politics was often played in a garden and even the graver business of war was transacted. In the Temple Garden in London, if we may believe the traditional story, were exchanged the white rose of the House of York and the red rose adopted by the House of Lancaster, floral symbols of those warring factions.

Even after the victorious Lancastrian Henry Tudor, in 1485, put a definite stop to the building of fortified castles, life in those garrison-homes continued in pretty much the same old way for many a year. It was not until well into the Elizabethan Age that the dark days of feudalism really ended. Since the garden was practically a second home in summer, the owner spent a good deal of time in adornment of the outdoor rooms with space too limited to allow for much experiment. But, however small, there were the center fountain, tree, turfed seats and wild flowers irregularly dotting the grass.

As time went on, people came to feel reassured that barons' wars belonged to the past. Gardens, instead of timidly hugging the walls of the houses, now confidently made a place for themselves somewhat apart but conforming to the architectural lines of the manorial hall. Even in the gardens of the great, any adventurous spirit of the gardener was checked by lack of space and particularly of variety of flowers after the spring and summer blooms had gone. Early in the sixteenth century, however, a remedy for the baldness of the garden was found in the ingenious device of the "curious knotted garden," as Armado calls it in *Love's Labour's Lost*.

The knot was not our conception of a string or ribbon looped and tied into a hard lump, but was a geometric design made on a raised square garden plot by the interlinking of lines of low growing herbs or of "dead material," and emphasized by filling the space with colored earth or flowers.

There were the closed and the open knots—the former the conventional curious knot, as we have come to picture it; while the latter was simply a group of low-bordered flower beds arranged geometrically in a square form, but separated from each other by paths often covered with colored earth. In the *Countrie Farme* (1616), we may read of both in the chapter on the placing of sweet herbs and flowers. . . . "Other some are set in proportions [patterns] made of beds interlaced and drawn one within another; or broken off, with borders, or without borders."

"Closed" or "open" depended on the gardener's purpose. If he wanted to achieve an intricate pattern that would offer interest to the eye of the beholder in winter as well as in summer, he would lay out a closed knot, the design formed by evergreen herbs and emphasized by colored sand in the spaces within the loops. "Because the open knots are more proper for these Outlandish flowers," Parkinson preferred them since there was little space, he said, for the flowers inside of the borders that outlined the closed knot. We may add, from a practical standpoint, that cultivation of the plants was thus facilitated by the easy access to them from the paths.

Knots were usually made in groups of four—one in each corner of the garden, traditionally square, or all four grouped together forming one huge plot. A garden not exactly square in form could often be made to appear so

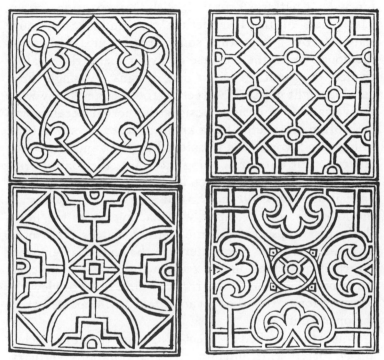

Knot Forms
from Lawson, *The Country House-Wife's Garden,* 1617.

by the skilful arrangement of the four knots. All four quarters might be laid out in a different pattern, all might be alike; or instead of a knot there might be a design in herbs or in colored earth, of heraldic animals, such as "rampande lyons" or "dragons of marvaylous likenes of dyvers floures made ful craftely." These were "to be seen in the Gardens of Noblemen and gentlemen which may beare coate armor." Today we see them now and then in public parks and city gardens.

Comparatively simple in design in their medieval infancy, knot patterns kept pace with the expansion and expansiveness of the Elizabethan era, and became more elaborate often repeating some architectural feature of the house. With the increase of living space, the wealthy rivaled one another in garden designs. A single knot quarter might measure 25 feet by 100 feet and many were the variations in design. Besides the herbal heraldic animals often substituted for a knot in earlier days, would be found scroll work done in colored earth, a small maze or labyrinth, the date of building the house, the coat of arms of the owner, or a living sundial like the one made in the garden of New College, Oxford. Anyone can appreciate the loveliness of the latter who has ever seen the floral clock that keeps perfect time in the Gardens of Princes' Street, Edinburgh. The patterns in the knot quarters were the chief attraction in the garden to those of our early ancestors who enjoyed the fresh air and liked to view the prospect long after the last marigold had departed from the open knot.

Round their walled or sweet-hedged gardens of pleached alleys, turfed seats, mounts, streams, fountains, statuary, topiary work, the Elizabethans strolled and finally rested in the flower-covered arbors for "tea." In *The Gardeners Labyrinth* (1577), we may see three gentlemen seated about a table set in a flowery arbor enjoying refreshment. In London huge gardens were impossible but came into their own in the countryside from which the inhabitants seldom stirred, and who could blame them? Roads little more than crudely made paths were impassable most of the year, so that London was seldom achieved. Neighbors were so far apart that frequent visiting was impossible. Consequently families were thrown upon themselves to a great extent, and as in medieval times many hours were spent in the gardens. What painstaking care was given to the placing of ornaments, flowing streams, and knots. Often were they enjoyed from a distance or from the vine-covered arbor on the mount where daily meals or elaborate banquets were often served.

Knotted patterns were featured not only in private estates of the wealthy but in royal palace and college gardens. In the ten separate wall-inclosed gardens on the grounds of Holyrood Palace in Edinburgh were several knot gardens; two of which on the north side of the palace were in the design of the fleur de lis of sunny France, and were dear to Mary Stuart, homesick in bleak unfriendly Scotland. At All Souls College, Oxford, much of the adornment was due to knot patterns, one of the larger ones representing a design from the arms of the founder Archbishop Chicheley.

But the average Englishman had his garden surrounded by a hedge in which was set a door. There were knots, too, of simple design with borders usually of dwarf lavender carefully trimmed flat across the top. It made a fragrant rack for drying clothes through which the fresh air could circulate.

However much the knots were enjoyed by the majority of Elizabethans, gardening writers in the best standing of the times were contemptuous and regarded them merely as displays of ingenuity, unsubstantial novelties not to be treated seriously. Cynical Francis Bacon was as scornful of knots as he was of "images cut out in juniper or other garden stuff—they be for children."

As for the making of Knots, or figures, with divers-colored earths, that they may lie under the windows of the house on that side on which the garden stands, they be but toys: you may see as good sights many times in tarts.

Parkinson in 1629 discusses knots merely to "satisfy the desires" of his readers, while Leonard Meager in 1670 says, "I have for the ease and delight of those that do affect such things presented to view divers forms or plots for Gardens."

But in spite of the disapproval, knots retained their popularity. Great was the competition to excel one's neighbor in intricate or unusual design. Since the only rule to be observed was to make the pattern conform to a square, gardening writers simply threw up their ink-stained hands at the thought of exhausting the possibilities of design. Parkinson, in the *Paradisus,* including but six knot patterns, says,

And because many are desirous to see the formes of trayles, knots and other compartiments . . . . I have caused some to be drawne, to satisfie their desires, not intending to cumber this worke with over manie, in that it would be almost endlesse.

In the edition of the *Maison Rustique* edited by Markham in 1616, it is said,

I cannot set thee downe an universall and as it were inviolable prescript and ordinance seeing the fashion of proportions doe depend partly upon the spirit and invention of the Gardener, and partly upon the pleasure of the maister and Lord unto whom the ground and garden apperuaineth: the one where of is lead by the hops and skips, turnings and windings of his braine; the other by the pleasing of his eye according to his best fantasie.

But we do find given fourteen designs, "that you may have the means to chuse those which shall most delight you and best agree with your good liking."

For the most part the writers left the gardener to his own devices in planning a knot. Stephen Blake in *The Compleat Gardeners Practise* (1664) offers a few designs of his own but advises the gardener to make his own,

Method and Form of Knots
from *Countrie Farme,* 1616.

"which probably may please your fancy better than mine."

Parkinson figures that a gardener may invent what he pleases so long as he observes "this decorum, that according to his ground he do cast out his knots with convenient room for allies and walkes." He is speaking, of course, of open knots. Lawson, in *The Country House-wifes Garden* (1617) says,

The number of formes, mazes and knots is so great and men are so diversely delighted, that I leave every House-wife to herselfe, especially seeing to set down many, had been but to fill much paper; yet lest I deprive her of all delight and direction, let her view these few choyse, new formes and note this generally, that all plots are square, and all are bordered about with Privet, Raisins, Fea-berries, Roses, Thorns, Rosemary, Bee-flowers, Isop, Sage or such-like.

Lawson then gives eight designs which he names as Cink-foyle, Flower-de-luce, Tree-foile, The Fret, Lozengers, Crosse-bow, Diamond and Ovall, and seems quite proud of them, for in the Preface he writes,

The Stationer hath (as being most desirous with me, to further the common good) bestowed much cost and care in having the knots and models by the best Artizan cut in great variety, that nothing might bee any way wanting to satisfie the curious desire of those that would make use of this Booke.

The Elizabethan gardener's life might have been a happy one, but we are certain he was very busy whether he was the owner of a small place or employee on a large estate. Lawson says, "If you are not able nor willing to hire a Gardener, keep your profits to yourself, but then you must Take all the pains." Francis Bacon says of hired gardeners:

Gardeners should not only be diligent and painful, but also experienced and skilful; at the least, one of them to have seen the fine gardens about London and in Kent; to be able to cast out the Quar-

ters of the garden as may be most convenient, that the Walkes and
Alleys be long and large; to cast up Mounts, to tread out Knots
in the Quarters of arms and fine devices, to set and sow in them
sweet-smelling flowers and strewing-herbs.

In the household accounts of the Duke of Buckingham
in 1502, we find that three shillings, four pence were paid
to "John Wynde, gardener, for diligence in making
knottes" in the Duke's garden. "Diligent and painful"
would certainly seem to be the necessary qualities for a
knot-making gardener when we learn what was involved
in producing the elaborate device in the garden.

In the *Countrie Farme* Markham says, "First, cast
what is the space and whole contents of your garden
wherein you meane to draw your proportions," so that
you could choose or make a design suitable for the allotted
space. Then the gardener, possibly with his master near
at hand, offering his own ideas to add to the problem, sat
down, equipped with paper and crayon. Knot-planning
was not a matter to be treated lightly, a design sketched
out casually as you were trying to decide whether to en-
large the dairy or sell off some cows. It required your
concentrated attention. As Markham said of knots,
"Their whole beautie and commendation doth consist in
a well framed and proportioned forme."

The designer with mathematical precision measured off
a framework and worked out a symmetrical design on it.
Markham gives two background diagrams, one indicating
the "manner of using and platforme, shewing the practise
of handling the lines for the laying out of a simple quarter
without any border." The form of the diagram is a square,
divided into quarters in each of which are drawn diagonal
lines, and an inscribed square made in the larger one.
Markham also makes a diagram for a more complicated

knot, dividing the square into thirty-six smaller ones and diagonals drawn across it. You will see from the illustration how the design is worked out. Simple or intricate, the knot is divided into quarters absolutely symmetrical in pattern.

Then came the problem of what kind of border to use for outlining the knots. As mentioned, Parkinson went into the question quite thoroughly for both "living and dead material" noting their "commodities and discommodities." There was lead that could not be readily bent and not easily injured but was over-hot for summer and over-cold for winter; "oaken inch boards" only for long straight beds because of their inflexibility but not lasting since the ends of the boards would rot; shank bones of sheep which when bleached "prettily grace out the ground" but are apt to heave out of it in winter, are easily broken, and "because they are but bones many mislike them"; tiles easily adjusted to the curving forms of a knot but also too readily broken by feet and frost. For flat ground, the latest invention of smallish pebbles was most durable and beautiful and easy to handle.

Of the living material for marking out the pattern, gardening writers were pretty much in agreement on most of the herbs, Markham stating what others also recognized. "All the sweet-smelling hearbes and others for nosegaies . . . are not fit and good to make proportions of" as, for example, thrift (*Armeria maritima*). Parkinson thinks it is lovely but it spreads and also dies out in spots in summer. Markham also mentions in 1613, "It is much subject to be slaine with the frost, and will also spread upon the earth in such sort that without very painefull cutting, it will put your knot out of fashion."

In *Maison Rustique* we find recommended pennyroyal,

lavender, hyssop, thyme, rosemary, rue, sage, marjoram, chamomile, violets, daisies, basil. Markham in his *English Husbandman* (1613) advises "Germander, Issope, Time, Pinke-gilly flowers, but of all hearbes Germander is the most principallest best for this purpose."

Parkinson discusses as possibilities thrift, germander, hyssop, marjoram, savory, thyme, lavender cotton, yew, juniper, and French box. Of the latter he says, "I chiefly and above all other herbes recommend [this] unto you"; in spite of "the unpleasing sent which many mislike and yet is small." Leonard Meager in *English Gardner* (1670) and John Lawrence in *Clergyman's Recreation* (1726) both testify to the worth of box because of its durability, but "as for boxe," Markham says, "Inasmuch as it is of a naughtie smell, it is to be left off and not dealt withall."

It was too bad he could not have read John Evelyn's entry in April of his *Kalendarium Hortense* (1664):

> Here to take off a Reproach which Box may lie under (otherwise a most beautiful and useful Shrub, for edgings, Knots and other Ornaments of the Coronary Garden) because its Scent is not agreeable to many: if immediately upon Clipping (when only it is most offensive) you water it, the smell vanishes, and is no more considerable.

For July he writes, "Clip Box, etc. in Parterres, Knots and Compartiments, if need be, and that it grow out of order; do it after rain."

For the "border of the whole square or knot about, to serve as a hedge thereunto," Parkinson says, "Everyone taketh what liketh him best," and goes on to suggest privet or sweet brier and thorn interlaced with a few roses or lavender, rosemary, sage, southernwood, lavender cotton.

Having set the lines of the knot pattern, the gardener was next faced with the problem of how to treat the spaces within the loops. He could use colored earth to produce a solid color effect or he could make a representation of his master's coat of arms in several colors, as described by Markham:

> And these armes being drawne forth in plaine lines, you shall set these plaine shadowing lines either with Germander, Issop or such like hearbes; and then for the more ample beautie thereof, if you desire to have them in their proper and lively colours (without which they have but one quarter of their luster) you shall understand that your colors in Armory are thus to be made.

Metal was to be imitated by yellow clay or Flanders tile, powdered; white by chalk, well burnt plaster or lime; black by coal dust; red by brick dust; blue by a mixture of chalk and coal dust; green by chamomile. After the material was arranged on the ground, "with a flat beating Beetell, you shall beate it, incorporate it with the earth."

Flowers planted within the spaces were set off well by the background of green "living material" kept trimmed low. In early days, flowers of one color were not massed together but planted in such a way that the bed resembled a tapestry or mosaic, so that, "far off, the eye could not the Manner of this mixture spy." Lawson mentions roses, cowslips, primroses, violets among other flowers for the knots.

> And all these by the skill of your Gardiner, so comelily and orderly placed in your borders and squares, and so intermingled, that one looking thereon, cannot but wonder to see, what Nature, corrected by Art, can do.

In Markham's *English Husbandman* we read of the exception to the custom of mingling colors, for he gives directions for a flat color effect with flowers:

In one thrid [of the knot] plant your carnation Gilly-flower, in another your great white Geli-flower, in another your mingle-coloured Gilly-flower, and in another your blood-red Gilly-flower.

Markham mentions several "outlandish" flowers of various colors to be massed, a different hue in each space, . . . "the grace of all which is, that so soone as these flowers shall put forth their beauties, if you stand a little remote from the knot, and anything above it, you shall see it appear like a knot made of coloured ribans, most pleasing and most rare."

At last the knot is completed and the gardener, we think, must feel pretty well satisfied with his work of art. Now all he has to do is to keep it in order. As Lawson says, "When Summer cloathes your borders with greene and peckled colours, your Gardener must dresse his hedges and antike workes" [topiary work, knots, mazes, laby-rinths].

In the Household Accounts of the Earl of Northumber-land, we may read of the employment of a gardener "to attend hourly in the garden for setting of erbis [herbs], and clipping of knottes and sweeping the said garden cleaner hourly." That task, I should think, the gardener would treat as a real holiday after the work involved in setting the knot.

The "Lover's Knot" was a favorite design. Stephen Blake portrayed one in *The Compleat Gardeners Practise* (1664) and underneath wrote:

> Here I have made the true Lovers Knott
> To try it in Mariage was never my Lott.

Although as early as 1613, Markham wrote, "The Knot Gardens are already being given up by the wealthy in favor of novelties," yet these designs enjoyed a long and popular life until the middle of the eighteenth century. By 1757 when Sir John Hill wrote *Eden; or, A Compleat Body of Gardening,* knots were practically outmoded in favor of those novelties or parterres. Hill writes:

> True Lovers Knots of Box are banished with clipped Yews and Holly Pyramids; nor is the plain strait Border the proper form for the Flower Ground. No edge becomes a Flower-piece like that of the Grass walk, and they never appear so well as when they follow meanders and rise in little clumps or clusters.

By the middle of the eighteenth century, England was well under the influence of France—in clothes, coiffures, manners, habits of thought. After the Spanish Armada and following the explorations, Englishmen began to feel a sense of individual pride. They traveled more, and as young men returned from the Grand Tour on the Continent they realized the crudity of English living conditions compared with what they had just seen. Charles II after his return in 1660 from exile on the Continent introduced many customs which the nobility and lesser ones eagerly seized upon.

Gardening was affected, too, by the foreign influence. More and more "outlandish" flowers were imported. English gardeners and gardening writers, John Evelyn for one, toured the continent and returned with their heads full of the "new style." Jean De la Quintinye, famous French gardener attached to the court of Louis XIV, visited England, and though the much disputed visit of Le Nôtre may never have taken place, it is certain he suggested plans for the gardens at Hampton Court. Englishmen adopted the plans of French garden designers— such as Claude Mollet who evolved many parterre patterns for Louis XIII; Boyceau who introduced curved lines in garden plots; De Vries famous Dutch architect-

English Form of Parterre
from Liger: *Le Jardinier Fleuriste*, 1763.

gardener who was influenced greatly by Italian horticultural design. French gardeners were employed by Charles II, among them André Mollet, son of Claude Mollet.

The extensive gardens of the great were now given over entirely to the Continental manner, newly made gardens with rarely a trace of an English trait in them; the old ones made entirely over in the new manner. A garden of five to eight acres was considered "as much as any gentleman need design and will furnish as much of all that is expected from it, or any nobleman will have occasion to use in his family." We recall seventeenth century Bacon's writing of thirty acres as the minimum then for a prince's garden.

Fortunately for the comfortable English tradition, the average Englishman had not the financial wherewithal to adopt the new style, and so he carried on in the old way.

French parterres seized the imagination of the eighteenth century gardeners as knots had fascinated the horticulturally minded sixteenth century Englishmen. These innovations were rectangular beds laid out in flat scroll work resembling crewel embroidery, in various colored earth, not in raised plots as had been the custom in knot gardens, but "par terre" on the ground. Sometimes borders were made of low growing herbs such as dwarf box, thyme, marjoram, dwarf lavenders and gaily colored flowers. The effect could be appreciated only at a distance and from a height because of the large area which the pattern covered. Philip Miller of eighteenth century *Gardener's Dictionary* fame, says:

In a fine garden the first thing that should present itself to the sight is a parterre, which should be next to the House, whether in the front or on the sides, as well upon account of the openings it affords to the House, as for the Beauty with which it constantly entertains the sight from all the windows on that side of the House.

Parterres can be divided into four classifications: Parterres of embroidery, parterres of English style, parterres of compartments, and parterres of cutwork. The ingenuity of the eighteenth century gardener was taxed fully as much as that of his ancestor in the effort to materialize the elaborate parterre design which, with the exception of the parterres de compartiments, were symmetrical on the longitudinal axis only, and the pattern was thus much more difficult to work out than the most complicated knot patterns.

On a large scale, the French gardener Le Nôtre had evolved many intricate designs for parterres de broderie, an inspired solution to the problem of what to do with the wide open garden spaces at Versailles. The area was much too extensive to hope to fill with flowers, which did not survive the winter anyway. To avoid having the inevitable empty, cheerless plots, he planted dwarf box in intricate lacy patterns with inspiration for design derived from the province of the jeweler, woodworker, upholsterer or embroidery worker. Frequently, in the same bed, would also be small knots and scrolls of grass work. The background of earth was covered with ordinary sand or gravel, while the paths next to the grass might be of red sand. The embroidery itself was indicated by black earth or iron scalings. The boundaries were borders of flowers with yews and shrubs placed at intervals and perhaps cypress trees set in the corners. This elaborate type of parterre of embroidery was considered the most beautiful of all the types, but as a rule too ornate for the simpler

French Parterre (embroidery)
from Liger: *Le Jardinier Fleuriste,* 1763.

gardening taste of most Englishmen, strive as they did to like the French customs they had adopted.

The parterres á l'Anglaise, therefore, were much more to their liking, a design in various shaped grass plots edged with box. Surrounding this pattern was a flower border separated from the grass by a path filled with colored sand, while white sand often covered the earth under the flowers. Gardeners fully inoculated with French ideas considered this type too plain, but were entranced by the foreign ornateness of style, particularly by the parterres de compartiments.

This type differed from the embroidery type, mainly in this feature: that the scroll work was repeated in each of four quarters, though reversed in two of them, and thus like the knot, was symmetrical on two axes. Often a fountain was set in the center of the large square, thus bringing together the four compartments. Here we find the background filled with sand, and the pattern between the compartments covered with red powdered tiles.

In the parterre of cut work we find no grass, no delicate scroll work, but a design made of flower beds bordered by dwarf box and cut into small sections, "quaint geometrical snippets," by red sanded paths not to be trod on but to indicate the design. The paths for walking were filled with yellow sand.

The whole design was brought together by a border perhaps five feet wide. It was often one long continuous flower border rising slightly in the middle. Or, again, it might be a flat border of grass with two narrow sanded paths one on each side. On the grass were often placed yew trees or urns of flowers. Finally, the border might be just a flat sanded strip, edged on the inner side with box and on the outer side with grass. Monotony was avoided

French Parterre (compartiment)
from Liger: *Le Jardinier Fleuriste*, 1763.

by tubs of orange trees and yew trees set at regular intervals.

Since the goal to be achieved in making a parterre was to present a design pleasing to the eye and since plants were too independent to conform to such whims of mortals, out went the growing things from parterres to prevent their detracting from the precise geometric patterns. Suppose then, at that unfortunate but happily short period of years, a visitor in a certain little girl's garden had asked,

> Mistress Mary, quite contrary,
> How does your garden grow?

She might well have answered that it didn't grow at all but had been merely laid out,

> With plaster and coal and brick and chalk
> And yellow clay all in the walk!

Batty Langley, in his *New Principles of Gardening* (1728), bitterly opposed the formal designs of knots and parterres but, ironically enough, introduced features against which modern taste would rebel as incongruous in the extreme, for a garden. Under the influence of the Gothic revival in architecture and literature, Langley filled his garden landscape with brand new ruins made to appear old—grottoes, obelisks, statuary, scores of objects and architectural constructions—which would surprise a visitor, unpleasantly we would think, at every turn in the garden. But, how he scored the designers of knots and parterres!

Since the pleasure of a Garden depends on the variety of its parts, 'tis therefore that we should well consider ot their disposition to present new and delightful scenes at every step which regular Gardeners are incapable of doing. Nor is there anything more shocking than a stiff regular Garden; where, after we have seen one quarter thereof the same is repeated.

Langley lays the fault to

the late Mr. London and Mr. Wise, who being then supposed to be the best Gardeners in England were employed by the nobility and Gentry of England to lay out and plant their Gardens in that regular, stiff and stuft up Manner in which may yet appear . . . stuft up with trifling flowers. Knots, Parterres of cut-work, Embroidery, Wilderness of Evergreens and sometimes of Forest trees . . . Their Parterres of Embroidery that consisted of Grass, Sand, Shells, Brick dust and crowded with Ever-greens were the first cause of these stiff Regularities . . . The plainer Parterres are, the more Grandeur, for when they are stuffed up with so many small ornaments, they break the Rays of Light and the whole appear a confusion.

Yet Messrs London and Wise translated *Le Jardinier Solitaire* with which they seemed to be in accord in ideas and there we may read:

In my Opinion there's nothing more ingenious belonging to a Garden than the different ways of making our different Figures in a Parterre especially when the design happens to be well contrived, and the execution of it performed by a Skilful Hand.

This was the general feeling of Englishmen throughout the eighteenth century, that if man cooperated with Nature it was remarkable what wonders could be accomplished in a garden. From four hundred years previous, they might have heard echoes of another lover of gardens, in these lines from Chaucer's *Franklyn's Tale:*

> And craft of mannes hand so curiously
> Arrayed hadde this gardin, trewely
> That never was ther gardin of swich prys,
> But if it were the verray paradys.

CHAPTER V

MAZES AND LABYRINTHS

The Labyrinth of old, in winding walls
A mazy way inclos'd, a thousand paths
Ambiguous and perplexed, by which the steps
Should by an error intricate, untrac'd
Be still deluded.
                        —Virgil, "Aeneid"

Mazes or labyrinths? If you like puzzles, a maze is excellent to keep you guessing outdoors. If you like a long walk without going far while you "think things out," with no fear of losing your way, a labyrinth is the place.

Do you remember the mythological story of your school days concerning Theseus' experience in another sort of labyrinth where he was forced to keep all his wits about him? It all began with the unfortunate death of King Minos' son, while the son was traveling in Attica. Terrible was the revenge on Athens which Minos planned, with the aid of a court engineer Daedalus, who constructed a circular building with winding passages along which lurked the minotaur, a monster half-man and half-bull, to whom every seven years, seven youths and seven maidens from Athens were sacrificed.

Theseus, son of King Aegeus of Athens, confident of his ability to put an end to this situation, made himself one of the fourteen victims at the next sacrifice. At Minos' court, he and the King's daughter Ariadne fell in love, and together they devised the now famous plan. At the entrance to the labyrinth Theseus fastened one end of a ball of thread which he unwound as he penetrated the winding passages where he came upon and slew the monster, rescued his thirteen companions, and wound his way out safely.

Although the scene of Theseus' adventure is always called a labyrinth, it was really a maze, for in the former you simply continue along one path, while in the latter you are given choices in turning, designed to confuse you. Strangely enough, this time-honored tale has a shadowy setting of reality in the winding passages discovered in the remains of a building uncovered in Crete during succeeding centuries.

Herodotus, Greek historian of the fifth century B.C., tells about his visiting the great Egyptian Labyrinth, built probably about 2000 B.C.—as we reckon time. The building was constructed to commemorate the union of the twelve divisions of the country, and here was the center of religious worship and of government administration. It contained 3000 rooms, 1500 on each of two floors, with courts, winding passages and corridors of such bewildering intricacy that a person starting without chart or clue at one entrance would be hopelessly lost before he could reach the exit.

Many other buildings in early times contained winding passages of a confusingly labyrinthine character, such as the one in the tomb of the far-famed Lars Porsena of Clusium, sixth century B.C. Another was in the so-called bower of Fair Rosamond, beloved of the twelfth century Henry II, whose wife finally found her way to the center of the labyrinth and gave her rival choice of knife or

The forme and ſhape of Bilboquet, which
is an inſtrument to take the meaſure of rounds, as we
haue declared before.

The forme of a Labyrinth.

This is truly a maze for you can get lost in the upper right square.

from *Countrie Farme,* 1616.

poison, the latter chosen by the unhappy girl. This labyrinth, Michael Drayton in 1631 wrote, was formed by
"vaults arched and walled with brick and stone, almost
inextricably wound one within another," and as John Aubrey wrote in his "Remaines" (1686) :

> Most curiously that Bower was built
>   Of stone and timber strong.
> An hundred and fifty dores
>   Did to this Bower belong,
> And they so cunningly contriv'd
>   With turnings round about
> That none but with a clew of thread
>   Could enter in or out.

Since Theseus' experience, more than one situation has
been saved by a length of thread.

Every labyrinth of the early days so far found was in a
building, practically all of which was occupied by the bewildering passageways. However often such a contrivance may be called a labyrinth, it still is not a labyrinth but
a maze. We may say that labyrinth is the generic term
while maze is a special kind of the general class. The
simplest route of a true labyrinth is for the path—after
a certain distance within the entrance of a circular structure—to turn, follow the main wall until nearly around
the entire circuit and opposite the first curve, then to turn
back and continue, parallel to the path just made, and repeat until the center is reached. So, no difficulty is experienced, but a good deal of boredom, I should think.
One of this elementary kind, very rare indeed, was found
in the house of Lucretius of Pompeii.

The maze type of labyrinth is frequently pictured in
various forms of art in ancient days: on coins, vases,
jewelry, and other ornaments. This type of labyrinth was

also common in early continental churches, usually as a
mosaic, circular in shape and several feet in diameter,

Proper Mazes to Be Cast in the
Quarters of a Garden
from *The Gardeners Labyrinth*, 1652.

and resembling the design of the Theseus Labyrinth. These were found in the pavements or on the walls of the buildings. Supposedly the earliest labyrinth of this kind and dating probably from the fourth century A.D. is set in the pavement of a basilica in Algeria. It is eight feet in diameter and may be a pagan remains simply used as ornament for the Church. A wall labyrinth with what is thought to be the design of the Theseus route, was discovered in the Church of San Michele Maggiore in Pavia. The purpose of these early church labyrinths is uncertain, whether for ornament or religious use, but by the twelfth century, the religious significance of the church labyrinth is certain.

The French cathedral labyrinths, dating from the twelfth and thirteenth centuries, are quite large, one of the pavement type at Chartres, in blue and white stone, being 40 feet in diameter, while one originally in the cathedral at Amiens was 42 feet. The labyrinths in Rheims and in the Abbey of St. Bertin at St. Omer were ordered destroyed because of the noise made during church services by children—and often by adults—as they traced the course when they should have taken their places among those following the ritual.

Many have been the theories about the religious significance of these church labyrinths. One is that the course represents the path to Heaven. We have choices of right and wrong all through our lives. If we make an unwise decision, we are kept so much longer from our goal. Some paths look attractive, but they may be the kind about which Macbeth's porter speaks, "the primrose way to the everlasting bonfire." But if we choose our way through life wisely, keep going on or turn back to the right way even though we find ourselves sidetracked temporarily by alluring temptations, we shall at last happily find our goal.

Another theory is that instead of going on the Crusades to fight the heathen Saracens in the Holy Land, or making holy pilgrimages—as did Chaucer's friends of the *Can-*

Church Labyrinth

terbury Tales—to faraway shrines in "sondry londes," those penitents who were too poor or too weak or too lazy to undertake such a venture made a substitute lesser pilgrimage at home with as "ful devout corage" as stronger and wealthier sinners did who traveled to far places to do penance. On his knees the penitent would trace the course on the pavement labyrinth or with his finger follow the route on the wall mosaic, and, at certain places indicated, repeat penitential prayers.

It has been thought that many of these church labyrinths were so laid out as to require a period of two hours for the penitent on his knees to reach the goal, in commemoration of the time taken by Christ for the journey to Calvary.

In England there have been found only a very few pavement labyrinths, but many "turf labyrinths." Whereas the pavement and wall types always had, after the beginning of the Christian era, a deeply religious significance, the turf labyrinth was solely for the purpose of offering a lively outdoor recreation to children and adults alike. Such labyrinths were found on the sites of ancient churches, but this is thought to have no significance since such sites were formerly occupied by Roman camps, and furthermore, camp sites where no churches have been built still show traces of turf labyrinths. It seems clear that they were used for sport by the Roman soldiers to whom they had the same significance as the baseball diamond near any modern army post.

These ruins are now in rural districts and in early days were kept up, being cut annually and used at the climax of several days of fair and feasting for a revival of what is still called "treading the maze" or "Game of Troy Town," the course of the maze being just complicated enough to add zest to a run of 400 or 500 yards.

Those medieval fairs were of much more importance in the life of the community than the country fair so common in the United States some fifty years ago. In those early days, not much buying and selling took place in the

town during the year for the simple reason that there
were but few shops and no wholesalers or jobbers sending
goods to be retailed. But at various places once a year
at least, was held a fair by charter grant from the King
to bishop, baron, or to the town. The Bishop at Winchester had a grant from William II (1087–1100) for an
annual fair to last two weeks, held on a hill near Winchester. Booths were temporarily erected and rented to merchants from England and even from the Continent. During
that time nothing but food was permitted to be bought or
sold for many miles around Winchester, except at the
rented booths. Thus the Bishop made a good thing of his
concession since he received a "rake-off" on every transac-
tion, even to the ribbon Johnny bought for his sweetheart's
hair. There was the usual quota of swindlers, pickpockets
and rogues, even then. Most important, it was a general
good time for all, and at the end, the big day of feasting
and drinking. In towns on the site of some old Roman
camp, the turf labyrinth had been put in order by sharpen-
ing up the sod paths, and the celebrants of the fair flocked
to this old recreation ground to watch the fun, and fun it
was for both onlookers and participants who found perhaps, after several rounds of liquor, that even the simplest
pattern of the maze labyrinth was difficult to follow.

The dimensions of these outdoor games differed widely,
forming a circle of from 24 feet to 90 feet in diameter,
with a turf path ranging in width from nine inches to
three feet. The sod was cut to a depth of six to eight inches
and removed to leave the path raised. I have wondered
whether, perhaps, the wider paths did not indicate a variation for the Roman soldiers who might have made it an
equestrian performance, for even a pretty well wine-be-
fuddled Roman could have easily trod a path a yard wide.

After the Romans departed from England in the fifth century, the labyrinths were neglected because the Celts, left to their own devices, were occupied by a hopeless, frantic effort to defend themselves from attacks on all sides by barbarians who had been waiting for just such an opportunity to take over Britain. Not until the last long Danish boat had brought its men from the north to settle down peacefully in England, did anyone again "tread the maze." During that period of five hundred years or so, the labyrinths not only became overgrown but clumsy cart wheels rolled over the paths, utterly putting them "out of fashion." With the coming of the Normans, English life which had become practically moribund was revived and once more the Troy Game was played. Of course, in many places the labyrinths had disappeared beyond all signs of existence, but in some towns, enough was left to enable the course to be traced. On these few remaining labyrinthine paths, the village children played during the year until the big day when the grown-ups took them over for their own games.

In the sixteenth century, the custom of treading the maze was still popular; several contemporary authors refer to it. In *Midsummer Night's Dream*, Titania, Queen of Fairies, accuses the jealous Oberon of being the cause of abandonment of sport, that the fun had all gone out of the place because of his glowering attitude:

> And the quaint mazes in the wanton green
> For lack of tread are undistinguishable.

But Roman turf labyrinths were not the only ones trod. The idea goes back to an undated time, for in some sea-coast countries such as Finland, Sweden, Iceland, there are the remains of labyrinths near the shore with the paths marked out by pebbles. We only hope the participants did not have to run the course barefoot.

In Wales in early days, shepherd boys used to cut their own labyrinths, which they called "Troy Towns," in the hillsides where they watched their flocks. There, perhaps on moonlight nights, they kept themselves awake by competitions in treading the maze, involving speed in reaching the center.

In London, in the thirteenth century, were laid labyrinths, and every Sunday during Lent children of the royalty played the Troy Game with the King and courtiers cheering the participants on. But for the antiquity of this game, we can go still further back in history—to Rome where the boys of high social standing played the "lusus Troiae." The ancient Romans maintained that this game was brought to Italy after the destruction of Troy, 1184 B.C., by the "pius Aeneas," who from the shores of Troy was driven by fate to Italy. And now, finally, the name of the game is obvious enough. To conquer Troy was a stupendous task—a city with a practically impregnable citadel surrounded by seven walls. The comparison is still clearer when it is noted that in most of the Troy games, there are seven circuits of the maze path to be mastered before reaching the center. So, whenever you tread the maze, you are unconsciously commemorating the Fall of Troy, more than three thousand years ago.

Not until the Middle Ages did maze labyrinths appear in gardens, low mazes traced by evergreen herbs and, later, hedge mazes set in box or compact shrubs. They might well have originated in the idea of making a most fragrant pilgrimage in one's own garden, in the fresh air among green-growing things. Such an atmosphere would certainly be conducive to things of the spirit. There one's prayers would be carried aloft on fragrant air.

But we find a more prosaic use which the labyrinth served for the gardener at his wits' end. Labyrinths were used to fill a large space and to give the garden a point of interest in winter. They were particularly valuable in such expanses as Versailles and Fontainebleau—a gardener's nightmare. As he tossed and turned, he must many a time have muttered, "What shall I do with this four acres in the forest clearing?" At last one morning the answer came crystal clear, "a maze-labyrinth." In *Hortorum Viridariorumque* (1583) Jan De Vries gave labyrinth designs he had worked out high sounding names, such as "Ionica" and "Corinthia." In a very short time these new ideas crossed the Channel with English travelers and soon became so acclimated to the gardens among the knots, parterres, fountains, arbors, mounts, and topiary work that one would have thought they were indigenous to English gardens. That the English had not earlier adapted the turf labyrinth for garden adornment is not strange. The idea probably never occurred to the early English gardeners whose problem was one of limited, not extensive, area; but the Elizabethan gentleman with more space in his garden welcomed the idea of a meandering leisurely stroll between alleys of sweet smelling herbs, such as savory, thyme, marjoram, lavender, chamomile, lavender cotton.

So when Markham in 1613 says, "Of all the best ornaments used in our English gardens, Knots and Mazes are the most ancient," he really is referring, not to the turf labyrinths of Roman origin, but to the more recently acquired French importations, quite different in construction—and why he should call them "most ancient" is a mystery.

At first these hedge borders were low enough to enable the visitor to look over the whole design. As in the case of knots and parterres, the beauty was appreciated only at a distance and somewhat above. Thus, the early garden mazes were not primarily puzzles, but designs to set off plants in a pleasing manner. They offered merely a whimsical method of walking about and enjoying the herbs, for a child all by himself could negotiate a path between borders not over a foot and a half high. It was the later high hedge mazes to which Goldsmith refers in *The Traveller* (1764):

> . . . . Dames of ancient days
> Have led their children through the mirthful maze.

Thomas Hyll in *The Gardeners Labyrinth* (1577), said that in his pages of designs for knots and mazes, his aim was to beautify the garden. In the Markham edition of *Maison Rustique* (1616), Chapter III, "Of the disposing or appointing of the Floores of the Kitchin Garden," whole beds are devoted to certain herbs, one being of "Camomill, for to make Seats [the medieval turfed seats still] and a Labyrinth."

In connection with this reference, I came across an interesting point. Markham's book (1616) is simply the edited work of Richard Surflet's translation (1600) of the French *Maison Rustique,* by Charles Estienne (1573), and happening to have by me the three editions for comparison, I noticed that in the latter book in this section regarding the advisability of planting whole beds of useful herbs, the author wrote, "une de camomile pour faire les sièges et labyrinthes, que l'on nomme Daedalus."

Thus the old Theseus adventure again—the labyrinth constructed by the court engineer Daedalus. However, in Markham's edition, the final clause, "which people call Daedalus," is omitted. Horticulturally of no importance, but to me it is interesting that Markham thought fit to omit this classic allusion.

In Thomas Hyll's *Profitable Arte of Gardening* (1568) the author gives a labyrinth which is circular and one that is square; the latter design is also found in Lawson's *Country House-wife's Garden,* (1617), with a tree instead of a boy in the center. All the world loves a puzzle and anyone can make quite a game of tracing these labyrinths, following through the various routes. They are also fun to invent, a good competitive game, the best result of which you may want to imitate in herbs in your own garden if space permits. Hyll writes so quaintly of his designs that I describe them in his own words. Of the round maze:

Here by the way (gentle Reader) I do place two proper mazes . . . as proper adornments upon pleasure to a Garden, that who so listeth, having suche roomth in their Garden, may place the one of them, which liketh them best, in that voide place of the Garden that may beste be spared, for the onelye purpose, to sporte them in at times, which mazes being workmanly handled by the Gardner, that much beautifie them, in devising four sundry fruits to be placed in each of the corners of the maze, and in the middle of it, a proper Herber decked with Roses, or else some faire tree of Rosemary, or other fruite, at the discretion of the Gardener.

Of the second maze,

it may eyther be set with Isope and Time or with winter Savory and Tyme: For these so well endure al y winter through greene. And there be some which set their mazes with Lavender Cotton, Maierome, and such like. But let them be ordered in this point, as liketh best the Gardener and so on end. For I doe not here set forth this, or the other Maze afore expressed, for any necessarie commoditie in a Garden, but rather appoint eyther of these (which liketh you best) as a beautifying unto your Garden: For that Mazes and Knots aptly made, do much set forth a Garden, which nevertheless I referre to your discretion for that not all persons be of like abilities.

In another hundred years, borders were high indeed. In *The Retir'd Gard'ner* (1706) this feature is mentioned:

The Palisades, of which Labyrinths ought to be compos'd, should be ten, twelve or fifteen foot high; some there are that are no higher than one can lean on, but these are not the finest.

At Theobald's, not far north from London, were Lord Burleigh's wonderful gardens under the care of Gerard, who had thus for twenty years served that Secretary of State to Queen Elizabeth. Those that, in the course of years, saw the gardens were many and famous. Bacon was prompted by their beauty to write his essay, *Of Gardens*. The much-traveled Hentzner in his visit there in 1591 was delighted by the labyrinth, and James I on his way from Scotland to receive the crown of England after Elizabeth's death in 1603 stopped at Theobald's, where in the labyrinth he

recreated himself in the meanders compact of bays, rosemary and the like over shadowing his walk.

The vantage point from which to view this square-shaped labyrinth was from the Mount of Venus, as it was called, built within the labyrinth itself. Theobald's eventually was given by Lord Burleigh's son to James I in return for Hatfield House, a royal residence where Princess Elizabeth had received news of her accession to the throne in 1558. Still one of the show places of England, Hatfield House today boasts of a true hedge maze nearly two hundred feet long, formed of yews and provided with an entrance at each end. Theobald's has long since been destroyed.

As estates finally became extensive in area, toward the end of the sixteenth century, another importation had gradually insinuated itself into English private parks. This was the "Wilderness," a large inclosed area with disorderly planting of thickets of sweet brier, honeysuckle, grape vines, mounds of earth bright with flowers. By the late seventeenth century, it had been reduced to a systematic arrangement, the space becoming ovals, squares, oblongs, thickly set with yews, lime trees, and tall shrubs with walks cut into these blocks of planting. Sometimes along the gravel paths would be a row of hornbeam with branches plashed, that is, interlaced to form an impenetrable wall to anyone who might have preferred to cut the corners in his stroll through the Wilderness. In the center of the block thus formed by the walks would be a single lime or elm tree, while along the paths might be statues, fountains or seats.

Hampton Court, fifteen miles from London, is now a place for "trippers" to go on Bank Holiday or for tourists any day, a lovely spot full of historic ghosts and gardens. The one you can see but in your mind's eye, but the other you can really see and enjoy. First of all, Hampton Court was a priory of the Knights of St. John, then in 1515 it was taken over by Cardinal Wolsey, then Henry VIII coveted it and got it as a present for Anne Boleyn. In the late seventeenth century, William III took the place in hand and began to remodel the palace and remake the gardens upon the plan of Versailles. He died, however, before much was ruined. One feature still remaining is the Wilderness. It is roughly in the form of a square, the paths forming diagonals and an inscribed square. In the northwest corner is the maze made for William III by the famous gardeners, London and Wise, of whom Batty Langley wrote so contemptuously. The maze is said to be on the same spot as one which was there during Wolsey's ownership of the palace. Statistics of measurement show that it is about four feet high, two hundred and twenty-two feet on the longest side, and the paths make a stroll

Hampton Court Maze, dates from 1690

of about a half a mile. The fun is in tracing the course, and not in finding the goal; for at the center there are only two seats shaded by a tree!

This particular maze has been game for many a writer of detective and love fiction. There is a gate opposite the entrance but the visitor cannot escape that way since it is only for the use of the busy gardeners who do not have time to follow the half mile of path when the center of the maze needs their services. The hedge was once entirely of hornbeam but when renewal has been necessary here and there, substitutions have been made of yew and holly and other material. Admission is one British penny, two cents to us, but its popularity is shown by the annual receipts of about $3800, indicating an attendance of nearly 200,000.

William III also had near the maze in this Wilderness, a labyrinth or Troy Town, with walks bordered by espaliers, that is, fruit trees trained flat on a lattice, making a good screen as they matured. The siege of Troy seems to have possessed this English King for he also had in his gardens at Kensington, green living topiary work representing all sorts of defenses and regular fortifications of that city.

The path in nearly every maze and labyrinth led to some artistic attraction at the center, but a few were constructed so that you simply came to a dead end. Such a one, roughly oblong in shape with three connected units of meanders or alleys, is found in a design in *Le Jardinier Solitaire* (1706). Having walked the course you find yourself face to face with a wall of hornbeam, not even a shady covered bench, a fountain or a statue. All you can do is to try to find your way out again. Some gardeners objected to the puzzle feature; others disliked merely a long course wound into a small area. One wanted a design for the bewilderment of the visitor, another desired an attractive display of flowers and plants. This difference of viewpoint led to pointless arguments and bitter recriminations.

Batty Langley in his *New Principles of Gardening* (1728) thought little of a design just to puzzle the visitor but placed the emphasis on varied features of interest for him as he took a pleasant stroll of comfortable length. Stephen Switzer, however, in his *Ichnographia Rustica* (1718) claimed that the purpose of a labyrinth was, in taking a walk, to give

an intricate and difficult Labour to find out the Centre, and to be (as the vulgar commonly like it) so intricate as to lose one's

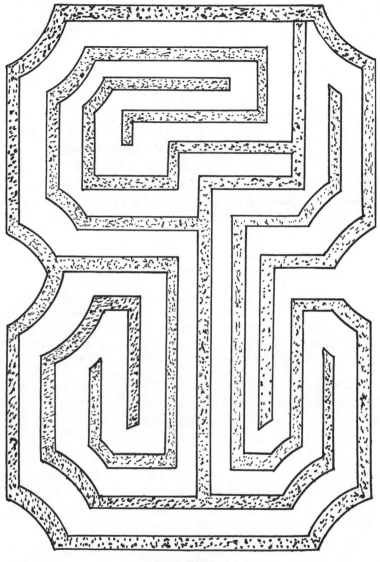

A Labyrinth
from Gentil, *The Solitary Gardener*, 1706.

self therein, and to meet with as great a Number of Stops therein and Disappointments as possible.

In his design a grass plot and statue at the center, which you reach directly after you begin the adventure, is not the goal. It is a covered arbor just a few feet away but with the only entrance on the other side of an impassable barrier. Before you can leave the center really to start on the course, you have, as Switzer says, a "dubious choice" of six entrances or paths opening from the center, "whereof is but one that leads to the centre [goal] and that is attended with some difficulties and a great many steps."

In *The Retir'd Gard'ner* (1706) is expressed practically the same attitude as Switzer's.

A Labyrinth is a Place cut into several Windings, set off with Horn-beam, to divide them one from another. In great Gardens we often meet with them; and the most valuable Labyrinths are always those that wind most, as that of Versailles, the Contrivance of which has been wonderfully lik'd by all that have seen it.

This "Labirinthe de Versailles," constructed for Louis XIV in the latter part of the seventeenth century, was the *ne plus ultra* in garden architecture, a labyrinth to end all labyrinths. At each of thirty-nine points was a fountain, each group of statuary figures indicating one of Aesop's fables; the streams of water issuing from the mouths of the animals, indicating their speech. Although a visitor might go through part of the maze and reach the exit, there was but one route he could take and see all the fountains. The water was brought from the River Seine by a complicated system containing fourteen water wheels with two hundred and fifty-three pumps and cost about forty million dollars. This elaborate affair was destroyed

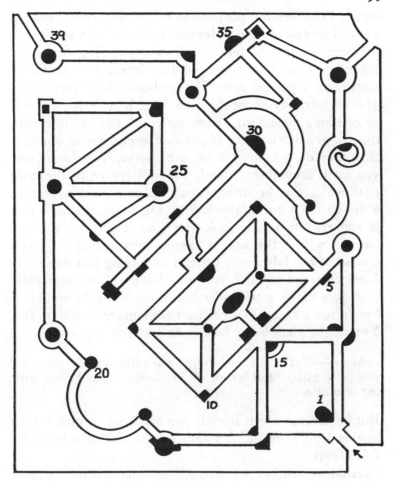

The Labyrinth of Versailles

in 1775 but the pattern was used in the Dial Garden near
Henley in England, thirty-nine sundials set at the points
occupied by the startling animal groups of the original.

In constructing a maze, there are but few rules to observe. Whether the purpose is to display your herbs in a novel way or to take a pleasant walk within a small area between borders of box or of sweet-smelling herbs, let there be at the goal some point of interest, a sundial, a statue, or a garden seat. There should be a certain degree of intricacy about the plan. In a labyrinth there will be one long meandering path with "islands" at intervals, that is, geometric plots of grass, flowers, herbs, but such that they do not put you off the course. Whichever way you walk around the island, you will return to the main path which may be straight, curved, or a combination. In a design for a floral labyrinth by De Vries, the main plot is square, but as you look down on it you see a round pattern within the square frame constituting the main course of the labyrinth. Instead of having just one route from entrance to goal, you may have an alternate path.

A low maze with walks bordered by herbs would be lovely for a fragrant stroll; a hedge maze would be fun. You might plant berry bushes as Lawson suggests:

Mazes well framed a man's height may perhaps make your friend wander in gathering of berries, till he cannot recover himself without your help.

But be careful which friends you send out to pick berries in this kind of maze. It might be the end of a beautiful friendship.

Another caution in constructing a maze is not to make the course too long or uninteresting. Add an attraction, such as a statue, but do not let it be so high or of such a nature as to furnish a clue to the puzzle. If the maze is a low herb-maze, make the pattern symmetrical and at the same time artistic. If the maze is a high hedge maze, you may want a spot along the course where someone familiar with the puzzle may guide a hopelessly stuck visitor, but any piece of statuary, tree or other obstacle designed to furnish a clue, must be so placed that the visitor cannot catch the idea.

Having drawn the pattern on paper with dimensions scaled to that of the actual space to be devoted to it, you will lay the design out in the garden by the same sort of device used in the *Maison Rustique* (1600). "For round workes, you must have an instrument, commonly called the Gard'ner's Bilboquet." This was nothing more than little stakes and a long length of rope to help designate the curves.

If you have a hedge maze, prepare the ground well before setting yew, holly, arbor vitae, or box to prevent later patching up of died out places. For a year or two, keep the hedge well trimmed, and the old writers advise with a knife rather than with shears, until the lower part has thickened up well. Keep the lower part somewhat broader than the top to prevent the dying out of branches because of lack of sun.

With so many good models, with such precedents of noble and royal examples, we may have a replica of some famous maze-labyrinth where, perhaps, on some moonlight night, historic lovers may have plighted their troth as they wandered through the meanders, heedless of any goal, but content just to be together. Perhaps it may be an herb-maze where Titania and Oberon have become reconciled in their skipping along the winding, velvety path of chamomile, where perhaps, because they did not care, they

　　. . . found no end, in wand'ring mazes lost.

CHAPTER VI

A GARDEN OF SIMPLES

The root of Solomon's seale stamped while it is fresh and greene, and applied, taketh away in one night, or two at the most, any bruise, blacke or blew spots gotten by fals [falls] or womens wilfulnesse, in stumbling upon their hasty husbands fists, or such like.
—GERARD's "Herball" (1597)

Always the same troubles of humanity, the "thousand natural shocks that flesh is heir to."

From early times herbs not minerals have been the main source of healing. The ancient Chinese had a sort of herbal anaesthesia in their "soporific sponges" containing henbane, hashish and other herbs of a narcotic nature. We find on the old clay tablets, records of mints, henbane and licorice used by early Semitic races pioneering in the Mesopotamian regions, while ancient Egyptians used caraway, saffron and many other herbs.

Primitive peoples made no medical preparations at all, but learned by trial and error that one plant when chewed or laid on wounds would produce a certain result, while another plant would have a different effect. By the fifth century in England, the Anglo-Saxons were using perhaps five hundred herb plants which country people still use in the same sort of remedies concocted by their ancestors. There were the usual troubles of broken heads, bleeding noses, sore eyes, bites of mad dogs, old wounds. The

Saxons used remedies almost entirely from herbal simples such as betony, mugwort, yarrow, sage, pennyroyal, either alone or in combination with other herbs.

A simple is a plant supposed to have one single or simple remedial virtue, peculiar to it alone. Often many simples were combined for a remedy—the system of poly-pharmacy—so many herbs sometimes that the effect of one simple counteracted the action of another. The pre-

Clubbing a Denizen of the Forest
from Lyte: *A Nievve Herball,* 1578.*

scriptions were transmitted by word of mouth, but ac-cumulated so much pagan lore in connection with herb gathering, remedy making, and dose administering that by the time the oral information was written down in "herbals" by the monks, the Church forbade such heathen proceedings. The resulting herbals, however, showed a purely pagan trend of mind hidden behind the Christian phraseology.

The Saxons lived in constant fear not only of physical ills but of many creatures of darkness, particularly the

* A translation of Dodoens: *Cruydt-Boeck,* Antwerp, 1554.

"elves," not our little sprites that we lovingly connect with fairies at the bottom of the garden, but ill-intentioned beings who dwelt in those dense forests which men were gradually felling so that the elves would have no homes. They were constantly pursuing human beings and it was a common thing to be "elf shot." Close kin to these were goblins and night mares. Then there was the "worm" (dragon) that insinuated itself into the body, the teeth for instance, and terrible demons that entered the mind and soul. Flying demons, blown by the wind where it listeth, were greatly to be feared by the Saxons as modern flying venom, those elusive germs, are dreaded by us. Those recent converts to Christianity, often but nominally, still cherished their old beliefs and although the Church had forbidden the pagan rites, they did not forget the Goddess of the Dawn when herbs were harvested, nor the Earth Mother who had been so gracious.

Amulets were much in vogue against rheumatism, against being barked at, against weariness on a journey. When the remedy called for was the application of a fresh herb, the plant was bound on with red wool, sacred to Thor and hated by the creatures of darkness. Now-a-days some among us wear a four leaf clover in the sole of the shoe, or carry a rabbit's foot when we are particularly desirous of success. Then, too, in those days there were charms for transferring the disease from the sick person to something inanimate. One prescription gives a most elaborate process for preparation of the remedy which, however, was not to be given to the patient but must be thrown into running water. There were salves with herbs for baldness as well as for too thick hair. An ointment for sunburn was made of tender ivy twigs boiled in butter and smeared on the affected parts.

In the early centuries, herbs were sought far and near in the fields and forests, but by the Middle Ages, medicinal plants were also cultivated in well ordered gardens. Within monastery precincts certain priests were delegated to tend the herbs for the care of their brethren or strangers within their gates. Within castle walls the ladies were eager for good crops, especially of those herbs used as healing applications for wounds. In times of peace which unfortunately did not extend over long periods the fashionable affliction of gout had to be taken care of, often by rosemary leaves boiled in water and bound on the offending part perhaps with red flannel—reminiscent of the old Saxon custom! Unseen monsters still prowled about, and as in the early days, betony was effective against "wykked sperytes," monstrous nocturnal visions, and "frightful visions and dreams." Then, as now, people were "seein' things at night" and afraid of things that go bump in the dark. We all recall the ancient Celtic Litany:

> From Ghoulies and Ghosties
> And long leggetty Beasties
> And things that go bump in the Night
> Good Lord, Deliver us!

By the sixteenth century we hear less of spooks but more about melancholy and over much sighing. There was the full quota of remedies for weak brains, for "bytings" of both man and beast, for gunshot wounds. William Turner at this time cautions against taking too much of an herb. "Hemp seed if it be Taken out of measure Taketh man's wyttes from them as coriander doth." The idea of a definite dose is quite modern.

We find beauty preparations such as complexion washes, yet our ancestors were a bit distrustful of water. "Many

folke that hath bathed them in cold water have dyed"
and it is "impossible for them that drynketh over much
water in theyr youth to come to ye age that God hath
ordeyned them." In Ram's *Little Dodoen* (1606) in the
gardening calendar we find for practically every month,
advice about bathing. In January, you shouldn't wash your
head, nor in November should you bathe the body. In
February, bathing is not hurtful, is advised for April, while
in May washing the face with fair running water was
good, and bathing in June is good if the person doesn't
tarry in it.

The Doctrine of Signatures was highly in favor at this
time, the belief that Nature had by the appearance of certain herbs, indicated to mortals their healing properties.
William Coles in *The Art of Simpling* (1656) said:

> The mercy of God maketh herbes for the use of man, and hath
> not only stamped upon them a distinct forme, but also given them
> particular Signatures, whereby a man may read, even in legible
> characters, the use of them.

Lungwort, for example, with white spots on the leaves
and distinctive shape, showed it would cure diseases of
the lungs. Viper's Bugloss, with stalks mottled like a snake,
was an antidote for poisonous snake bites.

There were certain general rules by which the labels of
diseases could be distinguished on plants, these based on
the major premise that the part of an herb resembling
some part of the human body in shape, color, quality and
consistency, possessed medicinal virtues especially suitable
for afflictions of that part. In early times a popular belief
was held that the body is made up of four humors, melancholy, phlegm, blood and choler; a vestige of that belief
is still kept today in describing people as melancholy, phleg-

Brewing an Herbal Remedy in the Apothecary's
Laboratory, 1500

matic, sanguine, or choleric. Ill-health of individuals resulted when one of these humors increased or decreased
too much. The remedy for such a condition was an herb
with the suitable color of flower, or proper consistency of
juice resembling the humor which was out of balance.

Edible flowers of yellow caused the normal flow of yellow bile, those of dull color decreased black bile. White flowered plants that have a thickish juice and grow in a damp place increased the humor of phlegm; but such a plant native to dry places was used to moderate phlegm. Some red flowered plants caused an increase of blood flow; others tended to check it. Flowers of mixed color had more than one medicinal virtue. Plants with certain peculiarities could be used to produce similar effects in people; as sterility or fecundity.

There were natural developments and outgrowths of the simple belief that the picture of the disease was stamped on some part of a plant to indicate its suitability to cure that ailment. Sometimes a plant indicated what harm could be prevented by having it about one. A plant growing in marshy sections called Shaking Grass or sometimes "Quakers" because of its almost constant quivering, was not only used for the patient suffering from ague but also kept in the houses in swampy places to prevent the disease. Hound's Tongue (*Cynoglossum officinale*) named from the shape and texture of the leaf was believed to be efficacious if placed in the sole of the shoe, in preventing dogs barking at you.

An herb was often used because of its external appearance, not only for its medicinal qualities but as a symbol. In *Apparatus Plantarum* by the German, Peter Lauremberg (1575-1624), we find: "The seed of Garlic is black; it obscures the eyes with blackness and darkness." This is to be understood of healthy eyes, but those which are dull through vicious humidity, garlic drives the viciousness away. The tunic of garlic is ruddy; it expels blood. It has a hollow stalk, and it helps affections of the windpipe. But garlic, an Anglo-Saxon word "gar" meaning spear, was the symbolic plant of warriors of Northern Europe in early days; the name was derived from its narrow tapering leaves.

Often it was felt that human beings could learn lessons in conduct and virtue from studying the habits of plants. Robert Turner tells that Charles I, imprisoned on the Isle of Wight before his trial, felt this as he considered the bright flowers that turned toward the sun all day long and the deserted King wrote:

> The Marigold observes the Sun
> More than my subjects me have done.

However much we may smile at the old belief in the Doctrine of Signatures, it is interesting to know that many of the herbs used centuries ago because of their supposed signatures are still used for those very ailments, not now from fancy but as a result of scientific experiments. The willow, growing near wet places naturally conducive to development of rheumatism, was early used for that disease. Now we get salacin from the bark of the white willow as an ingredient in a modern remedy for rheumatic troubles. In some European countries, red roses were used as a cure for hemorrhage if the dose was accompanied by these words: "Abek, Wabek, Fabek; in Christ's garden stand three red roses—one for the good God, the other for God's blood, the third for the angel Gabriel. Blood, I pray you, cease to flow." Today roses are still used in medicinal preparations for their astringent qualities.

In the seventeenth century we find an abundance of herbal remedies for melancholy, sadness, strengthening the memory, helping weak brains, quickening the senses, increasing delight. But we also find amazing and elaborate

concoctions of herbs for very real physical troubles—
broken bones, corns, gout, rupture, bruises, coughs, fevers,
jaundice, vertigo, indigestion, drawing splinters from the
flesh, toothache, eye inflammation, poisoned weapons, and
above all, cures for and preventive measures against the
dreaded plague. One curious remedy for toothache that
John Parkinson offers in *Theatrum Botanicum* (1640) is
for the victims to rub the bruised root of crowfoot on to
their fingers; by causing "more paine therein than is felt
by the toothache it taketh away the pain." There was an
ointment made with lupin mixed with the gall of a goat
and some lemon juice which would remove small pox marks
and make the user "look more amiable."

This was the age in which we hear so much of Nicholas
Culpeper who based his cures on the old belief that each
plant was dedicated to a planet which presided over a
special part of the body. So, in prescribing, Culpeper
would use an herb under the planet presiding over the
imperfect part or organ. There were benevolent planets
which cured without a doctor, and malevolent planets
which caused a change for the worse. Plants under Mercury were bright and vigorous and cured ills caused by
violence; flowers under the sun and moon were yellow
and cured eye troubles.

In the eighteenth century many of the early fantastic
remedies for human ills still held in spite of the great
advance in medical science. In the old manuscript books
of prescriptions, we find scientific formulas next to weird
concoctions, some of them quite ghoulish in nature. Sir
John Hill in his *Family Herbal* (1755) says: "mosses
have been supposed good against disorders of the head,
when gathered from the skull, but this is all fancy." In
towns and cities drugs were sold in open booths by grocers,

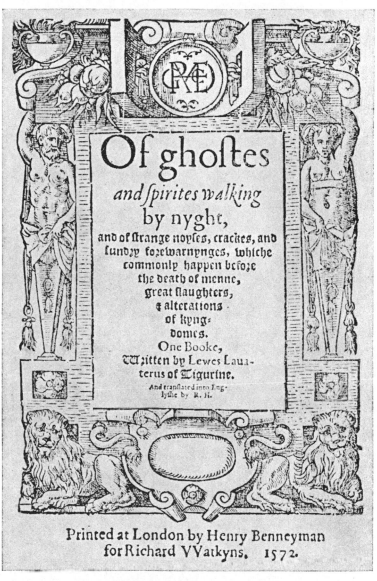

Of ghostes

and spirites walking
by nyght,
and of strange noyses, crackes, and
sundry forewarnynges, whiche
commonly happen before
the death of menne,
great slaughters,
& alterations
of kyng-
domes.
One Booke,
Written by Lewes Laua-
terus of Tigurine.
And translated into Eng-
lyshe by R. H.

Printed at London by Henry Benneyman
for Richard VVatkyns. 1572.

Goblins and nightmares were real in the olden days.

that is, sellers in gross, but James I finally allotted the drugs to the apothecaries and by that time practicing physicians were required to have passed some sort of examination before the Bishop of London or the Dean of St. Paul's and four approved physicians. But in the coun-

Cranium Moss
from Gerard's *Herball*, 1597.

try manors the welfare of the family and household depended not on physicians but upon the women folk trained from girlhood in the art of distillation, the formulas cherished in family still-room books.

In the tower of the thirteenth century Schloss Weinberg in Austria is the little pharmacy which the Countess Maria Anna found already begun when she went there as a bride. The gray walls of the room, made light by three windows overlooking the countryside, are lined with powder blue shelves containing pale blue glass bottles labeled in delicate scroll work, pots of blue and white porcelain,

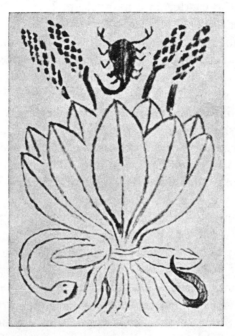

Plantain. Illustrating that it cures snake bites and the stings of scorpions.
From an edition printed in Rome c. 1480 of the 11th century Saxon herbal of Apuleius Platonicus, 500 A.D.

and jars of painted wood. We find glass retorts, sieves, mortars, crucibles, scalpels, scissors, spoons, and such utensils, and there is a portable case with bottles as in a modern doctor's kit. Though the room might resemble a boudoir, the serious business of healing wounds, setting broken bones, curing deafness, as well as relieving headaches and heart palpitations, was studied and practiced here by the good Countess who did not stop with caring for her own family, but went about the entire estate helping the retainers of the castle. The manuscript book with its 1141 recipes contains a treatise of midwifery, directions for broken limbs, treatment of sprains and wounds, all written out carefully by her. There is another book containing treatments for sick animals and recipes for medicines, ointments, soaps, perfumes, beauty preparations.

In the nineteenth and early twentieth century, before the improvement of roads or the common use of telephone and automobile, farms were pretty well isolated, and the good wife and mother had to be physician as well. She had no lovely blue and gray pharmacy in a castle tower, but the farmhouse kitchen many a day and night was redolent with the brewing of herb teas, the making of poultices, salves and ointments, the drying of many herbs against the winter's ills. As Miss Jewett says in her *Country of the Pointed Firs* of the herbs grown by Mrs. Todd, "Some strange and pungent odors that roused a dim sense and remembrance of something in the forgotten past." Some of the herbs were found by searching in woods and fields. Our grandmothers on the farms knew always the best place to gather coltsfoot or pennyroyal, while the youngest generation went along to carry the basket—but grandmother always did the snipping of the herb, just so far down the stalk.

Many of the old fashioned herbs are still used in such quantities in medicines that they are grown on a commercial scale and many groups earn a livelihood from crude drug crops such as pennyroyal, boneset, coltsfoot, comfrey, elecampane, horehound, tansy, wormwood, yarrow, peppermint. Although we ourselves in either town or country may have no thought of growing the medicinal herbs in a large quantity, yet for sweet sentiment's sake, let us plant a "physick garden," those perennial plants which were favorite remedies from ancient times to the present day.

As with the culinary garden, described in Chapter IX, the space need not be large. Both the old time kitchen garden and the physic garden were traditionally rectangular. You might have the physic garden as companion to the culinary garden on the other side of the kitchen door if that is where your culinary herbs are grown, or out in the main garden separated by a path from the kitchen plot. If you have twenty culinary herb plots, you might add any four you choose to the sixteen simples I have chosen, perhaps foxglove (digitalis), angelica, lungwort, larkspur. You would be surprised to find how much of your flower border really is a physic garden in good standing now— as it has been from ancient times—iris, anemone, lobelia, poppy, peony, lily of the valley, hollyhock, sunflower, roses, violets.

Of course all your twenty culinary herbs, except chives, are on present day crude drug lists. Of chives, Culpeper is greatly opposed. "If eaten raw, they send up very hurtful vapours to the brain, causing troublesome sleep and spoiling the eyesight." But onions a relative of chives was looked upon with favor by Gerard for baldness. "The juice of onions annointed upon a bald head in the Sun bringeth the haire againe very speedily."

The other nineteen culinary herbs have been used in medicine from early times and are still used for the effects, in many cases, that were vaguely hinted at in the old uses.

ANISE. This was used to avert the evil eye. Romans ate aniseed cakes to promote digestion. In the reign of Edward I (fourteenth century) anise was one of the taxable drugs when carried across the Bridge of London. Aniseed balls were used for coughs. Today we have anisette, a liqueur warming to the stomach. Anise is also used in dentifrices and in medicines to conceal their disagreeable flavors.

LEMON BALM. Pliny said balm was of so "great virtue that though it be but tied to his sword that hath given the wound, it staunceth the blood." Parkinson also recommended it for its astringent quality. Gerard said that "Bawme drunke in wine is good against the bitings of venomous beasts, comforts the heart, and driveth away all melancholy and sadnesse."

BASIL. It was sometimes used for reducing. An old belief was that at meal time women would not eat anything from dishes under which basil had been put without their knowing it.

BENE (sesame). The oil, mixed with that of myrtle and olive, was recommended by the Arabian Ibn Baithar (thirteenth century) for dandruff.

TARRAGON. The same Arabian botanist claimed it sweetened the breath, was soporific and if chewed before taking medicine, dulled the taste.

BORAGE. It is by now proverbial as a remedy for driving away melancholy. John Evelyn said it would revive the hypochondriac. If that could be done now-a-days with so much fear psychology used in advertising preparations and with so much discussion of symptoms by laymen, many nice cups of borage tea could be used to advantage. It was also given to cheer the hard student. Sir John Hill in his *Family Herbal* (1755) said, "Borage procureth gladsomnesse, it helpeth the giddinesse and swimming of the head, the trembling and heating of the heart, it encreaseth memorie and removeth melancholy and the King's evil, it doth only comfort."

BURNET. This was greatly valued as a vulnerary herb as the name of "sanguisorba" implies. Culpeper claimed it was a "most precious herb, little inferior to betony, a special help to defend heart from noisome vapours, and from infection of the pestilence, the juice thereof being taken in some drink, and the party laid to sweat."

CARAWAY. The seeds used to be served with roast apples at the end of a meal to promote digestion. It is sometimes added to bitter medicine to make the taste more agreeable.

CHERVIL. It used to be applied on bruises. Pliny said hiccoughs could be stopped by drinking vinegar in which the seeds had been soaked. Parkinson claimed that the candied roots warmed and comforted a cold "phlegmaticke stomack and a good preservative in time of plague."

CORIANDER. The seeds were considered by the Chinese to confer immortality. William Turner in his herbal of 1551 said that "Coriandre layd to wyth breade or barly mele is good for Saynt Antonyes fyre," that is, erysipelas.

DILL. It was mentioned in a medical botany of 1869 as effective in preventing obesity if the victim or patient were given a drink of the herb boiled in a broth. Culpeper said, "It stayeth the hiccough, being boiled in wine, and but smelled unto, being tied in a cloth."

FENNEL. This was recommended by Gerard and Parkinson for preserving the eyes. Gerard says, "The powder of the seed of Fennell drunke for certaine daies together fasting preserveth the eye-sight." William Coles in *Adam in Eden* (1657) is also interested in the too, too solid flesh. Fennel is advised to be used in drinks and broths "for those that are grown fat, to abate their unwieldiness and cause them to grow more gaunt and lank."

MARJORAM. Gerard highly recommended it. It "easeth the tooth ache being chewed in the mouth. The leaves dried and mingled with honey put away black and blew markes after stripes and bruses, being applied thereto." Gerard also advised a drink made of the leaves for those that "are given to over much sighing."

PARSLEY. William Turner (1551) said that parsley scattered over fish ponds would cure the sick fishes therein. It was also considered a cure for baldness if the seed were sprinkled over the head three nights every year.

ROSEMARY. It had myriad medicinal uses in the olden days. The leaves of rosemary and coltsfoot crushed made a smoking mixture for asthma sufferers. In *Bancke's Herbal* (sixteenth century) we read, "If thou have a cough, drink the water of the leaves boyled in white wine and ye shall be whole." Halitosis was a matter of consideration even in the time of Gerard, who says, "The distilled water of the flowres of Rosemary being drunke at morning and evening first and last, taketh away the stench of the mouth and breath, and maketh it very sweet, if there be added thereto, to steep or infuse for certaine daies, a few Cloves, Mace, Cinnamon, and a little Annise seed." William Langham in his *Garden of Health* (1579) makes a rosemary bath practically equal to a dip in the Fountain of Youth. "Seethe much Rosemary, and bathe therein to make thee lusty, lively, joyfull, likeing and youngly." Who could expect more of an herb?

SAGE. The ninth century Walafrid Strabo in *The*

A Mad Dog

from Matthioli, 1565.

Little Garden says, "Amongst my herbs, sage holds the place of honour; of good scent it is and full of virtue for many ills." Gerard said it "is singular good for the head and braine, quickeneth the sences and memory, strengthneth the sinews, restoreth health to those that have the palsie." He speaks of putting it "up into the nostrils" to clear the head. An early snuff.

SPEARMINT. Gerard considered it to be "marvelous wholesome for the stomacke."

SUMMER SAVORY. The fresh leaves were laid on wasp or bee stings to relieve the pain.

THYME. Always the symbol of strength, it was a favorite herb for aromatic baths. Still widely used in medicine. In the old days an infusion of creeping thyme was considered a sure cure for "that troublesome complaint, the nightmare."

Now we come to the physic garden itself, and the choice of only sixteen simples is difficult but I have noted their continual appearance in lists of medicinal herbs from early to modern times. John Evelyn in his *Directions for the Garden at Says Court* advises: "Physical plants should be set in Alphabetical order for the better retaining them in memorie." So, I give you: betony, chamomile, coltsfoot, comfrey, elecampane, fumitory, horehound, lavender, lovage, marshmallow, pennyroyal, peppermint, tansy, thoroughwort, wormwood, yarrow.

BETONY. *Betonica officinalis*—has been highly regarded from the time of the ancient Greeks. An old Italian proverb advised, "Sell your coat and buy betony." Anthony Musa physician of Augustus Caesar wrote a long treatise showing cures by betony for forty-seven diseases. In later times it was diligently cultivated in the gardens of apothecaries and monasteries for many physical ailments and was eagerly sought by laymen against those intangible evil spirits and was commonly planted in churchyards. In the *Grete Herball* (1516) we find that "For them that be ferfull, gyve two dragmes of powder hereof wt [with] warme water and as moche wyne at the tyme that the fere cometh."

CHAMOMILE. *Anthemis nobilis*—named Roman chamomile by the German Joachim Camerarius who found it growing in abundance near Rome and thus distinguished it from the German chamomile. One of the oldest of the "soothing" remedies. Culpeper said: "The flowers boiled in lee [lye] are good to wash the head and comfort both it and the brain." William Turner said, "It will restore a man to hys color shortly, yf a man, after the longe use of the bathe, drynke of it after he is come forthe oute of the bath."

COLTSFOOT. *Tussilago Farfara*—has always been used for any disease of the lungs. As early as the first century, Dioscorides recommended the dried leaves to be burnt and inhaled, while Pliny instructed a person suffering from a cough to burn the dried leaves and roots and the smoke to be drawn into the mouth "through a reed and swallowed, wine being sipped between inhalations." Gerard also says, "The fume of the dried leaves taken through a funnell or tunnell, burned upon coles, effectually helpeth those that are troubled with the shortness of breath, and fetch their winde thicke and often." Not long ago the writer of an article on coltsfoot told how, as a soldier in the World War, he dried the leaves and smoked them when he could not get tobacco.

COMFREY. *Symphytum officinale*—because of its muci-laginous juice this, too, has long been used in lung troubles. Culpeper says, "It has not its equal in the cure of whooping cough in children when all other medicines fail." In old time prescriptions, the white-flowered variety was used in an ointment for women while the red-flowered formed the basis for an ointment for men. The leaves were used as a poultice for sprains.

ELECAMPANE. *Inula Helenium*—is still another herb long praised for its virtue in curing colds, the most common of all man's ailments, apparently, since time began. Besides recommending it for coughs, asthma, and short-ness of breath, Pliny says the root chewed tightens loose teeth. Gerard thought it was particularly good for "short-

nesse of breath" and an old cough and for "such as cannot breathe unlesse they hold their neckes upright."

FUMITORY. *Fumaria officinalis*—the name "fumaria"
meaning "earth smoke" comes from the resemblance of the
plant to rising smoke. From the first century prized for its
purifying value, often being smoked for head disorders. In
the Nun's Priest's Tale of the *Canterbury Tales,* Dame
Partlet scorns Chanticleer's terrible forebodings springing from bad dreams. The good hen-wife says that all he
needs is a purging of his system with spurg, laurel, cen-
taury, fumitory or hellebore. Parkinson claimed that the
juice of fumitory dropped in the eyes "will take away redness and other defects, although it procure some paine for
the present and bringeth forth tears."

HOREHOUND. *Marrubium vulgare*—a time honored
herb for diseases of the chest. Walafrid Strabo in his
Little Garden (ninth century) praised horehound tea
above most other herb remedies. In the *Toilet of Flora*
of the eighteenth century we find horehound used as a snuff.

LAVENDER. *Lavandula vera*—a narcotic poison in large
doses, Culpeper says the oil is of a fierce and piercing
quality and ought to be carefully used, a very few drops
being sufficient for inward or outward maladies. Gerard said that "distilled water of the herb smelt and
the temples and forehead bathed is refreshing, but when
there is abundance of humours, it is not then to be used
safely or any composition infused with spice." William
Turner in his Herbal gives a headache cure which may not
be looked upon with favor by our modern men: "I judge
that the flowers of Lavender quilted in a cap and dayley
worne are good for all diseases of the head that they comfort the braine very well." In the World War lavender
was valued as an antiseptic for swabbing wounds.

LOVAGE. *Levisticum officinale*—was recommended by Samuel Johnson to Bennet Langton for rheumatism and much used from medieval to Stuart times for soothing, aromatic baths. Culpeper claimed it removed spots and freckles from the face while "the leaves bruised and fried in hog's lard and laid hot to any blotch or boil will break it."

MARSHMALLOW. *Althaea officinalis*—takes its place as a medicinal herb because of the mucilaginous quality of the root. Pliny said, "Whoever shall take a spoonful of the Mallow shall that day be free from all diseases that may come to him."

PENNYROYAL. *Hedeoma pulegioides*—American or mock pennyroyal or *Mentha pulegium* (English pennyroyal). Our grandmothers made many a cup of pennyroyal tea for measles and whooping cough or concocted a lotion of it and other herbs and cream, to be smeared over the face and arms to discourage insects when the family went a-berrying or fishing. Gerard mentions a sort of amulet, reminiscent of the Saxon customs: "A garland of pennyroyal made and worn about the head is of a great force against the swimming in the head, the paines and giddiness thereof."

PEPPERMINT. *Mentha piperita*—was known even to the Chaldeans as a healing herb having a good effect on the digestive organs. Parkinson recommended its use in "Baths with Balm and other herbs as a help to comfort and strengthen the nerves and sinews and weak stomachs," while Culpeper mentions forty uses.

TANSY. *Tanacetum vulgare*—was brought by the colonists from Europe and has been considered a remedy for such varied ills as bruises, freckles, sunburn, hysteria, sprains and rheumatism. The people in southern England used to wear the leaves in their shoes as a charm against the ague.

THOROUGHWORT. *Eupatorium perfoliatum*—commonly known as boneset. When children, if feeling a little droopy, our restoration to health was almost instantaneous upon the suggestion of boneset tea. So just for old times' sake—our personal old times' sake—let's grow boneset.

WORMWOOD. *Artemisia Absinthium*—was declared by Dioscorides to be a good remedy against intoxication. An old time remedy for gout, rheumatism, indigestion and sluggish livers. It was a great favorite as a strewing herb in those days of unsanitary conditions. Thomas Tusser in 1573 considered it excellent, as we see in his advice for July:

> While Wormwood hath seed, get a handful or twaine,
> To save against March, to make flea to refrain:
> When chamber is sweeped, and wormwood is strown,
> No flea, for his life, dare abide to be known.

YARROW. *Achillea Millefolium*—was called, in the old days of tournaments, "soldier's woundwort" or "knight's milfoil" because it was the basis of a healing ointment made in every castle and monastery, as the men came straggling back home wounded, sometimes to the death. The Indians used it for earache and swollen tissues. Our grandmothers sometimes made a tea of the leaves for a feverish cold or when grandfather's rheumatism was particularly bad.

In planting these sixteen simples, all perennials, we must be sure to set them out early enough to get a good start before the heavy frosts begin. When spring comes, the plants will be coming up as though they had always lived in their rectangular plots. The tall herbs will be at the back and the shorter ones in front. As William Lawson in the *Country Housewife* (1617) described the height of his plants, so I would arrange these simples:

Of Great Growth—comfrey, elecampane, lovage, marsh-mallow, tansy;

Of Middle Growth—betony, chamomile, horehound, peppermint, thoroughwort, wormwood, yarrow;

Of Smaller Growth—coltsfoot, fumitory, lavender, pennyroyal.

As I read over these pages, I feel that the Preface of William Coles, *The Art of Simpling*, 1656, would be appropriate for this chapter, too:

I have in it communicated such Notions as I have gathered, either from the reading of Severall Authors, or by conferring sometimes with Scholars, and sometimes with Country people; to which I have added some Observations of mine Owne, never before published: Most of which I am confident are true, and if there be any that are not so, yet they are pleasant.

CHAPTER VII

A GARDEN OF SYMBOLISM

To him who in the love of Nature holds
Communion with her visible forms, she speaks
A various language; for his gayer hours
She has a voice of gladness and a smile
And eloquence of beauty, and she glides
Into his darker musings, with a mild
And healing sympathy, that steals away
Their sharpness, ere he is aware.
—WILLIAM CULLEN BRYANT, "Thanatopsis" (1817)

"The Language of the Flowers," *Flora's Dictionary*—
Some rainy day when you are browsing in the attic among
the old books long banished from your library, I am sure
you will come across at least one such title reminiscent of
mid-Victorian sentiment. You may laugh, but that will be
from lack of real understanding of those slow moving
days of our grandmothers and greatgrandmothers when
the accepted reality of Hollywood romances was not
theirs to take seriously as we do now. There was a simplicity of life that we may smile at, but that we should
not scorn.

What romances were begun, and carried to happy or
unhappy endings through the sweet language of flowers
rather than by cold prosaic words composed of dull letters
of the alphabet. What a help to shy Victorian lovers and
others who often hated to call a spade a spade!

A little fragrant bouquet, in the seventeenth century called a tussie-mussie or nosegay by John Parkinson in his *Paradisus* (1629), was often sent not only for "Sight and Smell" by the lover but for a message to his lady love. The old-fashioned tussie-mussie was a cluster of flowers with the center one the most important in sentiment as well as in fragrance. The intended message was emphasized by surrounding flowers and fragrant leaves of similar import. The bouquet was placed in an elaborate filigree holder which, in later ages, became the prim little lace paper doilies.

A man might send a maid a nosegay composed of a dwarf sunflower (your devout adorer); Austrian rose (thou art all that's lovely); scarlet ranunculus (I am dazzled by your charm), and pelargonium quercifolium (Lady, deign to smile). A bit gaudy, to be sure, but the love-sick suitor would at least get his ideas across that way. Or he could send a red tulip (declaration of love) and jonquils (I desire a return of affection). If he chose to send a valentine not complimentary, there was always the Queen's Rocket (you are the queen of coquettes) or lady's slipper (capricious beauty). The lady could answer by a single flower denoting the status of her feelings—spiderwort (I esteem but do not love you), yellow rose (the decrease of love on better acquaintance), dogwood (indifference), or a single China aster (I will think of it). If the lady downright rejected the suitor, she could send him a variegated pink or the iceplant blossom. Perhaps the lover overdid the sentiment, protested too much, and she raised her eyebrows in suspicion. Then back would go a yellow hyacinth (the heart demands other incense than flattery).

Do not think for a moment that the language of flowers had its origin in the sentiment and sensibility of the mid-

Victorians. It boasts of an etymology and philology with stems and roots extending to the earliest of all chronicles, those of the Chinese. Plants were given names according to their outstanding peculiarity of form, odor, habits, and it was but a short step to making those names the symbol for the characteristic. Thus, the significance of the mandrake with its roots supposedly resembling the form of a man, and uttering a terrifying shriek as it was uprooted, soon became synonymous with horror. Definite use was made of these plant symbols long before the appearance of other symbols, words made up of letters to express what we would like to say. Primitive people, close to nature, said it in flowers and herbs—a lovely way of running the whole gamut of emotions, from the aesthetic, spiritual feelings to grim earthy hatred.

We have many evidences of this symbolism in the simple representations of plants in old temples, monuments, walls of caves, wherever there are relics of the ancient days of India, Assyria, Egypt, Persia, Japan, China, Greece. The lily with yellow anthers removed signified virginity. The lotus flower in which it was believed Brahma was born, became the symbol of reproduction. In the Far East the rose stood for virtue; in Egypt for silence; in Rome for festivity, while in later centuries it has always symbolized love. In general white flowers represented light and innocence, dark ones denoted sinister deeds and death, while blue flowers were for loyalty —"true blue," as we have come to say.

Both the Chinese and Japanese have long had an elaborate system of communication by floral signs, called "florigraphy." In the Arabian peninsula every object in life has a significant meaning, every plant stands for some attribute, but the basis for their symbolism is unusual. It does not lie within the plant, but takes its meaning from that of a word with which the plant name rhymes. An orange, for instance, is a popular gift because their word for "orange" rhymes with one meaning "lucky." The English translation, "I, Borage, bring alwaies courage" of the Latin rhyme "Ego Borago, Gaudia semper ago" is reminiscent of the system. In this case, however, the qualities of exhilaration and merry spirits produced by borage concoctions tend to produce courage and this, rather than the rhyme among the English, no doubt, accounted for the symbol.

The Romans have never seemed to go in for plant symbolism to any great extent, but the Greeks had a system of florigraphy carried out in fine detail. They could thereby not only express their personal feelings of joy, gratitude, happiness, hatred, but also carry on the affairs of state, religion and sports by sending floral messages of national or international importance. In Turkish harems, too, communications were often made by floral code.

In early days the French emphasized the use of color for symbolic meanings in their daily life, and since the language of flowers was important in France as elsewhere, the color of flowers took on a special significance. Since the color red was symbolic of love and the flower rose was also, a lover sending his sweetheart a red rose expressed his sentiments with a double force. Knights literally bore their feelings on their sleeves by wearing a certain flower or a nosegay of many colored ones. Sometimes the number of petals or leaves indicated the symbolism, three being important because of its representing not only the Holy Trinity, but also the whole of life—beginning, middle, and end. The shamrock with three leaves was sacred, and the pansy with three petals was sometimes called Herb

Trinity. The plants of the family Cruciferae, those with flower petals arranged in the shape of a cross—mustard, cabbage, turnip, radish—were considered signs of the Redemption.

Flowers of the daisy type were symbols of the sun, and later were considered as good omens for fortune telling. It is still practiced by staid adults, presumably old enough to know better, as they pull off the petals of a daisy one by one with the traditional chant, "He loves me, he loves me not."

Sometimes flowers symbolic of abstract qualities, virtues and vices, were used by maids and swains to determine the character of the loved one. The lover perhaps would draw a slip of paper from several on which were written names of flowers, and whichever one he drew, he would definitely know by its significance the outstanding characteristic of his sweetheart. If he drew the flower wild pink, she was silly; blue cornflower indicated she was loquacious; jasmine, cheerful; lily, sincere. Perhaps that is as sure a system as any for a lover to determine the true, inward qualities of his sweetheart.

From early times much attention to the language of flowers has been paid by poets who have attached symbols of their own invention to suit their purpose in poetry. Between lovers have been personal secret floral codes. Still others have composed dictionaries of flower language. I have come across a *Lexicon of Ladies' Names—162 Names with Their Significations,* each name represented by some flower with symbolic meaning. Another dictionary was *The Bouquet: containing the poetry and language of flowers.* But too many such books have departed far from the traditional symbols that have been in common flower parlance for centuries. It is all too much in the manner of

Humpty Dumpty who said to Alice, "When I use a word, it means just what I choose it to mean."

We find the true origin of the symbolism of some herbs and flowers obvious from their color and nature. Sometimes it lies far back in mythology, ancient folklore or medieval personages or events. Some plant language is so plain that it needs no further explanation, such as "usefulness" the symbol for grass, "frugality" for chicory, "oblivion" for the opium poppy, "true love" for forget-me-not. In the East aloe is a religious symbol for bitterness and grief, and the Mohammedans rooted a plant of it by the graves of loved ones.

The symbolism of many herbs is not quite so obvious but is still readily understood. Patriotism has long been the symbol for the nasturtium with leaves shield-like in shape and flowers resembling tiny burnished helmets. Balsam stands for impatience, that seeming irritability shown by the seeds as they burst forth from the dried pod at the touch of your fingers. The lily-of-the-valley is easily accepted as the symbol of "Return of Happiness" because of its early blooming in spring, when our hopes are renewed along with the new vigor of the vegetation all about us. Sweet brier or eglantine means pleasure mixed with pain, naturally enough from the delightfully sweet appeal of the leaves to the nose and the many tiny pricks painful to the touch. I wonder whether a pun was intended in the symbol of "Flee away" for pennyroyal, used for centuries to drive away fleas!

The significance of certain herbs is a little more subtle but still easy enough to understand when one learns the characteristics or uses. If you have ever smelled the rank odor of the fresh plant and seeds of coriander, you would never believe that the dried seeds are so fragrant that they were practically always an ingredient of Elizabethan sweet bags and pot pourri. Experiencing the odors of both fresh and dried seeds, you can easily imagine why the plant is symbolic of "hidden merit." Chamomile was "sweetness of humility" from its characteristic of rising serenely again in a path after being flattened by footsteps. In a play, *The More the Merrier* (1608) we find:

> The Camomile shall teach thee patience
> Which riseth best when trodden most upon.

St. John's Wort was early called the herb of war. In medieval tournaments, before the knights engaged in combat, each one was obliged to take an oath that he had no bit of St. John's Wort about his person. Since it was a vulnerary herb, it was thought to be able to call down the evil spirits and invite the wounds that the herb would heal. We would call it "tempting Providence."

Dyer's Bugloss obtained the symbolism of falsehood after it was discovered that the red coloring matter obtained from the roots was excellent for the rouge used by court ladies to give a deceitful color to cheek and lip. Dame's Rocket also stands for falsehood or deceit because the odor, like white nicotiana, is wafted on the air only in the shadows of the night. The symbolism of rosemary followed readily from the old belief that the plant not only restored physical energy, but as Culpeper says, "It helps a weak memory," and thus one would be more fitted to remember. Hence, a symbol for remembrance and constancy. Sir Thomas More said, " 'Tis the herb sacred to remembrance and therefore to friendship, whence a sprig of it hath a dumb language that maketh it the chosen emblem of our funeral wakes and in our burial grounds." But sprigs of rosemary were also carried and worn at weddings by both bride and groom. Robert Hacket (1607) said in his sermon to a couple he was marrying, "Let this Rosmarinus, this flower of men, ensigne of your wisdom, love and loyaltie, be carried not only in your hands, but in your heads and harts."

Repentance as the symbol of rue seemingly resulted from an uncertainty about its botanical name, *ruta,* which never has been satisfactorily explained—some say that it came from a Greek word "to free," because of its almost universal use for freeing from contagion. Indeed, the family of *rutaceae* contains trees and shrubs of over 100 genera which have medicinal properties. Whatever it may have originally meant in the classic language, "ruta" to the English sounded like "rue," their word for remorse or repentance and especially appropriate for such a bitter tasting plant. After awhile from being an herb of Repentance, it became the herb of Grace.

When we think now of heliotrope, we picture "cherry pie," the very sweet scented plant found in all old-fashioned gardens. But in early days the name heliotrope ("helio" from the Greek word for "sun," "trope" from the verb "to turn") was used to apply to many plants with flowers turning toward the sun all day. Such were marigolds and sunflowers. From that constancy came their symbolic meaning of "constancy in love."

Fennel was one of the herbs used in the ancient rites in celebration of Adonis, spirit of vegetation. On that particular day in midsummer, among all the quick germinating plants that had been cherished for the celebration, fennel was quite spectacular but withered before nightfall. This characteristic of "here today and gone tomorrow" made it the symbol of flattery. A Roman expression for flattery was "dare finocchio," to give fennel. In the seven-

teenth century, in Ben Jonson's *The Case Altered,* we find
Christopher saying, "No, my good lord," and the Count
resenting it: *"Your* good lord! O, this smells of Fennel!"

The symbolism of many herbs seems to be unknown in
origin, sometimes quite opposite or different in meaning
according to the country. In Greece parsley was the herb
for great occasions, and the plants were made into wreaths
for banquet guests—to discourage intoxication—and at
the Isthmian games to reward victors. Yet parsley also
was strewn over the bodies and graves of the dead. An
interesting bit of symbolic language came from the custom of planting parsley and rue along the edges of herb
beds. It became a common expression to speak of the be-
ginnings of an enterprise as "being at the parsley and
rue."

Basil is symbolic of love in Italy, of hatred in Greece.
It has been thought by some writers that basil came to
mean hatred from the old custom in painting to represent
poverty by a seated figure of a woman in rags with a plant
of basil near by.

The symbolism of several herbs is fascinating because
of religious or romantic associations. Broom was long regarded as an herb of humility from the belief that as
Christ was praying in the Garden of Gethsemane, the
guards under cover of the noise made by the motion of
the stiff branches of the plant, were able to come unnoticed
upon Him. Because of Christ's sorrowful chiding of the
plants, broom ever afterwards was the embodiment of
humility.

In classic days myrtle was sacred to Venus whose temples were in myrtle groves and became so commonly a
symbol of love that for many centuries myrtle was used
with roses in wedding ceremonies. Ivy was a symbol of

constancy from its habit of clinging to old ruins of buildings long after they had been abandoned by people. The thought of the constancy of ivy has been embodied in the story of Tristram and Iseult—the tragic lovers unhappily parted by death but buried side by side. Over each grave a plant of ivy began to grow and continued toward the other until the vines became entwined. So the two lovers were again united by the constancy of the ivy.

Much use was made of the language of herbs not only by the "courtier, soldier, scholar," but by the master of drama Shakespeare. In *Hamlet* heartbroken Ophelia with her pitiful imaginary basket of flowers distributed each herb deliberately with meanings that no Elizabethan would fail to recognize. Apparently in her disordered mind, mistaking her brother for Hamlet, Ophelia offers Laertes rosemary for faithful remembrance and pansies for love's sad thoughts or troubles—

Ophelia: "There's rosemary, that's for remembrance; pray you, love, remember: and there is pansies, that's for thoughts."
Laertes: "A document in madness, thoughts and remembrance fitted."

Then to Claudius she presents fennel to represent the dissembling and flattery with which he beguiled not only the queen, but Polonius, her father recently murdered perhaps, Ophelia thinks, by the king. She also gives him columbine because of his seducing the queen. To her, Ophelia offers rue to be worn by the queen as a sign of contrition but by her, herself, as a symbol of grief over the death of her father. The daisy represented the wantonness of the queen. The violets may have been blue or white; if blue, for loyalty; if white, for innocence of guilt. Small wonder they withered!

Ophelia: "There's fennel for you and columbines; there's rue for you; and here's some for me: we may call it herb of grace o' Sundays: O, you must wear your rue with a difference. There's a daisy: I would give you some violets, but they withered all when my father died: they say he made a good end."

If you are casting about for something especially novel for your herb garden or a part of it, a plot of symbolic herbs would be the thing. One of my friends, with the roots of happy memory deep in the lovely recollection of childhood hours spent among her grandmother's fragrant herbs, started a garden of remembrance for a dear relative when he went off to the World War. She began with borage for courage, an inspiration, I think. As time went on, the herbs increased to some two score varieties.

I have appended a list compiled from numerous sources of the "Language of the Herbs." From this list you could choose the thoughts and feelings you would like to perpetuate and group them together in perhaps just a corner of your garden. The labels you can make as simple or as elaborate as you like. You could have a rather wide oblong label with the name of the herb at the top and its significance written underneath. Or you could do as the Countess of Warwick did in the nineties. She made a label in the shape of the two wings of a bird; on the left side the name of the herb; on the other wing the symbolism.

You will find this garden a delight to plan and work out and later to be of utmost interest to herb lovers. Wandering through the garden, they will discover with joy that they are truly in an enchanted spot,

Where more is meant than meets the ear.

CHAPTER VIII

A GARDEN OF HERBS
OF A GOOD SMELL

If odours, or if taste may worke satisfaction, they are both so
soveraigne in plants, and so comfortable, that no confection of the
Apothecaries can equall their excellent vertue. But these delights
are in the outward senses: the principall delight is in the minde,
singularly enriched with the knowledge of these visible things, setting foorth to us the invisible workmanship of almightie God.
—GERARD, Preface to the "Herball" (1597)

From the time man first breathed—perhaps in the fragrant Garden of Eden where his Creator had placed him—
sweet odors have been most comfortable delights both to
the outward and inward senses. When Gerard wrote his
Preface, he was uttering convictions not only arising from
intuitive feelings of the untaught of ages past but on which
was based scientific research of centuries yet to come.

In early days, it was thought that disease was caused by
foul odors, a vaporous contribution of "wykked sperytes"
to man. In an effort to nullify or ward off the evil effects,
people enveloped themselves in an aura of sweetly aromatic scents by the use of perfumes and clouds of incense
so remarkably refreshing and stimulating to body and
spirits that no disease could penetrate. In ancient Greece
the living rooms opened on beautiful gardens where the
most fragrant plants were planted near the windows in

the belief that the scent had a salutary effect on the occupants of the house. In medieval monasteries the monks planted near the infirmary sweet smelling herbs for the benefit of their patients, and now modern science has given us reason to believe that health-giving ozone is developed from the sun's shining on the aromatic plants.

What with the universal lack of sanitation and an amazing insensitiveness to the crude methods of housekeeping, we may well wonder that anyone survived the primitive way of life in medieval England. But many a community and isolated household were often saved from devastating plagues and epidemics by perfumes, spices and strewing herbs used lavishly to spite the old Debbil, Disease.

The early doctors advised the continual smelling of aromatic herbs and they themselves in visiting patients carried nosegays of herbs. In later years they carried walking sticks with the top, a perforated metal ball, pressed full of herbs and spices. Bunches of rue and rosemary were placed on the Judge's bench to ward off possible contagion of jail fever. People in mingling with crowds carried handfuls of herbs in which they buried their noses, or held in their hands spicy pomanders of which they took long breaths.

When you were a child, did a playmate ever say to you as you were breathing in deeply the fragrance of a lovely rose, "You'll take all the smell out of it?" I used to wonder about it myself but quite recently science has given me an answer. Indeed, I did take in actual molecules of a fragrant flower. An experiment was made by sprinkling talcum powder over a small pool of mercury, and when a rose petal was held above the surface without touching the talc, the latter moved to the edge of the pool. This, the scientist said, was caused by the odor of the rose spreading over

Moat Between Castle Walls
from Gerard, 1597.

the mercury. When with two glass rods he pushed together the sides of this "odor layer" which was invisible, the odor of rose was definitely noticed. When the one molecule layer collected into a sort of pile, some of the odor rose again into the air. Since science has thus shown the odor to be a material part of the plant and herbs are known to have antiseptic qualities, the early doctors have been thus vindicated in prescribing herbs of a good smell to be applied to the nose.

Many a time in olden days, meats became long over-ripe before being used and consequently smelled "to high heaven." The cook, however, in preparing the meat used an abundance of aromatic herbs and spices, which thereby diminished to a great extent the harmful effects and rendered the food more palatable.

In our sanitary age of living, we do not use food with the kind of odor that has to be masked before it can be eaten. On the contrary, we season dishes in order to bring out the original flavor, which is enjoyed by us as an olfactory sensation in the process of exhalation when food is in the mouth. Around meal time, have you ever heard the outside door open and shut and then an enthusiastic voice, "My, something smells good! I'm hungry"? Then we often say, "I hope it will taste as good as it smells." As cooks, we should not undervalue that two-fold pleasure of the sense of smell that can be enjoyed in a culinary dish, properly seasoned with sweet herbs.

Certainly these delights of herbs are in the outward senses. But what about the "principall delight" which is "in the minde?" Ralph Austen in his *Treatise of Fruit-Trees* (1653) said, "Sweet perfumes work immediately upon the spirits for their refreshing; sweet and healthfull ayres are special preservatives to health and therefore much to be prised." Truly, the old herbalists believed in the healing effects of aromatic herbs upon ills of the spirit as well as those of the body. We read of scores of herbs to make one merry, to drive away heaviness of mind, to cure overmuch sighing, to strengthen the memory. Although we do not hold with such miraculous cures for sick minds and hearts now, we do appreciate the stimulating effects of sharp odors on fainting spirits as is attested by a whiff of smelling salts, or of quieter odors upon tense nerves. If you seem to be in for a sleepless night put a drop or two of perfume on your upper lip just under your nose; after that the sheep will have to count themselves as they go over the fence.

The sense of smell is not only the only one of the five senses to which man reacts without conscious effort but is the only one which he cannot refuse so long as he lives. He may close his ears to music, shut his eyes from fine paintings, stay his hand from the textures of silks or velvets, refuse to taste the specially prepared delicacy. But odors are received whether he will or not, and only if he is aware can he escape and then but temporarily.

Odors grasp and hold our imagination and memory. Above all others, the fragrances of green growing herbs, not gaudy or showy, but comfortable and homey, have the power to cast a spell over us so that we recall only the pleasant past, with all the sharp hard corners of grief and sadness softened. *"And there came a smell off the Shore like the Smell of a Garden."* Thus John Winthrop wrote in his Journal after those dreary, dangerous weeks on the Stormy Atlantic in the little boat with the brave band of Pilgrims. What nostalgic memories for those garden-loving English. What pictures rushed to their minds of those formal walled gardens fragrant with flowers and herbs! "The Smell of a Garden!" From all the old unhappy days they had left in their homeland, the dear memory of their beloved gardens remained beautiful and to be perpetuated. We find the first entry in the Plymouth records to be an assignment of meresteads *and* garden plots. Beautiful memories, high hopes for the future— these are the "principall delights" of what Richard Sur- flet in his *Maison Rustique* (1600) calls the "Garden for hearbes of a good smell."

Our Puritan ancestors were so harried clearing wilder- ness, building shelter, growing food and making clothing, that they never did materialize their plans for replicas of the lovely Elizabethan gardens they had left. They or we could never wholly duplicate such havens of delight, but even in this far removed century we may catch and hold in a garden of our own making somewhat of the spirit. The Elizabethan garden was a long time a-grow- ing, a climax of centuries of gardens, an unbroken con- tinuity of fragrant tradition.

In the far-away and long ago, there were but few varieties of flowering plants in comparison with the be- wildering number we see advertised in our beautifully illustrated modern catalogues. Those precious flowers were jealously protected, often as offerings to the gods, and grave was the punishment for anyone bold enough to smell of the sacred gifts, thereby robbing the deities of some of the fragrance. True enough the bold criminal sniffer actually with one good inhalation might have robbed the deity of several molecules of odor intended for him alone!

Herbs and flowers were used lavishly in the decoration of temples and in garlands for priests on feast days, just as later in the Christian era they were raised for the adornment of churches and chaplets for churchmen on holy days. Within the limited space bounded by monastery walls besides the plots for vegetables, culinary and medicinal herbs, there was an area allotted to these fragrant plants devotedly tended for sacred use by the monks.

In early days of feudalism when castles were little more than garrisons, garden plots were but a few yards square, but how thriftly planted with aromatic herbs and anxiously tended against the time when they would be harvested— raw material for salves, sirups, electuaries to heal knights and vassals, home from just another fight. No space within those narrow walls for a garden of merely ornamental flowers but, for the most part, those useful necessary herbs were fragrant—lavender, rosemary, violets, lilies of the valley, roses. By the thirteenth century, however, within every castle wall or outer moat, where space permitted, was the nucleus of the later pleasure gardens—the pleas-aunce or orchard with a turfed area and fountain or tree in the middle, while along the walls was a continuous garden seat of banked-up earth, turfed and planted with uncultivated flowers. A circular turfed seat was sometimes built around a tree and held in place by wattles with projecting ends but in contemporary pictures, the people chattering together do not appear to be suffering. Dr. Crisp in his *Mediaeval Gardens* suspects "an unwonted cuticular toughness peculiar to the Middle Ages." The flowers scattered through the "flowery mede" or turfed area are not ground cover but daisies, corn-flowers, poppies. The people must have been of ethereal weight, or else the gardeners must have had a busy time the day after a garden party in propping up the flowers not hopelessly crushed!

After the War of the Roses when castles were no longer fortified, the gardens spread out somewhat, but a good share of the features characteristic of the Middle Ages lingered on well into the seventeenth century. The turf-covered seats, for instance, found as early as the twelfth century are still noticed in garden pictures of the Victorian Age. We still find wattle fences, inner boundaries of lattice work, raised beds, astonishing topiary work, central fountains. In the Elizabethan Age, that great period of expansion, commercial, intellectual, domestic, with the importation of new customs from the Continent, the narrow insular scope of thought broadened. With the defeat of the Spanish Armada (1588), the Elizabethan gentleman felt himself a vicarious hero, swaggering about physically, mentally, emotionally. Gardening was an excellent vehicle in which to "show off" and lucky was the man who had money. Elizabethan architecture had expanded with the times, and far from being a glowering garrison, the typical house spread out in the form of a letter E or H, all right angles. The plan of the garden conformed to that of the house.

From the terrace in front of the house, one could look over the whole garden which in the best gardening tradition was square or rectangular. "Forthrights" or broad walks connected house and garden and ran the length of the latter, while smaller paths connected sections within the garden and a fountain graced the center. The walks were usually of chamomile for its fragrant scent when trodden under foot. The seventeenth century John Evelyn in his *Kalendarium Hortense* for October advises:

It will now be good to Beat, Roll and Mow carpet Walks and camomile, for now the ground is supple and it will even all Inequalities.

Around three sides of the brick wall was a gallery (an "herber" as Thomas Hyll called it) covered by rosemary, jasmine or musk roses trained to grow over the framework. At the corners would be arbors, while on the fourth side would be a long earthen seat turfed with chamomile and fragrant herbs. Sections of the garden were separated, not only by paths but by low, well-clipped hedges of herbs such as lavender, sage, rosemary, southernwood or lavender cotton. The garden displayed a bewildering variety of adornment. Usually there was a "mount," simply earth banked up high enough to permit of a view from the jasmine or honeysuckle covered summer house on top. Through the garden might flow several little winding streams, or a fish pond might be unexpectedly discovered. There were mazes, labyrinths, parterres and knotted beds filled with colored sands to emphasize the patterns made by the ribbons of herbs. There were stone or lead vases, bits of colored glass mounted on sticks to shine among the green foliage, and probably a sundial, so popular at this time. Most astonishing, but greatly favored by Queen Elizabeth, were the life-size, carved wooden figures of animals—predecessors of the startling iron deer and dogs on Victorian lawns. Similar figures were evolved in topiary work and in Lawson's plan of a Yorkshire garden (1617) we see an unharnessed prancing horse with his master, the latter, however, in full armor and very long sword decidedly "rampant." (See Lawson's ideal garden Chapter III.)

In this glorious Elizabethan Age we find definite attempts at division of plants in the garden, in the isolation of vegetables, herbs, and now for the first time ornamental flowers, a difficult task since heretofore there had been little distinction between vegetables and herbs and between herbs and flowers. Lawson, in *The Country Housewife's Garden* (1617), recognized the difficulty in his confusing statement of explanation:

Herbes are of two sorts, and therefore it is meete (they requiring divers manners of Husbandry) that we have two Gardens; A Garden for flowers, and a Kitchen garden; or a Summer garden; not that wee meane so perfect a distinction, that the Garden for flowers should or can bee without herbs good for the Kitchin, or the Kitchin garden should want flowers, nor on the contrary; but for the most part they would bee severed: first, because your Garden flowers shall suffer some disgrace, if among them you intermingle Onions, Parsnips, etc.

Assailed on all sides by a blend of foul odors which they seemed to accept as inevitable, the Elizabethans perhaps felt they could draw the line at onions, quite mild, one would think, compared to the open sewage system in the city streets or no system at all in the country.

Parkinson in 1629 also felt that "the many different sents that arise from the herbs as cabbages, onions, etc. are scarce well pleasing to perfume the lodging of any house," and therefore he would place the kitchen garden on the other side of the house from the flower garden and away from "the best and choyse rooms."

During the early seventeenth century, along with the feeling of security of freedom from fears of "malice domestic or foreign levy" there was a general spiritual expansion and exuberance. The Elizabethan gentleman found a great outlet for his surplus energy in gardening. We see him eager for the new in everything, on the watch for new varieties of plants and flowers that garden minded explorers brought back from their voyages. Parkinson lists some of these "outlandish" flowers as being valued for "giving the beauty and bravery of their colours so early before many of our owne bred flowers—Daffodils, Fritillarias, Iacinthes, Saffron-flowers, Lillies, Flower de luces, Tulipas, Anemones, French Cowslips, or Beareseares, and a number of such other flowers—they are almost in all places with all persons, especially with the better sort of the Gentry of the Land." For these extra-special plants and the "floweryest" of the old time herbs, the Elizabethans now instituted an innovation, a plot for flowers

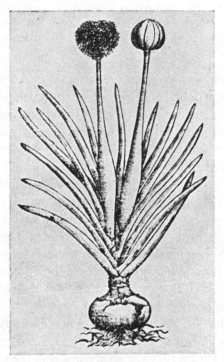

White Onions
from Gerard's *Herball,* 1597.

alone, variously named by gardening writers of that time as the *Summer Garden* by William Lawson, the *Garden of Pleasure* by Parkinson, *The Summer Garden* or the *Garden of Pleasure and Delight* by Thomas Hyll, *Garden for flowers and sweet smells* by Gervase Markham. A new era for gardeners began.

Richard Surflet in the *Maison Rustique* (1600) says:

The Garden shall be divided into two equall parts; the one shall containe the hearbes and flowers used to make nosegaies and garlands. . . . The other part shall have all the sweet smelling hearbes, whether they be such as beare no flowers, or if they beare any, yet they are not put in Nosegaies alone, but the whole hearbe with them . . . and this may be called the Garden for hearbs of a good smell.

Nowadays, our conception of a Garden of Pleasure and Delight would be just that with no thought for the morrow. The garden would be formed to feast your eyes and nose but with no ulterior, utilitarian purpose. As I read the books of Elizabethan and Stuart gardening writers, I always am impressed by the thought that there still lingered that old feeling of necessity for thrifty planting and harvesting of herbs, a feeling inherited from gardeners in those early garrison-castles where space was at a premium. Still unaccustomed to spacious garden areas to play with, the Elizabethan "moderns" did not yet feel easy about plots of flowers just to look at and to smell. They were not like Ferdinand! Their thoughts lingered on the usefulness of what was grown.

Unlike the *Theatrum Botanicum* definitely an herbal, Parkinson's *Paradisi in Sole* was largely devoted to the "Garden of Pleasure," yet so strong was the utilitarian instinct that the author suggests thriftily that the clippings of aromatic herbs used in borders, mazes, labyrinths, knots and parterres, could well be used for strewing. A good idea, so twentieth century-ized, and we can have a grand smelling open fire by drying such clippings and strewing them on the blaze. Most amusing to me about the *Paradisus* is the herbalist's routine in discussing each plant for

The Pleasure Garden
from title page of Dodoens, 1644.

the garden of pleasure—the kinds, the place, the time, and the "Vertues." Parkinson feels called upon to mention useful qualities, even though they be negative. Of basil, he says:

The ordinary Basill is in a manner wholly spent to make sweet, or washing waters, among other sweet herbes, yet sometimes it is put into nosegayes. The Physicall [medicinal] properties are, to procure a cheerefull and merry heart, whereunto the seede is chiefly used to that, and to no other purpose.

For the "Willowe flower" we read:

There is no use hereof in Physicke that ever I could learne, but is onely cherished among other sorts of flowers, that serve to decke and set forth a Garden of varieties.

But for snapdragon, "They are seldome or never used in Physicke by any in our dayes" and for Sweet William, "We have not knowne any of these used in Physicke."

William Lawson also seemed strictly utilitarian at heart though he accepted the ornamental flower plot. Here is what he says:

Though your Garden for flowers doth in a sort peculiarly challenge to it selfe a profit, and exquisite forme to the eyes, yet you may not altogether neglect this, where your herbs for the pot doe grow: And therefore some here make comely borders with the herbes aforesaid. The rather because abundance of Roses and Lavender, yeeld much profit, and comfort to the senses: Rose-water, Lavender, the one cordiall (as also the Violets; Burrage [borage] and Bugloss) the other reviving the spirits by the sence of smelling, both most durable for smell, both in flowers and water.

We can, however, appreciate this feeling of necessity for thrifty gardening when we realize the problems of the Elizabethan housewife. How she must have worried and wondered however she could raise enough herbs and flowers, in spite of extensive acreage and flowering hedges in addition to the formal garden near the house. It was a century for extravagant use of herbs for sweet scents— for perfuming shoes, gloves, jackets, linen, clothes, tobacco, snuff, candles, soap, but still it was long before the period of commercial manufacture. Consequently the housewife herself, with her maids, not only made these perfumes but all cosmetic, medicinal and household preparations, mouthwaters, hand lotions, cosmetic powders, bath powders, moth preventives, sweet bags, ointments, aromatic vinegars, sirups, electuaries. The Elizabethans, characteristic of the English of all centuries, shunned heavy oriental scents, preferring aromatic herb and refreshing flower scents from their own gardens.

In reading the lists of ingredients in some of the old recipes, we cannot even visualize the harvest necessary, especially as we contemplate the possible yield of our own modest gardens—four pounds of orange flowers for orange flower water, a bushel of roses for potpourri; 1000 damask roses for "sweet water of the best kind," a pound of rosebuds for oil of roses, a pound of violet flowers for sirup of violets. Can you imagine the fragrance of the Elizabethan garden?

We today can have a garden with "hearbes of a good smell," a potpourri of sweet odors. We would derive much more enjoyment from life if we cultivated our noses. We spend hours learning how to appreciate music or painting, we train ourselves to distinguish between textures of fabrics, to develop a taste for unusual foods, but the sense of smell we just take for granted and do nothing to sharpen or cultivate it. To satisfy flower growers new formations have been made in the shape of flowers, pointed petal petunias, shaggy zinnias, chrysanthemum-like marigolds. Great effort has been made to produce larger blooms, to add new colors, yellow asters, red morning glories. Infinite study has been made to produce disease-resistant flowers. No one yet has insisted that the hybridizers retain the scent of the flowers. There we have lost interest and what becomes of the old-fashioned scents? Where can they be found but in "old-fashioned flowers?"

You will find yourself vastly enriched by the time you devote to learning to discriminate odors in your garden. As your interest deepens, you will find yourself able to notice differences of which you had been unaware before. And what a really intelligent and aesthetic appeal your plants will have. You will be amazed during your pursuit of the fascinating study of plant odors, how different they smell in different locations in the garden, in dry soil or moist, in the morning and at night. The white flowered nicotiana, so sweet during the day, the red variety shedding its sweet perfume only at night. Night in a garden! And what an unforgettably sweet fragrance sweet brier has after a summer shower.

Your garden of "hearbes of a good smell," if you like, may be a fragrant retreat, distinctly yours, different from any other garden. It may be a haven, inclosed literally to be sure, by a hedge, fence, or wall, but more than that, spiritually it will be sanctuary from the world crowded with problems, worries, troubles, a peaceful haven in which to untangle tied up nerve strings from our modern way of hurry to do so much in so little time. William Lawson, back in the seventeenth century, asks and answers the question, "Where is the most delight" when people want to lose the world for awhile. "Whither? but into their Orchards! made and prepared, dressed and destinated for that purpose, to revive and refreshen their senses and to call home their over-wearied spirits." Could any advice be more fitting today?

Elsewhere the care and cultivation has been dealt with and so here we need discuss only the choice of fragrant plants. If area permits nothing would contribute more to making your garden a retreat, than a roofed over summer house covered with sweet brier or honeysuckle. What a lovely place to come on a broiling hot summer day or in a rain. There we may work and play. Darning socks might even take on romance or, if you are engaged in writing or study, what a guarantee of inspiration every minute, and what a perfect place for just dreaming dreams!

Plant the most fragrant plants near the house, according to the ancient Greek custom. For individual herbs

A Triumph of the Sixteenth Century Gardener
from Gerard, 1597.

you will have decided preferences, quite different perhaps from those of any of your friends. In different centuries certainly we find variations in popular favorites. Parkinson, for instance, in writing of the sweetness of Sweet Sultans, says it "surpasses the best civet that is." Civet, a substance of animal extraction, was much used in the seventeenth century as a fragrant fixative in potpourri, pomanders and sweet bags. Now we feel that a very little of the odor of civet goes a long way.

Thomas Hyll in *The Gardeners Labyrinth* (1577) lists angelica, lovage, fennel, anise, elecampane, hyssop, thyme, savory, mints, pennyroyal, chamomile, costmary, feverfew, oculus Christi [clary], sage, tansy, rue, marjoram, Dutch-box, rosemary. William Lawson in *The Country House-wife's Garden* (1617) mentions roses, rosemary, lavender, bee-flowers [borage], hyssop, sage, thyme, cowslips, peony, daisies, clove-gilliflowers, pinks, southernwood, lilies. Richard Surflet in the *Maison Rustique* (1600) lists southernwood, wormwood, pellitory, rosemary, jasmine, marjoram, balm, mints, pennyroyal, costmary, hyssop, lavender, basil, sage, savory, rue, tansy, thyme, chamomile, mugwort, wild marjoram, nepeta, sweet balm, Good King Henry, anise, horehound.

From these lists we will find many candidates for our own fragrant garden. Some of the herbs seem to be "must" choices if we judge from the old gardening writers' encomiums which smack of modern testimonials of good character. Thomas Hyll would certainly have cooperated with us to the fullest extent. He says,

What rarer object can there be on earth, (the motions of the Celestial bodies except) than a beautifull and Odoriferous Garden plot Artificially composed . . . But now to my Garden of Flowers and Sweet Hearbs and first the Rose . . . Of all the flowers in the Garden, this is the chief for beauty and sweetness.

But Parkinson's pets to which he devotes many pages in his *Paradisus* were the carnation and clove pink.

But what shall I say to the Queen of Delight and of flowers, Carnations and Gilliflowers, whose bravery, variety and sweete smell joyned together, tyeth everyones affections with great earnestnesse both to like them?

Hyll says, "Gilly flowers, carnations or July-flowers (so called because in July they are in their prime and glory) these for beauty and sent are next the Rose," while Stephen Blake in his *Complete Gardeners Practice* (1664) offers a pretty good testimonial for carnations which "for beauty and delicious smels and excellent properties deserve letters of gold."

As for lilies of the valley, we may agree with John Lawrence who says (1726):

The Conval-Lilly or Lilly of the Valley is esteemed to have, of all others, the sweetest and most agreeable Perfume; Not offensive or overbearing even to those who are made uneasy with the Perfumes of other sweet scented Flowers.

Violets are pointed out by Parkinson as "Spring's chiefe flowers for beauty, smell and use, both single and double, the more shadie and moist they stand the better." To us moderns, violets are more for the pure aesthetic pleasure than for ingredients of salads and sirups.

Lavender, of course, has always been an English favorite. Lawson says the flower "is good for bees, most comfortable for smelling except Roses; and kept dry, is as strong after a yeare, and when it is gathered." Rosemary also was a favorite. Parkinson says, "Rosemary is so well known through all our Land, being in every women's garden, that it were sufficient but to name it as an ornament among other sweete herbes and flowers in our Garden, seeing everyone can describe it . . . the whole plant as well leaves as flowers, smelleth exceeding sweete."

Meadowsweet (*Filipendula ulmaria*), which Gerard calls "medesweete" or "Queen of the medowes" was Queen Elizabeth's favorite strewing herb. The herbalist also prefers it, "The leaves and flowers far excell other strowing herbs for to decke up houses, to strowe in chambers, hals and banketting houses in the sommer time; for the smell thereof maketh the hart merrie, delighteth the senses; neither doth it cause headache or lothsomnesse to meate, as some other sweete smelling herbes do."

We also read in the old lists of "turnsole," or heliotrope, both names derived from words meaning "turning toward the sun." Our more immediate forebears called it "Cherry Pie" from the almond-like fragrance of its flowers, reminiscent of the odor of cherries. For our fragrant garden I would also add all the thymes that can be found, particularly the creeping varieties for placing between flagstones of a path or for ground covers. Parkinson mentions lemon thyme and golden thyme and his list continues with lavender cotton, hyssop, savory, sage, and clary sage, basil, sweet marjoram, burnet. Of burnet he says, "The whole plant is of a stipticke or binding taste or quality, but of a fine quick sent, almost like Baulme" and of the latter plant he approves, "for the herbe without all question is an excellent helpe to comfort the heart, as the very smell may induce any so to believe." "In all your Gardens," says Hyll, "Banks and Seats of Camomile, Penny-royal, Daisies and Violets are seemly and comfortable."

It would be impossible in so few pages to quote the high praises the early writers sang of all the sweet scented plants. Neither can I describe the odor of each one or what murmurs of disagreement would arise. The sweet scented pelargoniums, introduced into England at the end of the seventeenth century from South Africa, are a particular delight, with as many kinds of odors as there are varieties of plants. And this is true of mints, as it is of thymes, all fragrant and impossible to select because of individual preferences.

I would introduce certain few fragrant shrubs for their "reminiscent" odor. Each one will recall certain scenes from an individual past, not distinctly perhaps, but as a pleasantly vague background. You may already have them in your garden: Carolina allspice (*Calycanthus floridus*) or as commonly called, strawberry shrub, with reddish little fruit which, as children, we tied in our handkerchiefs and bruised for the perfectly delicious odor. Then I would include the sun-loving *Daphne Cneorum, Daphne Mezereum* and *Viburnum Carlesi.*

CHAPTER IX

A LITTLE CULINARY HERB GARDEN

> In March and in April, from morning to night,
> In sowing and setting, good huswives delight:
> To have in a garden, or other like plot,
> To trim up their house, and to furnish their pot.
>
> At spring (for the summer) sow garden ye shall,
> At harvest (for winter) or sow not at all.
> Oft digging, removing, and weeding, ye see,
> Makes herb the more wholesome and greater to be.

These are seasonable thoughts from the *Five Hundred Points of Good Husbandry* suggested by Thomas Tusser to English gardeners of 1573, yet familiar to gardeners of all nations from the beginning to the end of all earthly gardening.

This culinary herb garden, small or large, that you are going to arrange and plant this spring, "in March and in April, from morning to night" is described in words or pictures from earliest times. The setting varies with the centuries and the nations, but all are outstandingly alike in two features, compactness and orderliness, essential for practically the same reasons as most of us consider—limited space and efficiency of management. These gardens, arranged in geometrically rectangular plots, not only facilitated the irrigation of the garden and economized

A Farm of the Elizabethan Period
from Matthioli, 1565.

space, but also produced an aesthetic effect, appreciated by Ralph Austen a seventeenth century gardener. In his gardening dialogue he said: "Decent formes and order of things are pleasant to the Eye."

Going back in gardening history to the ancient Egyptians, Babylonians and Assyrians, we find contemporary records describing gardens arranged in orderly plots, with central and cross paths through which streams of water flowed for irrigation purposes. The Persians had no different arrangement except that of walling in the channels of water between the plots.

In Greece and Rome whether in town or country each house had, as a matter of course, its formal compact kitchen garden traversed by irrigating streams. We usually picture the great orator Cicero, purple with rage, denouncing his victims and shouting, "How long, oh Cataline, will you abuse our patience?" Instead, imagine the gardener Cicero, sowing carefully in the little formal plots the seeds of those herbs so much used then, borage, chervil, coriander, rue, parsley, basil, fennel and hyssop. Then picture him ten days later, perhaps, inspecting his garden after a strenuous day spent in thoroughly flaying some obnoxious senator. Cicero is bent over, peering intently at one of the plots, then suddenly straightens up and with toga flying, dashes into the house and quite unrhetorically shouts to all within, "The basil is up!"

During the long period of the Middle Ages roughly from 500 to 1500 A.D., we find the same plan of squares or oblong plots. Compactness and economy of space were particularly important in this age of fortified castles, especially in the smaller castles where the gardens was forced to be grown within the limits of the courtyard. In this period we begin to see the confusion of art and "artyness." The

plots are now raised one or two feet from the ground level
and banked up by stones, bricks, or often by bones from the
animals consumed at those heavy banquets. The paths are
sometimes covered with colored sands, a treatment later
carried to excess and much scorned by true gardeners, particularly the Elizabethan Francis Bacon, who claimed that
"they [sanded paths] be but toys, you may see as good
sights many times in tarts." Rare and unusual flowers were
cherished in special beds protected by elaborate trellises
or woven wicker fences. Sometimes the beds are simply
turfed over and upon them are set pots of flowers. The
channels of water are supplemented or sometimes replaced
by a fountain in the center of the garden. Turfed seats,
supported by a low wattle fence, surrounding a shady
tree, made a lovely place to rest and contemplate the effect
of one's labors, especially as these seats were often planted
with aromatic herbs. The garden itself was surrounded
by a double wattle fence.

Petrus de Crescentiis a lawyer of Bologna in his treatise
on agriculture in 1471, wrote that the garden should be
in accordance with the owner's financial and social standing. Whereas nobles and kings should have at least a
twenty acre garden, the middle class could do with three
or four. But even people of the lowest class could at least
have a small square garden with a lawn in the center decorated by a fountain, the edge bordered by sage, basil, mint
and marjoram.

Letters from Cortez to Charles V in 1500 tell about the
palace gardens of Montezuma at Iztapalapa. Again we
find absolute symmetry in their square plots with a central
fountain. In France we find the same orderly arrangement, and the garden divided in half by a row of trees, the
center marked by the usual fountain. One side, bounded

by a hedge, was a square space devoted to vegetables, pot herbs and simples, with a maze formed of chamomile at one end. In the list of much used herbs we find hyssop, lavender and rosemary. Erasmus the Dutch philosopher in his "Colloquia," followed the plan, by now traditional, of geometric plots irrigated by water channels between them.

John Parkinson, Elizabethan devotee of gardening, told how any space could be made rectangular in appearance by skilful arrangement of paths and knots in relation to the plots. These again were the same kind of gardens that Milton a little later suggested as one of the pleasures of the contemplative life.

> And add to these retirèd Leisure
> That in trim gardens takes his pleasure.

The medieval influence still persisted in the fountain and raised bed which now had a low railing instead of the complicated trellis. Persia is still faintly represented by shallow tiled canals which, however, contain no water except when pumped through. The garden was quartered by paths, the main one leading from the terrace in front of the house was called the forthright, broad enough for several people to chat together as they strolled through the garden. The smaller paths, called "covert walks," were sometimes covered over by a lattice into which vines were woven or climbing flowers were trained. Around the inside of the garden wall was a continuous gallery, which developed from a lightly covered lattice into solid wooden architecture with windows. These Tudor and later the Stuart gardens were characterized by all sorts of garden furniture. There were sundials, bee skeps, and topiary work, that is, hedge plants cut into forms, later developing

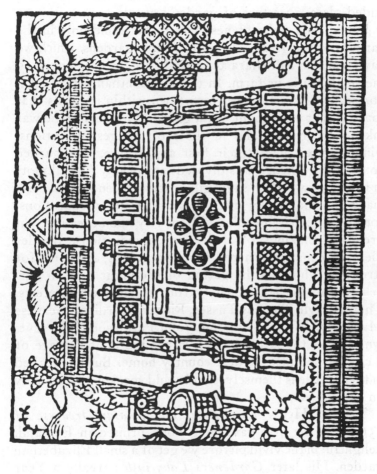

Sixteenth Century Outer Paling Inner Lattice
from Hyll, *Profitable Art of Gardening*, 1579. (From the rare copy
in Sterling Library, Yale University)

into wooden figures of animals. There were statues, lead ornaments, arbors, paths covered with colored sands and, placed in the flower beds were sticks hung with colored and gilded glass, ancestors of garden crystals.

But all this elaborateness was to be found only in the gardens of the great. The more simple gardens, which we have come to call characteristically English, belonged to the small house or farm. In this Elizabethan period London was so like an overgrown town within its walls that space was at a premium, yet a garden for every home was taken for granted and in the most congested sections, window boxes made their first appearance. The garden bounded by a hedge was divided into primly formal plots in which grew fennel, sage, gilliflowers, lavender and rosemary for the family medicines and toilet preparations, for even the "city people" did not rely upon chemists, but grew the makings of their own preparations. Besides these were many pot herbs, herbs for salads, and herbs for strewing. This was the period of the great English gardeners and herbalists who wrote about their interests, Thomas Hyll, Thomas Tusser, Richard Gardiner, Gervase Markham, William Lawson, John Parkinson, John Evelyn, all but the latter having either the limited space of a city garden or a modest country home. But all worked in their gardens themselves and could speak with authority on the subject.

Thomas Hyll's *Most Brief and pleasant treatyse of* 1563 was the first gardening book printed in England, delightful in the vivid picture we get of a small Elizabethan garden. His later *Gardeners Labyrinth* is really a Year Book treating of practically every phase of gardening.

Thomas Tusser a retainer at James I's court for ten years retired to his Essex farm where he completed in

Rectangular Beds
from Evelyn, *French Gardiner,* 1675.

1557 his rhyming gardening book which he called *A Hundreth good points of husbandrie*. By 1573 both his knowledge of gardening and his sense of rhythm had developed and he published *Five hundreth points of good husbandry*. In his list of the herbs he considered essential to the garden, he classifies them under seven heads: (1) 21 kinds of strewing herbs; (2) herbs and roots to boil or to butter; (3) 42 seeds and herbs for the kitchen; (4) 22 herbs and roots for sallads and sauces; (5) 40 herbs, branches and flowers for windows and pots; (6) 17 herbs to still in summer; (7) 28 herbs necessary to grow in the garden for physic. Capers, lemons, olives, oranges, rice, samphire, Tusser lists under herbs or sallads but never entertained any idea of raising in England for he says:

> These buy with the penny
> Or look not for any.

Space is so limited that we cannot begin to do justice to the contributions of these writers to the art of gardening, but Richard Gardiner of Shrewsbury, Shropshire, I just can't bear to omit. He published a list of the vegetables and seeds he sold, the earliest seed catalogue. His *Profitable Instructions for the Manuring, Sowing and Planting of Kitchen Gardens* (1603) is the only book specializing on kitchen gardens that does not include the potato. But the reason is perfectly plausible. Although John Gerard grew in his London garden "potato's of Virginia," as he lists them in his herbal of 1597, that vegetable had not reached as far west as Shropshire.

If we cross to America at a somewhat later period and consider our Colonial gardens, we find that our ancestors had brought with them on perilous Atlantic crossings many seeds, roots and plants and had established them together with plants found here, in gardens trim and formal as those they had left in England. We find in the Salem garden of 1620 square or rectangular plots with paths through the middle, with "parsley, sweet chervil, sorrel and other pot herbs on one side of the path; and on the other sage, spearmint, mullein, fennel and medicinal herbs." Besides these there were a score of others.

We now find ourselves confronted with the American culinary herb garden of today. The traditional formal arrangement used for centuries of experience can still be relied upon to bring satisfactory results. Choose a spot, sunny if possible somewhere near the kitchen door; a little plot 12 inches by 18 inches will grow enough of any one culinary herb to supply that particular flavor for the average family. So, determine how much space is available for your garden and figure out how many varieties of herbs you can have in that space. Whatever we do and however we may "express ourselves" in arranging the flower plots and borders, let's have this kitchen herb garden in the old time tradition, trim, tidy rectangular plots with square corners, straight paths and outlining borders, and spaced with mathematical preciseness. By planning ahead, your garden will not only be useful but a lovely fragrant spot offering you superlative satisfaction with far less work, really, than you now believe.

William Lawson the early seventeenth century Yorkshire gardener declared in his *New Orchard and Garden* that "whereas every other pleasure commonly fills some one of our sences, and that onely with delight, this makes all our sences swimme in pleasure, and that with infinite varieties ioyned with no less commodite."

Have enough herb plots to form a perfect rectangle and separate them by gravel, or by an edging of parsley or chervil. Have one central path leading to a focal point or sundial, old-fashioned bee skep, or perhaps a clump of one of the taller herbs, like sweet fennel that is not cut down when the seed heads are harvested. If the garden has many plots, you should have cross paths wide enough for convenience in working among the plants. William Lawson discusses these matters of the little kitchen garden and goes on to the sensible way of placing the herbs—again we go back to the early days of raised beds and water channels for irrigation.

"You need not here raise your beds as in the other Garden because Summer towards, will not let too much wet annoy you; yet must you have your beds divided, that you may go betwixt to weed, and somewhat forme would be expected: . . . . . . To which it availeth that you place your herbs of biggest growth by walles, or in borders, as Fennell etc. and the lowest in the middest, as Saffron, Strawberries, Onions etc."

In this chapter is a chart where you will find tabulated the heights of the twenty culinary herbs mentioned at the end. This will vary somewhat in different gardens. You will also find a column indicating whether the herbs are perennial, biennial or annual. Both columns should be studied in determining their position in the garden. I would let one half of the garden be devoted to perennials and biennials and the other half to annuals. Of the twenty herbs listed, ten are perennials or biennials, and the other ten annuals. If you let the central path be the dividing line or the path crossing the other way, it makes the cultivation easier. Once you have established the perennials you seldom have to dig up the plot again, but the annual beds must be thoroughly dug up each year. You would find it confusing, especially in a garden of small plots, to dig a

PLANTING COLUMN	Annual or Perennial	Germination Days	Height Inches	Number of Plants Needed	Large or Small Seeds	Distance Apart for Plants Inches		Annual or Perennial	Germination Days	Height Inches	Number of Plants Needed	Large or Small Seeds	Distance Apart for Plants Inches
Anise	A	10	18	12	L	8	Dill	A	8	30	6	L	12
Lemon Balm	P	14	18	6	S	10	Sweet Fennel	P	8	48	4	L	12
Basil	A	12	12	6	L	12	Sweet Marjoram	A	12	10	12	S	6
Bene	A	12	12	12	L	8	Mint	P	-	12-24	6	-	10
Borage	A	14	24	6	L	12	Parsley	B	21	12	24	S	6
Burnet	P	10	18	4	L	12	Rosemary	P	18	12-24	6	S	12
Caraway	B	12	18	12	L	6	Sage	P	15	18	6	S	12
Chervil	A	12	9	24	S	6	Summer Savory	A	10	12	12	L	10
Chives	P	-	12	6	-	12	Tarragon	P	-	12	12	-	10
Coriander	A	12	12	8	L	4	Thyme	P	10	10	6	S	8

bed here and one there. This confusion would be increased by the fact that in the spring before the plants have got a good start, it is really difficult to keep the plots separate unless you are a terribly systematic soul and have an infallible method for labeling in the autumn when you think you'll never forget. Even if you have it all down neatly in a diagram, I still think it simpler to separate the types of plants quite definitely.

On the diagram of a possible arrangement of a culinary herb garden I have indicated the division of annuals from the perennials and biennials by the central path. Chamomile sowed in that path will be soft as chenille if kept cut and rolled. However, in that main path and transverses, gravel is also good because it makes such a clear cut line of demarcation between the plots. A green line of parsley at the edges of the central path, if gravel, is lovely. Chervil makes a good edging too, though a little taller than parsley but since it needs a bit of shade, it is not practical for a wholly sunny exposure. John Evelyn apparently thought highly of it—"Chervil is handsome and proper for the edging of the Kitchin Garden bed."

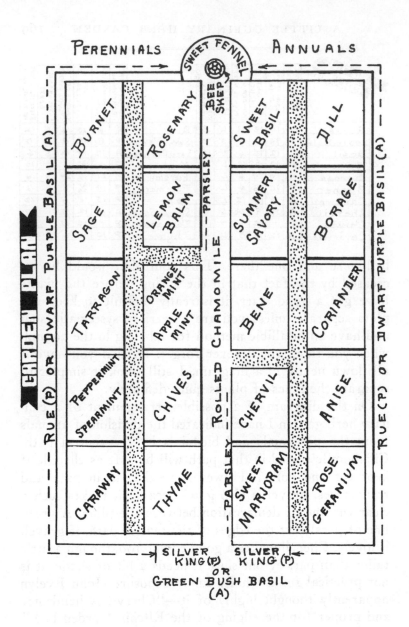

If you want to go outside the class of culinary varieties, the glossy germander is a good edging, or one of the short, erect thymes, like *Thymus nitidus*.

When we consider the boundary for the herb garden itself there are several possibilities. It might be a low fence of white pickets, woven cedar palings, or wire lattice. Or you might have a hedge of perennials herbs, hyssop or rue, with one plant of a taller herb, myrrh or silver king, on each side of the entrance. The purple dwarf basil, an annual, would make a striking hedge because of its peculiarly distinctive shade of purplish red. Plants of the sweet or curly basil would be effective at the entrance.

After you have determined the size of your garden and the number of herb varieties, there comes the exciting part of collecting the seeds and plants. Several herbs you either must or should buy as plants. Some believe that the best rosemary plants are those obtained from seed. Possibly so, but you are probably letting yourself in for discouragement. Incidentally, that holds true for lavender and lemon balm. The seeds of those three herbs germinate so slowly, and their growth during the first year is so slight, that frost may overtake them before the plants are strong enough to remove to the house for the winter. So I would start with plants. The true tarragon, *Artemisia Dracunculus,* has to be bought as plants since it does not produce seeds, and I can see no particular point in trying to raise chives or mints from seeds. Plants of chives are so inexpensive and increase so easily by dividing the clumps every year or so. Only a few plants of any of the mints or of lemon balm are needed because they will fill the bed before the end of the first summer if you "layer" them. This is done by pegging down a few ends, covering with soil, and after a few weeks when they have rooted, cutting them off from the main plant and so getting separate plants which later may also be layered.

From seed sown outdoors when there is no further danger of frost, I should raise all the annuals, the biennials caraway and parsley, and the perennials burnet, sage and thyme. The size of the seeds will determine the treatment for sowing. The large seeds should be sowed thinly and covered with about an eighth inch of soil. The heavier the soil, the thicker you sow the seeds and the less you cover them. The danger lies in getting them too deep in the ground. Some seed should be sown in the bed where they are to grow, particularly anise, chervil, coriander, dill and fennel, because the roots are such a network of fine threads that they do not recover easily from the shock of transplanting.

Small seeds should be mixed with sand for ease of distribution over the ground. Such are lemon balm, marjoram, savory, thyme, and parsley. Have the surface soil very fine, water before sowing, letting it drain off well, then sprinkle the seeds over the surface and then firm down the whole bed with a flat board but do not cover with soil. Keep these small seeds covered, however, during germination by paper or burlap to keep out the light. Water through the cover or with a fine spray to avoid washing the seeds about. If you soak germinating seeds in water for a few hours, drying the surface before planting, you will be helping them start swelling, particularly such seed as parsley which has the reputation of "going 9 times to the devil and back" before starting upwards. A prevalent belief among sixteenth century gardeners was that plants grown from seeds soaked in scented water would take on that sweet odor. Thomas Hyll wrote of soaking seeds of artichoke in rose water or lily juice or

An Early Gardener Laying Out His Plot
from *Countrie Farme*, 1616.

Garden Laborers at Work
from Lawson, 1638.

oil of bays, and then drying in the sun before sowing them
so that "the fruits will yelde the same savor as the licour
in which the seeds were soaked." Would an artichoke with
any other smell taste the same?

Hyll also naively advises two methods for protecting
the seedlings from "byrdes, antes, field mice and other
spoylers of the garden." One way is to sprinkle juice of
the house leek on the seeds before sowing them. The
other device is this: "The soote cleaving on the chymney
wych gathered a daye before the seedes in the earth, and
myxed with them doeth the like defende the seedes in
safety." Quite by the way, soot added to the soil about
parsley plants really helps their growth, whether or not
it keeps off "byrdes, antes, field mice."

As soon as the seedlings show four leaves, the weaker
ones may be thinned out or if the seeds have been sowed

in a seed bed, transplanting may take place. Be careful in transplanting, thinning, and weeding, to hold down the neighboring seedlings so their roots will not be disturbed and their growth retarded.

Maintenance of the herb garden is really quite simple. Keep the soil loose by cultivating about once in ten days and after a rain as soon as the soil can be worked. In hot weather a little cultivation will prevent loss of moisture. Weeding will have to be done more in the plots of slow growing herbs like anise, caraway, marjoram and parsley, but after the leaves of plants touch each other, they themselves are strong enough to keep down the weed growth. If you are the one elected to do the weeding, console yourself with the thought you were not earning your living as a garden worker in medieval times. A head gardener received sixty dollars a year, laborers from four to twelve cents a day. Women were hired for weeding and watering at four to six cents a day,—hardly enough to keep them in lipsticks!

Finally, since some annual plants, as basil and savory, are cut down when harvested in July or will have had their season, like borage, three successive sowings at four week intervals are desirable to prevent a bare spot. Each time give the soil a little humus before sowing. When much cutting back is done on marjoram or chives, fertilize the soil a little each time after cutting. When the flowers of the chives have passed, cut their coarse stalks to the ground. The taller plants, as dill and fennel, should be staked when eighteen inches high. Some plants try to spread beyond their limits—thyme may be clipped, but the mints have to be treated sternly. Here's the answer to the old question what to do with demoded license plates from your cars. Sink them, or other plates, into the mint beds on the boundary lines and it will quite effectually discourage underground runners.

Even if we had said all we could say about growing herbs, Thomas Tusser's advice of first reading and then experimenting is the best guide:

> Thus ends in brief,
> Of herbs the chief.
> To get more skill,
> Read whom ye will:
> Such mo [more] to have,
> Of field go crave.

A LIST OF TWENTY CULINARY HERBS

ANISE. *Pimpinella Anisum*—annual—from seed.
  SEEDS: bread, cake, apple sauce, stews, soups, tea drink.
  FRESH LEAVES: garnish, salad.

  TECHNICAL USES: ground seeds in curry powder and for sachets.
  Oil from seeds: flavors liqueurs, liquid tooth washes, soaps, perfumes, ointments, liniments, hair preparations, licorice extract, candy, and in medicine and as a vermifuge.

LEMON BALM. *Melissa officinalis*—perennial—buy plants.
  FRESH LEAVES: salad, in tarragon vinegar, soups, stews, fish sauces, iced beverages, hot infusions.

  TECHNICAL USES: Oil from plant: liqueurs, toilet preparations, particularly *Eau des Carmes,* furniture oil polish.

BASIL. *Ocimum Basilicum*—annual—from seed.
  LEAFY TOPS: garnish, vinegar.
  LEAVES (CHOPPED OR POWDERED): soup (bean, tomato, turtle), rich stews, salads, cream or cottage cheese, egg or tomato dishes, chopped meat, sausages, in butter sauce for fish, sprinkled over peas or boiled potato, in vegetable juice cocktails.

  TECHNICAL USES: oil from plant: perfumes of flower scents.
  HOUSEHOLD USE: basil plants in house to drive away flies.

BENE or SESAME. *Sesamum orientale*—annual—from seed.
  SEEDS (AFTER SHUCKING): bread, cookies, cake, confectionery.

OIL FROM SEEDS: for frying meats, etc.

TECHNICAL USES: seed oil as adulterant for olive oil.

BORAGE. *Borago officinalis*—annual—from seed.
YOUNG FRESH LEAVES: salads, pickles, iced beverages, as greens.
FRESH FLOWERS: crystallized for confectionery, cakes, and in potpourris.

BURNET. *Sanguisorba minor*—biennial—from seed.
LEAFY TOPS: gives cucumber taste to vinegar, salads, iced beverages.

CARAWAY. *Carum Carvi*—biennial—from seed.
SEEDS: rye bread, cake, cheese, German sauerkraut, sugar coated for confectionery, in apple sauce and baked apples, German and Hungarian cabbage soups, in goulashes, served to munch after meals.
ROOTS: boiled for vegetables.

TECHNICAL USES: Oil from seeds: of Tunis variety for mouth washes and cheap perfumes; of Russian variety for flavoring liqueurs (Kümmel), and for confectionery.

CHERVIL. *Anthriscus Cerefolium*—annual—from seed.
LEAVES (CHOPPED OR POWDERED): in soup (sorrel or spinach), fish sauce, egg dishes, French dressing, butter sauce with wine over veal cutlets, béarnaise and ravigote sauces, butter sauce for broiled chicken.

HOUSEHOLD USE: leafy tips (and seeds) formerly used in polishes to scent floors and furniture.

CHIVES. *Allium Schoenoprasum*—perennial—buy plants.
GREEN TOPS (CHOPPED FINE): soups, cheese, omelettes, potatoes, croquettes, sausages, tomato cocktail.

CORIANDER. *Coriandrum sativum*—annual—from seed.
SEEDS (CRUSHED): bread, gingerbread, biscuits, cookies, cakes, baked apples, sausages, cheese, sauce for wild game, poultry stuffing.
SEEDS (WHOLE): sugar coated for confections (comfits).

TECHNICAL USES: (Seeds) improve taste of cheap cocoa, flavors liqueurs, used in gin distilling, in curry powder, confectionery.

DILL. *Anethum graveolens*—annual—from seed.

SEEDS: apple pie, spiced beets, pastry, Scandinavian bean and beet soup, gravy.

SEED HEADS: pickles and vinegar.

YOUNG LEAFY TOPS (CHOPPED): cottage and cream cheese, fish butter, sprinkled over steaks and chops, in potato salad, cream sauce for chicken.

TECHNICAL USES: oil from seeds: to scent soap and perfume.

FENNEL. *Foeniculum vulgare,* var. *dulce*—annual—from seed. (Florence fennel or finocchio)

THICK PART OF THE BASE: boiled as a vegetable, used to flavor wine.

SEED OIL: used in soap.

Foeniculum vulgare—perennial—from seed (sometimes called *F. capillaceum*).

(Sweet fennel)

YOUNG STEMS: served raw as appetizer.

Carosella (*F. vulgare,* var. *piperitum*)—raw stems particularly popular with Italians.

Foeniculum vulgare—perennial—from seed.

(Bitter fennel)

SEEDS: pudding, soups, cakes, German sauerkraut, spiced beets.

LEAVES (CHOPPED OR POWDERED): soup, fish sauce, boiled or baked fish, garnish.

TECHNICAL USES: oil from seeds: to flavor liqueurs, in confectionery, scent for soap. Seeds: for hair dye.

SWEET MARJORAM. *Majorana hortensis*—annual—slow from seed.

LEAVES (POWDERED OR CRUSHED): sprinkled over roast beef, lamb or pork, in butter sauce for fish; used in vinegar, salads, cheese, puddings, chopped meat, stuffings, soup, egg dishes, peas, beans, spinach, tomatoes, in cocktails.

LEAFY TOPS: garnish.

TECHNICAL USES: oil from plant: to scent soap, perfume, and pomades. Flowering tops: in dye, potpourris, and sachets.

HOUSEHOLD USES: hot infusions; leafy tops formerly used in polish to scent furniture.

MINT. Perennials—buy plants or slips.

Spearmint (*Mentha spicata*) ; peppermint (*M. piperita*).

Applemint (*M. gentilis*) ; orange mint (*M. citrata*).

LEAVES (CHOPPED OR POWDERED) : lamb and fish sauces, apple sauce, fruit cup, iced beverages, confectionery, sprinkled over vegetables (peas, boiled potatoes, carrots, spinach, raw cabbage), in pea soup, in currant jelly.

LEAFY TOPS (fresh, if possible) : in vinegars, mint jelly.

TECHNICAL USES: oil from plant: tooth paste, mouth washes, liqueurs, chewing gum, soap, perfumes.

HOUSEHOLD USES: leafy tops (fresh) in hot infusions and scattered about to keep mice away.

Leafy tops (dried) in hot infusions and in moth mixtures.

PARSLEY. *Petroselinum hortense,* either *filicinum* (ferny leaf) or *crispum* (curly)—biennial—slow from seed.

LEAVES (FRESH) : garnish.

LEAVES (POWDERED OR CHOPPED) : sprinkled over soup, poached eggs, boiled potatoes, fish, mixed in butter sauces, fricasseed chicken stock.

ROSEMARY. *Rosmarinus officinalis*—perennial—buy plants.

LEAFY TOPS (FRESH) : garnish, summer drinks, pickles.

LEAVES (CHOPPED OR POWDERED) : in jams, sweet sauces, sprinkled over pork and beef roasts, in veal stews, soups, peas; added to deep fat for frying potatoes.

TECHNICAL USES: oil from plant: Hungary water, hair preparations, tooth washes, in perfumes and soaps.

HOUSEHOLD USES: leafy tops (dried) in moth mixtures.

SAGE. *Salvia officinalis*—perennial—from seed.

LEAVES (CHOPPED FRESH) : in cottage cheese, pickles.

LEAVES (CHOPPED OR POWDERED) : sprinkled over poultry, veal, pork; used in sausage, stewed tomatoes, string beans, cheese.

TECHNICAL USES: hair tonic.

HOUSEHOLD USES: leaves rubbed on teeth to clean them and strengthen gums; hot infusion for gargle; hot infusion for tea.

SUMMER SAVORY. *Satureia hortensis*—annual—from seed.

LEAFY TOP (FRESH) : garnish.

LEAVES (CHOPPED OR POWDERED) : in string beans, peas, salads, stuffings, meat cakes, croquettes, cocktails.

HOUSEHOLD USES: leaves (fresh) rubbed on insect bites to take out the sting.
Leaves (fresh or dried) for aromatic baths.

TARRAGON. *Artemisia Dracunculus*—perennial—buy plants.
LEAFY TOPS (FRESH) : for Vinaigre d'Estragon, in pickles.
LEAVES (CHOPPED OR POWDERED) : in salads, in mustard; in tartar, fish, cream and béarnaise sauces; with chervil in ravigote sauce; in cocktails; butter sauce for shell fish dishes; in egg, mushroom and chicken dishes.

TECHNICAL USES: oil from plant: perfumes and toilet preparations.

THYME. *Thymus vulgaris*—perennial—from seed.
LEAFY TOPS (FRESH) : garnish.
LEAVES (CHOPPED OR POWDERED) : with other herbs in vinegar, in sauces for meat and fish, cocktails, croquettes, chipped beef, fricassees; with pork, veal; in soups with onion; cheese, carrots, peas, scalloped onions.

TECHNICAL USES: oil from plant: in deodorants, anaesthetics, gargles, perfumes.
HOUSEHOLD USES: leafy tops in aromatic bottles, sachets, hot infusions.

CHAPTER X

A GARDEN OF SAVORY SEEDS

"Wife, some time this week, if the weather hold clear,
An end of wheat sowing we make for this year:
Remember thou therefore, though I do it not,
The seed-cake, the pasties, and furmenty pot."
—THOMAS TUSSER (1573)

Always at the end of autumn sowing in the fertile farming land of Essex and Suffolk in England, the farm hands were rewarded by great feasting. The housewife and her maids prepared an abundance of frumenty, a mixture of hulled wheat which had been boiled in milk with the addition of cinnamon and sugar. Many were the hearty pastries and appropriately enough, seed cakes.

Have you ever prepared days ahead for ravenous threshers on a farm? If you have you can imagine that those busy mistresses and maids gave not a thought to the significance of the traditional seed cakes as a part of the conclusion of grain sowing. Seed cakes had always been made, that was all. Never a close inspection of the peculiar and distinctive shape of the individual seeds from the crop they had gathered in their gardens. No conception of the many fascinating superstitions connected with them. No realization of the amazing way Nature has arranged them for self-sowing. How little were those sixteenth century mothers aware of the medicinal virtues

lurking in some of the seeds they used in cakes served at
the end of huge feasts, or given, at other times, to the
children who, they had learned from past experiences,
had been benefited by seed cakes! Little did those busy
women, flinging in seeds of one kind in the cake batter,
another kind in a crock of pickles, know that from ancient
times seeds have been held in the highest regard.

I don't suppose many people of the sixteenth century
would really have cared about the romance of seeds anyway. But to us of the twentieth century, with a flair for
happily combining romance, history and science, we would
find the study of them a most fascinating accompaniment
to their practical use in cooking. Moreover, many are the
dishes that would be pleasantly varied by the addition of
savory seeds. They have been known as far back, at least,
as the pyramids at Cheops in Egypt, for in a papyrus
found in one of the tombs, was the mention of coriander.
In Biblical times dill and cumin were considered so important that they were included in the payment of tithes.
In Roman days spice cakes, strongly flavored with aniseed,
were served at the end of their heavy feasts. Down
through the centuries all savory seeds have featured
greatly in the commerce of nations and the food of individuals. It will interest you to know that all the herbs
whose seeds are used for flavoring belong to the Umbelliferae.

The production of seed is the ultimate goal of plant
and tree. In many instances we use that seed as food.
Sometimes, as with fruit trees, we eat the casing that the
seed comes in—the apple or the pear. In the case of trees
bearing nuts, we use the meat of the seed itself—the wal-
nut or the coconut. As for the herbs bearing savory seeds,
we eat also the casing which so closely surrounds the seeds

that it cannot be separated from them, as is so often done with fruits or nuts.

While commenting on the fact that the housewives of Tusser's time probably had no interest in the fascinating

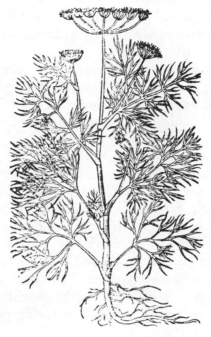

Dill
from Gerard, 1597.

seeds they used in cooking, we might also remark that they, however, did grow them in the kitchen garden. We moderns seem to be content to buy the few we use in containers perhaps long collecting dust on grocers' shelves because of the slight demand for them. Anise drops or caraway cookies we buy already baked. But, do let's enter adventurously into our cooking and go the whole way by growing our own herbs. Wouldn't it give you just a little inward thrill to have, by early autumn, a dozen jars of savory seeds that you had harvested from your own garden, fresh, redolent with the fragrant essential oils, clean seeds carefully separated from the chaff and the little stems commonly found in commercially packaged seeds of doubtful vintage?

You may grow the seeds discussed except the baker's dozenth—cardamom, of tropical nature and not truly a savory seed anyway. The flavor of it, however, is such a delightful addition to pastries that I couldn't resist including it. The dozen easily grown are: anise, caraway, celery, coriander, cumin, dill, fennel, black and white mustard, nasturtium, poppy and sesame.

When I say that far too few individuals raise these seeds in their gardens I am thinking of the millions of pounds of seeds imported to this country yearly, crops which could be easily raised at home. In 1935, for instance, some 146,000,000 pounds of sesame, over 6,500-000 pounds of caraway, over 1,500,000 pounds of coriander! Each one of these herbs would grow in your garden as easily as the ubiquitous spring radish and with greater joy to the cook!

Aside from the joy of the utilitarian harvest, you will be entranced by Nature's "wonders to perform," her art as designer of the seed house for ornament and use. Look closely at a carrot seed. You will notice it has two cells with seeds. When the pod is ripe it splits along the upper side into halves and the wind carries off the seed. The ripened pods of balsam seeds are the most exciting and are warranted to cause a startled comment or more if you place a ripened pod in the hand of one of your most trusting friends and tell her to close her hand slightly, squeezing the pod. It simply explodes and seems to writhe as it ejects the seeds. We have all noticed dandelion fluff carried away on the breeze, each seed borne by a tufted sail. All these processes are simply Nature's devices for getting her seeds re-sown.

Nature shows her artistry in shaping her seeds. Don't you always hold your breath a little when you open a seed packet of herb or flower you have never grown before? I do; I am always curious to see what it looks like, how it differs from all the other seeds I have ever seen. The poppy seeds take innumerable forms, and I truly believed it when I first learned that they are of every shape but square. The calendula seeds are little crescents with a latitudinal corrugation unpleasantly reminiscent of a caterpillar. The delphinium produces shiny irregular bits of black seeds resembling tiny chunks of coal, while the pods in which they are inclosed look like urns of classic design. And have you ever seen the seed pod of star anise?

Some of us unfortunately don't have gardens and several people have asked me what herbs can be grown indoors. Almost any of them, I should say. I know one lovely lady who raises as many as twenty-six herbs in beautiful window boxes, beautifully mounted. If you, however, are without benefit of garden, indoors or outdoors, do buy packages of a dozen varieties of savory seeds and really look at them. Study closely the individual seeds and see how distinct each variety is from the others, even from those of the same family, the Umbelliferae.

Then, by all means, experiment with the seeds in your cooking; and I mean experiment with the common sense of a cook. Don't, I beg of you, follow any recipe slavishly.

My own caution to you, as I pointed out about herbs in general is to use your dozen savory seeds sparingly until you feel really acquainted with them. Your object is to emphasize the original flavor of the food, not to disguise it. In each seed is the essential oil that characterizes its flavor, and it will take a few trials to discover how much oil there is in a given quantity of one variety. But don't be timid about experimenting. Your family do get so tired of food flavored monotonously with salt, sage or cinnamon. One flavor only is not much different from no flavor at all, and this makes for unappetizing food that just doesn't get digested.

If we were to enter many kitchens and observe the unimaginative routine of ordering the same old ingredients, and then were to watch these materials being combined, seasoned and cooked in the same old way, we might think we were back in the Middle Ages when variety of food was unknown. But here lies the difference in the culinary centuries. Now we have varieties of food from all over the world but use the same seasoning in all. In early days sameness was avoided by variety of flavoring, and many more herb leaves and seeds were used than we would dream of now. We find in the fourteenth century poem, *Piers Plowman,* that the Alewife cherished her herbs.

> I have pepper and paeony seed and a pound of garlick,
> And a farthingworth of fennel-seed, for fasting days.

Even in Hannah Glasse's *Art of Cookery* (1747) we read that the author recommended "paeony" kernels to be put into a dessert cream. In *The Closet Opened* (1669) we read of Sir Kenelm Digby's using the seedy buds of tulips in culinary recipes. Until recently, seeds of lovage were used in candy making, and even now in England, you may come across candied lavender fruit.

Grow some of the savory seeds, if possible, because the flavor of fresh seeds from which the essential oils have had little opportunity to escape, is so rich and delightful. Buy them, if necessary, but have them either way, make their acquaintance and use them to give such a flavor to the same old dishes that your family will say, "That's what I have wanted all my life."

ANISE, *Pimpinella anisum*

The word *pimpinella* developed in the Middle Ages from *dipinella,* because of its secondary winged shape leaflets. In the Gospel of St. Matthew, 23:23, we read,

Woe unto you, scribes and Pharisees, hypocrites! for ye pay tithe of mint and anise and cummin, and have omitted the weightier matters of the law.

In the marginal notes, "anise" is correctly interpreted as dill. Since John Wiclif's translation of the New Testament from a Latin version down the ages in other versions, the original Greek *anethon* has been rendered "anise." Possibly Wiclif was more biblically than botanically minded, and both the Latin *anethum* (dill) and Greek *anethon* sounded like anise to him! Dioscorides, first century herbalist, discusses dill under the Greek name, *anethon.*

Anise is a fragrant annual of the Umbelliferae, about eighteen inches high. The long white fibrous tap root makes transplanting difficult, so it is advisable to sow the seeds, which should be fresh, where the plants are to develop. The leaves are interesting in that the lower ones resemble those of celery, the higher ones grow more finely cut, until the top ones are thread like. The yellowish white umbels, spreading to one and one-half inches in diameter, appear about two and one-half months after planting. A month later, the fruit or seeds are ready to harvest, and if neglected will simply fall to the ground and re-sow.

Anise grows most happily in a warm, sunny, fairly dry spot, in light moderately rich loam. The only care it needs is thinning and a thorough weeding, necessary because of the slow growth of the herb.

The seeds are about one-eighth inch long and are really fruits with short bristles, each made up of two mericarps inclosing the seed. A tiny stalk or pericel usually remains attached to the end of the fruit. This fruit, oval in shape narrowing to a point, greenish gray when ripe, is definitely ridged. Aniseeds are fragrant with methyl-chavicol, the oil having characteristic anise-like flavor so much used commercially for soaps, hair preparations, dentifrices, perfumes, ointments, liniments, liqueurs, cordials, and curry powder.

Anise is indigenous to Egypt, Greece and Asia Minor. It was in great repute among the ancient Assyrians, as is found from the clay tablets in the library at Ninevah. Pythagoras of the sixth century B.C. valued anise as an ingredient of an antidote for scorpions, and claimed also that a spray of the plant held in the hand would prevent an epileptic attack. The herb was also used in early days to ward off the Evil Eye.

Among the Romans, cakes called "mustaceae" were served at the end of rich heavy banquets. These cakes were made largely of meal, anise, cumin and other aromatic seeds which, because of their carminative effect, prevented the necessity of large doses of whatever was sodium bicarbonate to the Romans. Pliny the Elder, of the first century A.D. in his *Natural History*, recommends anise as an ingredient in all seasonings, mentions that it is placed underneath the crust of bread, and gives more than three score remedies in which aniseed is the chief ingredient. According to Pliny,

this plant imparts a youthful look to the features and if suspended to the pillow, so as to be smelt by a person when asleep, it will prevent disagreeable dreams.

Halitosis was also considered by Pliny. He says that "anise has the effect of sweetening the breath and removing all bad odours from the mouth, if chewed in the morning" with a little sweetening and the mouth then rinsed with wine. Later in England, the sixteenth century herbalist William Turner also says that "Anyse maketh the breath sweter and swageth payne."

Hippocrates the first great physician, fifth century B.C., recommended anise for coughs and ever since it has been popular in cough mixtures because an essential oil, anethol, affects the bronchial tubes as to bring about expectoration.

By 1305 in England, anise was one of the drugs taxed upon reaching London Bridge en route to the city. But it was cherished as an ingredient for sachets by Edward IV (reigned 1461–1483) who had all the linen of the household perfumed with a mixture of anise and orris root.

In the settling of America, the colonists considered anise so important that the organizers of the Virginia group required every man to plant six seeds of that herb. In 1672, John Josselyn an Englishman who had traveled extensively in the northern colonies wrote his *New England's Rarities* in which he listed, "Such Garden Herbs (amongst us) as do thrive there, and of such as do not."

Perhaps he did not find a warm enough spot for the cultivation of anise for he claimed that although "Annis thrive
exceedingly, Annis Seed, as also the Seed of Fennel seldom come of maturity." He also says, "The Seed of Annis
is commonly eaten with a fly." I have never yet heard a
good explanation of that gratuitous bit of information,
but perhaps some New Englander can enlighten me.

Now, let us see how we can use aniseed in our cooking.
Scandinavians eat the seeds of umbelliferous plants to a
much greater extent than we Americans do, and many
are the hints we could take from them when we yearn for
culinary variety. A few seeds added to soups tone up a
too often tasteless liquid. Instead of always adding cinnamon or nutmeg to applesauce, aniseed will make a spice
variation. Beet salad with the addition of the seed is a
favorite Scandinavian dish.

You have often mixed chives with cottage or cream
cheese for sandwiches or for appetizers. Try a teaspoonful of aniseed to a cupful of cheese, spread on crackers,
and your cocktail guests will call for more. An interesting
commercial product I learned of recently, is the impregna-
tion of toothpicks with aniseed oil, also with peppermint
and other interesting flavors, to give that different taste to
the appetizer into which the tooth picks are stuck.

Aniseed may be added to any basic recipe for biscuit,
bread or cake. Cookies with the stomach-warming seeds
are particularly beneficial and satisfying to the younger
generation, as they rush into the house from school for a
lunch. Have one dependable basic recipe for a not-too-
rich sugar cookie, add what variety of seed your hungry
youngsters prefer, and you will find an answer to the after
school problem. The following is a good general recipe:

½ cup shortening   3 cups flour
1½ cups sugar   2 teaspoons baking powder
2 eggs   1½ teaspoons salt
Grated rind of lemon or orange ¼ cup milk or orange juice

Cream the butter and sugar, add the well beaten eggs and mix thoroughly. Sift flour, baking powder, salt and grated rind. Add this to the first mixture gradually, alternating with milk or orange juice. Then add one tablespoonful aniseed, crushed or whole. If you wish a blended flavor of anise, crush the seed, but if you like to bite through the seed to get the entire flavor, add them whole. After the ingredients are mixed thoroughly, chill the dough, roll out thinly on a slightly floured board, cut with cutter which has been dipped into flour, and bake about ten minutes in a moderately hot oven. The length of time for baking will depend on the thickness of the cookie. If you prefer drop cookies, add more liquid to the dough, drop from a teaspoon, about an inch apart, and let stand for a few hours in a cool place.

CARAWAY, *Carum Carvi*

This is a biennial plant of the umbelliferae family. There are several interesting explanations of the origin of the name. Pliny says that it comes from the Province of Caria in Asia Minor, to which it is native. Others derive the name directly from the Arabic name for the seed, Karawya. It is also asserted that the word comes from the Gaelic "caroh," meaning a ship, because of the curved shape of the seed.

To those of us not specialists in botany, scientific descriptions of plants strange to us are as bewildering as the definitions in the famous Dr. Samuel Johnson's "Dic-

tionary." Particularly naive, picturesque but quite clear are
the descriptions of plants by the early writers. I can think
of no clearer picture of the caraway plant than that written by John Parkinson in his *Paradisus* in the seventeenth
century. He says that it

hath many very fine cut and divided leaves lying on the ground,
being alwaies greene, some-what resembling the leaves of Carrots,
but thinner and more finely cut, of a quicke, hot and spicie taste:
the stalke riseth not much higher than the Carrot stalke, bearing
some leaves at the ioynts along the stalke to the toppe, where it
brancheth into three or foure parts, bearing spoakie umbels of white
flowers, which turne into small blackish seede, smaller than Ani-
seede, and of a hotter, quicker taste: the roote is whitish, like un to
Parsnep, but much smaller, more spreading underground, and a
little quicke in taste, as all the rest of the plant is, and abideth long
after it hath given seede.

The seeds are dull, very dark brown, about one-fourth
inch long, with five lighter colored ridges, rough in texture,
slightly curved, and tapering at each end. Since caraway is
a biennial, it doesn't complete its life cycle until the second
year when it blooms in early June and produces seeds a
month later. Because the flowers open so early in the season, the plant is not readily confused with wild carrot or
Queen Anne's Lace which is poisonous to eat. Caraway
will thrive best in a dryish, sunny spot in somewhat clayey,
enriched loam. Because of its long, delicate taproot, it is
difficult to transplant the seedling, so the seeds should be
sown where the plant will mature, in the open ground
when danger of frost is over, or in the autumn as soon as
the seeds ripen. The only care is to thin out the crowded
seedlings and keep clear of weeds, and avoid shade of
faster growing plants. Because of the biennial nature, to
secure a crop each year, seeds should be sown annually.

Caraway was used in ancient Egyptian medicine because the "spicie taste doth warme and comfort a cold weake stomacke." The seed has also been long used in love potions. In the second part of Shakespeare's Henry IV, V-3, we find Justice Shallow offering a favorite conclusion to an Elizabethan dinner:

You shall see my orchard, where, in an arbour, we will eat a last year's pippin of my own gaffing with a dish of caraways.

That custom is still observed in many of the Guildhall banquets in England.

Parkinson said that "the seede is much used to bee put among baked fruit, or into bread, cakes, etc., to give them a rellish, and to helpe digest winde in them [that] are subject thereunto. It is also made into Comfits and put into Trageas, as we call them in English, Dredges that are taken for the cold and winde in the body, as also are served to the table with fruit." The herbalist Culpeper also recognized the medicinal virtues of the seed. "Carraway confects, once only dipped in sugar, and a spoonful of them eaten in the morning fasting, and as many after each meal, is a most admirable remedy for those that are troubled with wind."

Dr. Fernie of the nineteenth century claims that in Germany caraway seeds are given for "hysterical affections, being finely powdered and mixed with ginger and salt to spread with butter on bread."

Aside from the commercial use of caraway seeds in perfume, soap, kümmel, etc., some of the great import is used by individuals. Most of our foreign born population still follow the cooking traditions of the mother country. Hungarians and Germans usually add caraway seeds to their goulashes and soups, while the peasants of Norway and Sweden make a black bread with caraway. An appetizing dish is created by adding bacon drippings to cabbage as it is boiling, then stirring in a half teaspoonful of the seed. A little added to the vinegar used to pickle beets gives a pleasing difference from the usual recipe. It may also be added to the dressing used for potato salad, or stirred into mashed turnip. As anise is used in cottage or cream cheese, so caraway may be treated:

Take one cup of cottage cheese, add salt and pepper to taste, one teaspoonful of caraway, and enough cream to soften the mixture for spreading.

On the Continent where such delicious Gorgonzola cheese is to be had, we find served with it, buttered bread on which is spread a mixture of caraway and sugar.

We often buy at foreign bakeries "salt sticks," most delicious for serving with salad. These sticks may be made at home from your pastry recipe. The dough is formed into short sticks, covered with white of egg, sprinkled with salt and caraway seeds and then baked quickly in a hot oven. Baking powder biscuits may be varied by the addition of caraway.

In the eighteenth century, we find many mouth-watering recipes in those informally written cook books which gave more than just recipes for food, even to hints on the whole art of living. One particularly charming *Receipt Book of a Lady of the Reign of Queen Anne* was written in 1711 by Elizabeth Wainwright, not at all hampered by spelling rules. Many recipes are marked by an X, which any housewife will tell you marks the spot of the formula for a tasty dish which has been especially praised. "To make a Caraway Cake" is thus marked, and I offer it for your approval. Think nothing of a pound of butter!

Take a large quart of fine flour, one pound of butter; rub the butter into the flower till it be luke warm: take the yolk of six eggs, one white, six spoonfuls of good cream, 5 or 6 spoonfuls of new yeast and when you have maid it into a past, set it before the fire half an hour till it be well Risen; then take it and work into it half a pound of Caroway Comfitts and when your oven is hot, butter your cake pan and worke up your cake as quick as you can and set it in a quick oven.

In the *Godey's Lady's Book* (February, 1862), I found a recipe for a rich seed cake which reminded me of Elizabeth Wainwright's for its ample quantity of those ingredients to which most of us nowadays give a second thought before measuring with such a lavish hand. We find a pound of butter for a little over a pound of flour, well dried, as we are warned, and eight eggs. There is no yeast or baking powder called for, and we are advised to bake the cake for two hours in a quick oven.

If you don't feel like plunging into the making of a rich seed cake, try a batch of caraway cookies. Simply use the basic recipe suggested above under Anise, and add a tablespoonful of caraway seeds in place of aniseed.

CARDAMON, *Elettaria Cardamomum*

The name "cardamom" or "cardamon," as it is often spelled, comes from the Greek word meaning "spice plant."

The seeds of very pungent flavor have an ancient and honorable reputation, having been known to the East Indians and Arabs of very early times, and are still much used in the East in curry powders, and chewed like candy to relieve colic. We find written records of their use as far back as the eighth century B.C. in Sanskrit manuscripts, and we read that cardamom was one of the four hundred simples valued by Hippocrates in the fifth century B.C. We also find it highly spoken of by later Greek and Roman writers and learn that it was supposed to have aphrodisiac properties and was a popular ingredient of love potions.

The Persians had a most elaborate routine for a charm to induce the return of an erring husband. According to a recent version of the process, you start with placing a mixture of cloves, cinnamon and cardamom in a large jar. Over this, read seven times backward the "Yasin" chapter from the Koran. (Obviously, not the Koran, but the sacred book of Persia must have been meant.) Then the jar is filled with rose water; a shirt belonging to the husband and a paper containing the name of that truant and of four angels, are both immersed in the liquid. The jar is put over a fire, and as soon as boiling begins the husband is on his way home. I imagine the contents must have to be in just the right proportion and every other condition met exactly or no husband!

Cardamom was much used in beauty creams and also in pomanders for the spicy perfume of the essential oils in the seed. The Portuguese navigator Barbosa, in 1514, claimed that cardamom was grown on the Malabar coast. There are some dozen varieties, as we know, all of tropical or semi-tropical climatic conditions, and growing also in Southern India, Ceylon and islands of the Netherland East Indies.

This perennial plant with thick fleshy rhizome has a smooth, jointed, hollow stem about one inch thick, rising to twice a man's height. It is sheathed at the lower part by leaves sometimes a yard long. Each leaf is shaped like a narrow pointed blade, smooth and dark green on the upper side and lighter underneath, the effect emphasized by the soft, short white hairs covering that surface. The flowering stems which rise from the rootstock are weak and tender and sprawl out perhaps two or three feet. They, too, are jointed, with green bracts at the joints, and bear many flowers, usually four in a group of loose racemes from the axils of the green bracts. The flowers resemble small, greenish yellow orchids that had a poor start in life but had succeeded in having one large violet colored lip. Each flower is followed by a fruit called the great cardamom, light colored, hollow, bluntly triangular, about one-half inch long. The pods are gathered before they are ripe and dried in the sun which bleaches them. The pods are not opened until the seeds are to be used, thus preserving the full aroma. When we do open the pod, we find three cells, each with two rows of seeds—very dark, reddish brown, known as the lesser cardamoms.

Commercially, the oil of cardamom is used with other oils for flavoring, sometimes combined with oil of orange, of cinnamon, of cloves or of caraway. It is also used in bitters, liqueurs, candy, fumigating concoctions, and in synthetic lily-of-the-valley perfume.

Medically, oil of cardamom is used for head disorders and for flatulence. Do you remember David Copperfield's experiences with Mrs. Crupp his housekeeper? That acme of all faithless servants, imposing continually on his innocence, would come the very picture of suffering and ask David if "I could oblige her with a little tincture of cardamoms mixed with rhubarb and flavored with 7 drops of the essence of cloves, which was the best remedy for her complaint, or if I had not such a thing by me, with a little brandy which was the next best." Having prowled through David's belongings many times, Mrs. Crupp knew full well that he had not a drop of the best remedy but a goodly supply of the "next best!"

Cardamom gives that characteristic flavor to Scandi-navian pastry. "Fattigman Bakkelse" or Poor Man's Pastry is a Swedish dainty good to serve with afternoon coffee, and made quite simply:

1½ cups pastry flour	1 teaspoonful vanilla
2 eggs	1 teaspoonful salt
2 tablespoonfuls heavy cream	¼ teaspoonful crushed carda-mom

Stir the sugar, cream, salt, vanilla and seeds into the eggs, lightly beaten. Add the flour, more or less of the suggested amount, to make a dough of a consistency to roll out thinly. Cut into fancy shapes, fry in deep fat and lay on brown paper to drain excess fat. Sprinkle with powdered sugar.

Cardamom cookies may be made by adding one tea-spoonful powdered seeds to the basic recipe for sugar cookies.

CELERY, *Apium sativum,* or *A. graveolens* var. *dulce*

A parsley, of the umbelliferae order, with the botanical name of *Selinon* (parsley) but ages ago the N changed to R, making it "seleron" and probably the Italian, "celeri." The early writers kept the S and as late as the eighteenth century John Evelyn in his "Acetaria" says that "Sellery" was formerly a stranger. The herb for its high and grateful taste is ever placed in the middle of the grand sallet at our great men's tables.

Our garden celery is a cultivated variety of wild celery or smallage, *Apium graveolens*. Dr. Fernie in his "Meals Medicinal" says that wild celery which is dangerous when growing as a plant exposed to the daylight becomes most "palatable and beneficial" when earthed up and bleached. So many wild plants become pleasantly fragrant when moved into the garden. The Romans made the Smallage (small ache) into garlands for the heads of guests to absorb the fumes of wine. From earliest times celery had been recommended for nerves, rheumatism, to purify the blood, and for many troubles of spirit, mind and body.

Sometimes the seed is produced the first year. It is really the dried fruit, divided into separate mericarps, each seed tiny, dark brown, and with five definite ridges of a lighter brown. The cultivation of the plant has been widely written about, Farmer's Bulletin 1269F "Celery Growing" (five cents) being helpful. Do not confuse celery seed with the commercial celery salt, which is a mixture of crushed seed and salt. The seed is used in pickles, catsup, soups, French dressing. It adds a particularly good flavor to boiled dressing for potato salad. Coleslaw is given a different taste by the addition of celery seed, crushed or whole. The amount depends on individual taste, but a heaping teaspoonful to a quart of cabbage would not seem to me too much.

CORIANDER, *Coriandrum sativum*

An annual known as long ago as the Sanskrit authors who referred to it as "kustumburu." The Roman Pliny called the plant *coriandrum* from the Greek "koris," meaning a bug, and a well deserved name, too, as you will agree if you have ever smelled the very rank odor of the fresh green plant and seed.

Coriander as Gerard writes, "is a very stinking herbe, it has a round stalke full of branches two foote long." The leaves are almost like the leaves of the parsley, but later

on become more jagged. And there you have coriander!
It is a plant of a soft green much cut foliage. The flower
umbels blossoming in late June are about one and one-half
inches across, of a delicate tint of rosy lilac. The little
florets composing each umbel are arranged in neat symmetrical clusters, more readily noticed a few weeks later
when the fruits have developed. These should be harvested as soon as they have ripened because they are so
heavy for their tiny slender stems that they will soon fall
to the ground and self-sow abundantly like weeds.

A magnifying glass (for the financial outlay of ten
cents), a few of each of the savory seeds, and you have
the makings of a grand evening's entertainment. I'll war-
rant that you become so fascinated by the study of these
little round seeds of coriander that you won't realize the
time passing until perhaps you are simply made to stop.
(Orphie, wherever he may be during the evening, promptly
at 11:16 after the late news flash, stalks into the library
and by insinuating ways, tells us to leave so that he can
go to bed—on his master's desk!)

The first time I really looked at, in and around the
coriander seed I was so thrilled I went about with my
magnifier and seeds making everyone see how marvelous
they are. The so-called seed is really the fruit, each one an
almost perfect sphere about one-eighth inch in diameter.
The outside is a dull brownish yellow with a tinge of
purplish red at one end and is rough in texture, with the
most interesting arrangement of ridges, a heavy straight
ridge between two indistinct wavy ones. The top is somewhat pointed and surrounded by little pin point knobs, the
remains of the calyx teeth, at the termination of each
straight ridge. Now, if you rub the seed between your
thumb and forefinger, you will find that it separates into

halves, botanically mericarps, and the thin outside shell or pericarp, drops off. In each mericarp is a seed, half globular and held in place by a hair-like strip of shell across the top of the flat section.

The odor of the dried seed has been described as a combination of sage and lemon peel but since I do not like the odor of sage, and I am entranced by burying my nose in a handful of freshly crushed dried coriander seed, I cannot hold with that description. Odors are so terribly hard to name and most of us describe them by comparison with pleasant or disagreeable odors, commonly known. I have had many friends name the odor that coriander suggests and the results have been camphor or lemon peel. Whatever its name, the odor is clean, refreshing and spicy, I think, and that fragrance seems to become more pronounced the longer you keep the seeds. That is my difficulty—I use up my supply each autumn all too soon for potpourri or in gingerbread, and in trying experiments on my friends.

The seeds which are said to retain their vitality for several years may be sown in the open ground in a sunny place having moderately fertile sandy loam and average moisture. Germination is so easy that you may sow quite sparsely and then thin out seedlings to stand eight or nine inches apart. Because of the taproot, transplanting is difficult. It is said that in India where a great deal of coriander is raised, the ripe fruit is rubbed between the palms of the hands until the mericarps separate and then it is broadcast in the open fields. By the fourth day the seeds have germinated, and by the end of the fourth week the harvest has been made. That process ought to be quick and interesting enough to suit the most impatient gardener. In the English shire of Essex, coriander seed is sowed with that of caraway, a very efficient plan, too, for a small plot of ground. The caraway, being a biennial, does not reach maturity until the second year, so the coriander can be planted, grown and harvested while the foliage of the caraway is still a pretty bright green rosette not yet lifting its stalks and serving to cover the plot otherwise left bare.

The seeds of coriander, one of the earliest known spice herbs, have been found in old Egyptian tombs. One of the bitter herbs at the Passover, it is mentioned in the Old Testament as so well known that the unfamiliar manna is described by comparison with the coriander seed.

And when the dew that lay was gone up, behold, upon the face of the wilderness, there lay a small round thing, as small as the hoar frost on the ground.

This, from Exodus XVI : 14 and in verse 31 we read:

And the house of Israel called the name thereof Manna; and it was like coriander seed, white; and the taste of it was like wafers made with honey.

Further on, in Numbers XI : 7,

And the manna was as coriander and the colour thereof as the colour of bdellium.

The "bdellium" is not known but thought to be a gum, rosin, precious stone or pearl.

Pliny claimed that the very best coriander came from Egypt, so it must have long been known to these early peoples. Today two-thirds of what we import comes from Morocco.

Marcus Varro, Roman writer of the first century B.C., is quoted by Pliny as recommending coriander seed crushed with cumin and sprinkled with vinegar to be spread over meat to preserve it in summer. We read of an early Emperor of China collecting plants from all over his kingdom for the royal garden and in that search, coriander was brought back as a great prize.

The plant was introduced into England by the Romans, along with many other herbs which died out in the deserted gardens of the villas after the departure to Rome or the murder of their owners early in the fifth century as the Saxon barbarians came pillaging and destroying. Many plants were reintroduced from the Continent in the Middle Ages by the monks for their monastery gardens. Coriander, however, since it reseeds and germinates so readily must, I think, have survived all the neglect and grown on happily in those deserted villa gardens.

In Ion Gardener's *Feate of Gardening* (1440), the oldest original work in English on gardening, coriander is recommended for cultivation. We also find coriander among John Josselyn's list of herbs grown in New England in the seventeenth century.

Many and varied have been the uses of coriander seed from ancient to modern times, medicine and magic, cordials and candy, perfume and pastries. It was an ingredient of many medicinal preparations among the ancient East Indians and Egyptians while in the fifth century B.C. it was much used by Hippocrates, the great physician. William Turner in his herbal (1551) said that "coriander layd to wyth breade or barly mele is good for Saynt Antony's fyre."

In the *Thousand and One Nights,* coriander was used as an aphrodisiac, and it was an ingredient, along with fennel, of an incense to summon devils. Other ingredients were of a definitely narcotic nature, black poppy, hemlock and henbane which acted on the nervous system to such an extent that terrible hallucinations would be produced. William Turner claimed that coriander if "taken out of measure" would "taketh men's wyttes." Strangely enough, science has determined the truth of this and coriander or caraway in excessive amounts—two ounces at least—will produce a narcotic effect.

The coriander seed was used in "hippocras," a spiced wine, as an ingredient of the famous Eau des Carmes which was taken as a pleasing cordial and used externally as a freshener of body and spirit, and was also a constituent of angelica water "for the stomach's sake." The seeds dipped in fondant, often colored pink, were a favorite comfit for children some years ago. Once in a while now we see various colored tiny sugar coated seeds of anise, caraway, coriander and celery for cake decorations. Just the other day I bought a few for old times' sake hoping to bite into lovage seed, an old favorite for candies.

At the present time coriander seed or oil is used to a great extent commercially. We imported nearly two million pounds in 1935. The pale yellow oil is used in medicinal preparations with senna and rhubarb because of the carminative effect, and in liqueurs and cordials for its stimulative reaction. Because of these virtues plus a pleasant taste, the crushed seed and oil are used in rich cakes, biscuits, custards, and jellies, and we read of its use to improve inferior grades of cocoa. The seasoning of French sausage includes coriander. In mixed spice it is about one-quarter the bulk and in curry powders it is about half.

At home we may use coriander seed to produce some pleasingly different culinary effects. The crushed seed gives a spicy flavor to chopped meat and beef stews, and as anise and caraway were recommended to be added to beet salad or pickles, you will find coriander also delicious. In the

Receipt Book of a Lady of the Reign of Queen Anne
(1711) Elizabeth Wainwright gives a "receipt" for Gingerbread Wafers which you might like to try.

Take one pound and a half of flower, a quarter of a pound of fine sugar, an ounce of beaten ginger, ten ounces of treakel, a small nutmeg, half a pound of butter rubd in ye flower, a few Caraway seeds and Coreander. Make yis into a past, and rowle it very thin and cut it wt ye top of a glass, a littel will bake ym.

A gingerbread recipe I follow is this:

2 cups flour	⅔ cup shortening
1¼ teaspoons baking soda	½ cup brown sugar
½ teaspoon salt	2 eggs, well beaten
3 teaspoons ginger	¾ cup molasses
1 teaspoon cinnamon	¾ cup boiling water
1 teaspoon coriander seed	¼ cup warm water

To bring out the flavors, that is, the essential oils of herbs that are to be used in fairly dry mixtures, soak the required amount of the leaf or seed in some of the liquid for half an hour before using. In this case, crush the coriander seed and soak in the ¼ cup warm water. Add this mixture when the boiling water is added.

Sift the flour twice with soda, salt, ginger. Cream the shortening with brown sugar until light and fluffy. Add eggs and beat well. Add ¼ of flour mixture and blend, then add molasses and beat until smooth. Add remaining flour mixture, beating well. Add boiling water (and spice water) gradually and beat until smooth. Turn into greased square loaf pan and baked in moderate oven 50 minutes.

Cumin, *Cuminum Cyminum*

The name comes from the Greek *"kyminon"* but of Semitic origin. An annual known from ancient times, much used in medicine, in superstitious practices and in cooking.

This delicate little plant, reaching not much more than a foot in height, divides into small slender stems having jagged leaves finely cut into threadlike divisions, giving a spidery effect at the tip ends. The flower umbels are a dainty rose color when fully blossomed out in July. The fruits are little ridged oblongs covered with the finest of little bristles. These fruits or seeds, as we call them, are flat on one side, about one-fourth inch long, light brown when ripe, about two months from planting.

Seeds should be sown in quite sunny, moderately fertile, well-drained soil, with average moisture, and more thickly than most herb seeds because the germination is not to be depended on. Do not try to transplant the seedlings, frail little bits of life; simply keep out the weeds which will come because of the very slow growth of the herb. If not harvested when ripe, the seeds will self-sow.

Theophrastus, fourth century B.C., writer and devotee of plant culture, said that, "One must curse and abuse it [cumin] while sowing, if the crop is to be fair and abundant." That would seem hardly necessary to us who do not dread the Evil Eye, from which the ancients tried to protect their harvests. It certainly would be amazing to see a fair lady strewing her seeds, cursing roundly each step of the way. Perhaps, though, that's the reason I receive such pathetic letters complaining of not being able to grow even the smallest crop of cumin! I would store up the curses for any rain falling after sowing, if we agree with Gerard that "a shewer of raine presently following [the planting of cumin] doth much hinder the growing thereof." Gerard boasted that the seeds he grew were "much fairer and greater than any that cometh from beyond the seas," and that seed he sowed in the middle of

May sprang up six days after and was ripe in the end of July!

Cumin was grown extensively in early days in the Mediterranean and in the Eastern countries, so highly valued that it was, in Biblical days, one of the tithes along with mint and dill. In Isaiah XXVIII : 25–27, we read of the plowman scattering the cumin seed and later, beating the umbels with a rod to thresh out the seeds. In December, 1937, George VI of England made a tour of the Duchy of Cornwall where he was personally presented with the symbolic quitrents, paid in early times in lieu of actual feudal service required of tenants. Among the gifts was a pound of cumin.

Pliny said that his contemporaries soaked the crushed seed in water and drank the liquid in order to make their faces pale, considered appropriate for hard students. Others smoked the crushed seeds to produce the proper paleness. Strangely enough, the actual qualities of the seed make it effective in overcoming the pallor of persons long ill.

To the Greeks cumin symbolized cupidity, and Marcus Aurelius is supposed to have been nicknamed "Cumin" because of his avaricious nature and it was not complimentary in financial arguments to be accused of having eaten cumin. In the olden days, too, cumin was supposed to have the power of retention. Fed to departing lovers or to pigeons it would insure their return. Many a loaf rich in cumin was baked for soldiers going off to the Crusades and many a final cup of wine was drunk in which some of the seeds had been dropped. There runs an old folk story about a peasant family that felt good luck had come to them because of the continued presence of a wood nymph near them. The wife made a loaf of cumin bread for the nymph who sensed the significance of the gift and, hurt that she was not trusted, abandoned the neighborhood. Sometimes just having the seeds about one was held effective. During German marriage ceremonies in the Middle Ages, both bride and groom carried cumin, dill and salt in their pockets, perhaps to make assurance double sure.

Because of the virtues of cumin as carminative and stimulant, the seed has been used from ancient times in medicine. Pliny recommended it for indigestion for which caraway was also used, but in England caraway was gradually substituted for cumin. We still find cumin on the crude drug lists today for the same virtues as in early times.

In medieval times cumin was used for dangerous wounds and we also learn that if you take the seeds, sugar coated, night and morning, "by the help of God you will obtain benefit." Gerard suggested a rather unusual use: "It stancheth bleeding at the nose, being tempered with vinegar and smelt unto." He possibly recognized its stimulating effects when he says that, "Being taken in a supping broth it is good for the chest and for colde lungs." Nowadays cumin is much used in liqueurs, such as kümmel and crème de menthe, because of the warm effect produced. The oils of cumin are used somewhat in making synthetic perfumes with the scent of violet, lily of the valley, and hyacinth.

In India cumin seed is an important ingredient of curry powder; in Spain it is used with saffron and cinnamon in many distinctive dishes. In Holland, Scandinavia and Switzerland the peculiar flavor of cheese is due to cumin. A Swedish friend tells me they use it crushed over boiled potatoes, in pickled cucumber or cabbage (with fennel also) and in many pastries. Oh, that we, too, could learn to cook adventurously!

Some day when you are just sick and tired of some variety of canned soup you frequently use, drop a few crushed cumin seeds into the boiling liquid just a minute or two before serving. I am sure you will be delighted with the toning up the flavor has assumed. Try a pinch of finely crushed seeds in part of a batch of sugar cookies. You never can tell until you experiment, how a different seasoning now and then makes all the difference in a dull dish.

CHAPTER XI

A PICKLING AND PASTRY GARDEN

DILL, *Anethum graveolens*

An annual unbelliferous plant. Many have been the opinions on the derivation of the word "dill," but the consensus seems to be that it is derived from an Old English word. Dr. Fernie says that it was named from *"dilla,"* a verb meaning to lull, because of the soothing effect on babies. To this day, water in which the seed has been soaked is given to children to lull them to sleep. In the modern Oxford Dictionary, we are told the word comes from the Old English *dili,* but that etymology is unknown. The root of "anethum" is the Greek word, to burn, probably so named because of the warming effect; and it is interesting to learn that dill was often called "Anet" years ago in the rural districts of England.

This "pleasant and fragrant plant," as the Latin poet Virgil called it although native to the East and Mediterranean regions, is very easy to grow and satisfying because of its decorative quality and its useful seeds. Many visitors to my garden are amazed that dill is something that grows. They have always taken dill pickles for granted, as they have stuffed olives or sage cheese, never stopping to think how pickles got their name, unaware that the peculiar flavor comes from fragrant seeds of a plant easily grown in any kitchen garden.

Parkinson describes the plant thus:

[Dill] is a smaller herbe then Fennell, but very like, have fine cut leaves, not so large, but shorter, smaller and of a stronger quicker taste: the stalke is smaller also, and with few ioynts and leaves on them, bearing spoakie tufts of yellow flowers, which turne into thinne, small and flat seedes: the roote perisheth every yeare, and riseth againe for the most part of it owne sowing.

The seed, which is said to retain its germinating capacity for three years, may be sown in the open ground after all danger of frost is gone. The plants will thrive most happily in a warm, sunny, rather sheltered spot, in sandy, well drained, moderately rich loam. Do not try to transplant, keep the weeds out by cultivating the soil frequently. If you cannot have a protected spot, you must stake the plants since they often reach four feet up.

I enjoy the dill at the beginning as well as at the end of the season. Not a thinned out seedling is thrown away, for I chop the delicate leafy branches, stir them into potato salad, or often sprinkle a tablespoonful over lamb chops when they are almost broiled, then some dabs of butter and finish the broiling. Many a time I have used the little dill tops this way and with what acclaim from everyone at the table.

When most of the seed heads have turned a brownish color in late August, cut off all the umbels, spread them out on a heavy cloth to finish ripening and to dry for about ten days. Then thresh out the fruit by rubbing the umbels one at a time between the palms of the hands, dry for a week more and store in closely covered jars. These dill fruits will surely be on your program of magnifying-glass study. They are little, brown, elongated ovals from one-eighth to one-fourth inch long, rounded through the middle on both sides. The individual fruit may be separated into mericarps, each having three light colored, longitudinal ridges and widish fins on each side, narrowing toward each end. Turning over one of the mericarps, you will find the interior slightly concave, cradling a seed held in by a thread of shell over the top, from end to end.

Dill was much valued in ancient days as is evidenced by its inclusion in the Biblical tithes. We read in the *Natural History* of Pliny (first century A.D.) of nine medicinal remedies with dill as the chief ingredient. Because of its soothing effect dill has always been much used medicinally. As the sixteenth century Gerard said it would stop the "yeox, hicket, or hicquet," so the seventeenth century Parkinson informs us that, "Some use to eate the seed to stay the Hickocke," all hiccoughs to us. Parkinson's contemporary, Culpeper, is more definite in his directions. Dill will

stay the hiccough being boiled in wine, and but smelled unto, being tied in a cloth. The seed is of more use than the leaves and used in medicines that serve to expel wind.

In early days dill was used by witches for their wicked potions, but it also was used against evil spirits. We find Meg Merrilies, in Scott's *Guy Mannering,* singing her gypsy chant just before the birth of Harry Bertram, to keep the newcomer from harm:

> Trefoil, vervain, John's wort, dill
> Hinder witches of their will.

Dill in the early days of our country was a "meetin' seed." During the long, dreary adult sermons every Sunday, when little legs began to jerk, the seeds were brought out and nibbled. Such occupation stopped the fidgets, although it is to be suspected that no more of the sermon was heard.

As far back as the seventeenth century at least, dill seeds were used in pickling. Parkinson said, "It is put among pickled Cowcumbers, wherewith it doth very well agree, giving unto the cold fruit a pretty spicie taste or rellish." John Evelyn in his *Acetaria* (1699) gives a fairly workable recipe for pickling "Collyflowers" (cauliflower) :

Boil them till they fall in Pieces: then with some of the Stalk, and most of the Flower, boil it in a part of the Liquor till pretty strong: then being taken off, strain it; and when settled, clear it from the Bottom. Then with Dill, Gross Pepper, a pretty Quantity of Salt, when cold, add as much Vinegar as will make it sharp, and pour all upon the Collyflower.

Instead of always buying your dill pickles from the delicatessen, why don't you this spring plant some seeds, both of dill and of cucumber, so they will ripen at the same time? Then "put down" your own dill pickles and "taste the difference!"

Cover the bottom of a good sized crock with a layer of fresh umbels of dill, then a tablespoonful of mixed spice, if you like, and a layer of well scrubbed cucumbers of a fairly even size. Continue this process to within a few inches of the top of the crock. Grape leaves, placed on the very bottom and over the top layer, will help to keep the pickles green. Then make up as much brine mixture as will cover the top layer, using this proportion of material: ½ lb. salt, ½ pint vinegar, 1 gallon water. Pour this mixture (the Agric. Bureau says it should be 86 degrees, and not hot since hot brine will prevent the desired fermentation) into the crock and cover with a weight which will keep the cucumbers submerged. In about two weeks they should be dark green in color and well flavored. When this state is reached, transfer the pickles to jars, add a little dill and spice. Make a new brine, or use the old mixture, bring to a boil, cool just a bit, fill the jars to overflowing, seal and keep in a cool place. The Dept. of Agric. Bulletin *Making Fermented Pickles* (five cents) is helpful. Ask for Farmer's Bulletin No. 1438.

A dill vinegar is good for variation with ordinary vinegars in French dressing. This may be made quite simply by soaking dill seeds in any good vinegar for 10 days. I use 2 tablespoonfuls of seeds to 1 quart of vinegar. Then strain, or filter if you want the vinegar quite clear, and bottle.

Scandinavians use dill a great deal, in pastries, as apple pies, in soups, gravies, potato salads and with fish dishes. A delicious hors d'oeuvre can be made with salmon. Spread fingers of toast with salmon on top of which run a narrow ribbon of mayonnaise. Sprinkle over this a few dill seeds.

SESAME, *Sesamum orientale* or *S. indicum*

An annual which is native to Eastern countries. Invaluable for many centuries for the oil found in great abundance in the seed. Sesame is also called "benne" or "bene" from the Malay word, *bene,* meaning grain or seed.

The plant ranging in height from two to four feet has just one stem, hairy, light green, round and ridged slightly. This is about the only plant of any height that I do not have to stake as it grows, a staunch and sturdy stalk. Although the plant has no branches, the leaves, opposite in position, are on such long stems that the general impression is one of innumerable arms. When you have seen one hairy leaf of this plant you have by no means seen them all. On the lower part of the stem the leaves are broad, some sharply toothed, others roundly lobed. As they ascend the stalk, the indentations diminish until the upper leaves are quite long, narrow and tapering almost to a point. In the axils of the topmost leaves in early August, come pretty little flowers, like miniatures of the foxglove flower, some a pale orchid, others cream colored.

The hairy, light green seed capsules are blunt oblongs with four rounding sides made by longitudinal grooves. When you open the rather hard, tough shell, you see that each of the rounded sides was a long cradle for a row of seeds, each one less than one-eighth inch long, coming to a point at one end, and whitish in color. The whole seed—because of its size, color and hard shiny surface—reminds me of tiny rice kernels. Some varieties of sesame produce pale yellow seeds, others almost black, but the kind we grow in our kitchen gardens have an ashy white color.

You will delight in raising a crop of sesame, if for nothing more than to amaze your visitors! Practically all will say, "Sesame? Do you mean the 'Open, Sesame' kind?" And sure enough, it is the very same ancient and honorable grain. The seeds may be planted in the open ground in May, in a sunny well drained spot. I have never fussed or bothered at all about the plants which I have had in various places in the garden. I simply thin out the crowded seedlings, remove the weeds, and harvest a good crop of seeds in September.

We may have first heard of sesame through John Ruskin's grand essay, *Sesame and Lilies,* in which he makes sesame the secret word that will unlock the treasures to be found in books. Most of us, however, as children enjoyed the old story of Ali Baba's brother, locked in the robber's cave and forgetting the "Open, Sesame!" which would have released him. Many will recall similar folk tales in which various magic flowers or plants were used to unlock treasures, the primrose in Germany, the Rasrivtrava in Russia, the fern, the mistletoe or the witch hazel branch which tells well-diggers where to look for water.

The East Indians, also, have faith in the magic powers of sesame to open secret places, and gave it the name of *Vajrapushpa,* meaning thunderbolt. Offerings of the seed are made to the god of death.

Sesame in classic times was an herb of magic, always associated with Hecate, queen of the witches, and with Medea and Circe, her daughters. It was much used for its medicinal virtues by the Greek Hippocrates, great physician of the fifth century B.C. and by all that followed him. The Great Mogul of India in the sixteenth century was passionately fond of perfumes and had all the flowers of a sweet scent in his garden steeped in the oil of sesame seed, because it held the odor so well. The thick liquid was then used as a fragrant bath oil and as a dressing for his royal hair. Many and varied are the uses of the seed and oil. The sticks of India ink, Chinese ink, are made from the soot obtained by burning the oil.

The Greek writer Theophrastus, third century B.C., highly praised sesame seeds for their flavor. In the satires of the Roman Petronius, first century A.D., well turned phrases are spoken of as being "sprinkled with Poppy and Sesamum." The oil, the first kind to be developed on a large scale, was and still is used much more than olive oil in Egypt, probably because of the fact that it doesn't readily become rancid. The flavor is delightful, like delicate tasting nuts. A most delicious confection is made by

mixing sesame seeds with enough sirup to hold them together, then molded into a form like a popcorn bar. Our
family is so fond of these sesame bars that we buy them
in wholesale lots in New York just for our own delecta-
tion.

We read of the seeds sprinkled on Sicilian bread, but
in America we use them for the most part in cake and
cookies. Try some cookies, and you will hear loud clamors
for more. To the basic recipe given, add a good tablespoonful of the seed slightly toasted to bring out the
nutty flavor.

FENNEL, *Foeniculum vulgare* or *f. capillaceum*

The Romans always regarded fennel as a kind of small
fragrant hay, and gave it the name of *foeniculum* which
means that. In the Middle Ages, the word became "fan-
culum" and later "fenkel" by which it is still known in
Sweden.

There are several varieties of fennel, three of them
used in cooking, but all derived from the perennial wild
or bitter fennel (*F.vulgare*). In early days as demand
for the plant grew, it was brought into gardens and cultivated. From that transplanting and care comes the garden
fennel. Another development was an annual dwarf variety,
F.vulgare var. *dulce* or Florence fennel, known on the
markets as "Finocchio." The plant has broad, overlapping
base leaves which form a slightly flattened ball. Soil is
heaped up around these swollen bases which thus become
blanched.

Still another development is the Carosella or *F.piperi-
tum,* with thickened fleshy stalks which are eaten raw like
celery. Some writers use the word "dulce" for the bo-

tanical description of finocchio while others apply it to Carosella.

Garden fennel is a tall perennial growing to a height of three to five feet, depending upon the soil. The stalk is bluish green, hollow, round and smooth; the leaves of a fine feathery appearance somewhat like carrot foliage. Culpeper describes the plant thus:

It has large, thick, white roots, which run deep into the ground, much dividing beset with small fibres. It has large winged leaves, of a dark green, divided into many segments, of long, slender, very fine, capilaceous parts. The stalk grows to four feet in height, much divided, and full of whitish pith. The flowers are found at the top in flat umbels, of small yellow fine-leaved flowers, each of which is succeeded by a couple of roundish, somewhat flat, striated brown seed.

As a matter of fact, the seeds, although on brownish tones, have also touches of yellow and of gray in them. Each seed is about one-fourth inch long, definitely concave, with a grayish ridged streak through the center and a margin of lighter hue. The convex side has three ridges coming to a blunt point at each end. The seeds, as well as the other parts of the plant, have a strong, sweetish anise odor and flavor. Milton in his *Paradise Lost,* Book IX, was aware of the fragrance of fennel:

> The savoury odour blown,
> Grateful to appetite, more pleased my sense
> Than smell of sweetest Fennel.

The seed should be sown very thinly in the open ground when all danger of frost is over. It is particularly important to scatter the seeds well apart to avoid losing plants by thinning, since transplanting is somewhat difficult because of the root. When finally left to grow to maturity, the plants ought to stand a foot apart. The soil should be light and limy, of medium fertility with no addition of manure. Fennel likes a sunny location and little moisture. If you stake the plants as they reach about eighteen inches in height, you will have given fennel all the care it needs.

The yellow umbels open toward the end of July, and the seeds will be almost ripe in September when they turn brownish. Then they should be harvested or they will fall to the ground and reseed. Cut back the stalk to six inches from the ground, cut off the flower heads and allow them to finish ripening for about ten days on a heavy cloth. Then thresh out the seeds by rubbing the dried umbels lightly between the palms of the hands. Spread the seeds out again on the cloth for about a week, then store in tightly closed jars.

John Josselyn in his *New England Rarities* (1672) says, "Fennel must be Taken up, and Kept in a warm cellar all winter," but I have never found that necessary. Without any protection at all during winter, the fennel plants survive and come up fresh looking and bright green early in the spring.

Fennel, probably introduced into England by the Romans, was much used by ancient Egyptians, Chinese and East Indians and was highly recommended by the Greek physician Hippocrates, fifth century, B.C. Many are the superstitions connected with it, with seemingly conflicting sentiments in various countries. An old saying, handed down from the thirteenth century Welsh physicians of Mydrai, is: "He who sees fennel and gathers it not, is not a man, but a devil."

In Southern England, the country people cannot be induced to give away fennel lest they be overcome by disaster. Yet there is the belief that "Sowing fennel is sowing sorrow." I have never heard an explanation of that. Perhaps the fact of fennel's being a symbol of flattery is the answer.

In classic pagan times, the plant was used to make the wreath for the victor, while later in the Christian era fennel, sacred to St. John, decorated doorways during holy days dedicated to him.

In Longfellow's *Goblet of Life,* we find assembled a few of the early superstitions:

> Above the lowly plant it towers,
> The fennel, with its yellow flowers,
> And in an earlier age than ours
> Was gifted with the wondrous powers
> Lost vision to restore.
>
> It gave new strength and fearless mood
> And gladiators, fierce and rude,
> Mingled it in their daily food;
> And he who battled and subdued,
> A wreath of fennel wore.

Among the Orientals, Adonis, symbol of great beauty in young manhood, later the spirit of vegetation, was worshiped, mourned in the autumn and saluted in the spring with due rites. Seeds of fennel and of other quickly germinating plants were sown in pots and carefully tended for eight days until the little seedlings were well on the way, watched hopefully until they bloomed. Then on the longest day in summer, the plants were cut and used to adorn housetops and statues of Adonis. The fennel with its feathery foliage withered quickly, and thus contributed to its symbolic reputation for undependability.

Besides the use in superstitious practices, fennel was valuable for medicine and food. It was one of the nine healing herbs of the Anglo-Saxons. In the early days

sponges were dipped in infusions of herbs having a soporific effect and applied to the nose of a patient to dull the
pain of an operation. Later he was restored to conscious-
ness by fennel juice administered on the sponge.

The ninth century emperor Charlemagne was such a
great believer in the benefits of herbs that he compiled a
long list that he recommended for every garden. For his
own extensive gardens, fennel was prominent among the
herbs he insisted should be grown. In the thirteenth century, the royal household accounts of Edward I show that
about nine pounds of fennel seed were used during one
month. The seeds of fennel as well as those of coriander
were given a coating of sugar and eaten as comfits because
of the warming effect on the digestive system. The seeds
were also eaten uncoated to overcome the pangs of hunger
on the many days laid aside for fasting. In a poor woman's
pocket in *Piers Plowman* of the fourteenth century, we
find fennel seeds reserved for fasting days. Many a poor
person, I imagine, tightened his belt and chewed fennel on
some days not devoted to fasting.

Since the effect was to dull the appetite, though not
furnishing food, fennel was a popular ingredient in recipes
for reducing. In the *Good Housewife's Jewel* (1585) we
read a formula, "For to make one slender":

Take Fennel and seethe it in water, a very good quantity, and
wring out the juice thereof, when it is sod, and drink it first and
last, and it shall swage either him or her. (Now-a-days, for her
alone, I fancy!)

Besides being taken alone, fennel seed was introduced
into many a culinary dish, as soup, bread, fish sauces,
and fruit pies. Parkinson says, "The seede is much used

to be put into Pippin pies and divers other such baked fruits, as also into bread, to give it the better rellish." In 1711, Elizabeth Wainwright in her *Receipt Book of a Lady of the Reign of Queen Anne* tells how "To Make a Biskit Cake":

Take a pound of flower well dryd, a pound and a quart of fine sugar fine seavet [sieved], an ounce of Caraway, Coreander, sweet fenel seeds, 12 eggs and egght whits. Beat ym very well and then strew in your sugar and seeds and then your flower and 5 spoon-fulls of rose water, beat ym very well together about half an hour; butter your tin, ym bake it.

The use of fennel depends on the individual taste for anise flavor to which it is very similar, though somewhat stronger. In practically any recipe that calls for leaves of fennel, the crushed seeds may be substituted. I have friends who like the taste in bread and in fruit pastries. I am awaiting the report from one friend who in canning apple sauce last fall, put fennel leaves in some of the jars and applemint in others, to prevent the canned flavor. This lady is a swashbuckling cook who comes upon grand dishes through her courage to experiment.

Fennel seems to be the one "must" herb for fish dishes and sauces. In boiling fish a delightful flavor will result if a few herbs, about one and one-half tablespoonsful in all, are tied up in a square of cheesecloth and dropped in the boiling liquid. Be sure to remove the herb bag before serving the fish! A good mixture is equal amounts of the leaves of sweet marjoram, thyme, basil and sage with coarsely crushed seeds of fennel. Another combination might be seeds of fennel and celery, chives, thyme, and winter or summer savory.

In broiling mackerel or steaks of halibut or salmon, you will like the delicious taste resulting from the addition of an herb mixture to the butter you spread over the fish before putting it under the fire. Take about ¼ cup of soft butter, add ½ teaspoonful of salt, ⅛ teaspoonful of pepper, 1½ tablespoonsful of mixed herbs, say basil, chervil, thyme, marjoram and finely powdered fennel seeds. Mix these ingredients thoroughly. Spread half on the fish, and after turning it over, spread the other side with the remaining mixture.

There are several kinds of sauce delicious for serving with fish having a tendency to be dry. One is a cream sauce with herbs added. Mix thoroughly a level tablespoon of flour and of butter, then smooth out with top milk or thin cream to the consistency you like. Add ¼ teaspoonful of salt, a pinch of pepper and 1½ teaspoonsful of mixed herbs—equal parts of basil, sweet marjoram and finely powdered fennel. From time to time vary the combination of herbs and thus avoid monotonous sameness.

One variation of the above sauce is to boil the herbs in salted water for 15 minutes, strain out the herbs by means of a cheesecloth fitted into a wire strainer and use this liquid instead of milk or cream to thin out the flour paste. Still another sauce is made by putting 1½ teaspoonsful of equal parts of powdered chervil, finely chopped mint and finely powdered fennel seed, the juice of one lemon, and one cup of butter in a small skillet. Place over a slow fire until the butter melts, then turn up the flame and let the mixture boil quietly for two or three minutes.

MUSTARD

Mustard took its place among the herbs in ancient days and still is outstanding even though we now seldom think of including it in our herb gardens. The name developed from the Latin word, *mustus,* the new wine with which the mustard-loving Romans mixed the pounded seeds, and the word, *ardens,* burning.

In ancient times the writers had no scientific system of botanical classification, so when they spoke of mustard, that's all there was to it. Since for years black mustard has been grown for the seed, and the white variety for a salad herb, we can but surmise and deduce what kind is referred to in the ancient books. The Biblical grain of mustard seed is probably the first thought that comes to our minds, and I am sure that we somehow associate these tiny grains both with the fields of yellow mustard and the can of mustard flour on our kitchen shelves. We find in St. Mark IV: 31–32.

> It is like a grain of mustard seed, which when it is sown in the earth, is less than all the seeds that be in the earth:
> But when it is sown, it groweth up, and becometh greater than all herbs, and shooteth out great branches, so that the fowls of the air may lodge under the shadow of it.

It has been thought by some students that the Biblical plant belonged to a botanical group found in Europe and Asia and called *sinapi,* which is the Greek word for mustard, the name used by Theophrastus. But the plant does not grow to the proportions of a tree, so a good many scientists believe the grain of mustard referred to an Arabian many-branched shrub, called *Khardal,* found growing luxuriantly near the Sea of Galilee. The seeds are tiny and when crushed resemble mustard in taste and odor.

There also is a field mustard called "charlock" (*Brassica Sinapistrum*) with which we are all familiar. This plant grows to two feet tall and is notably a weed. In Tennyson's *Idylls of the King,* in the Idyll of "Gareth

and Lynette," we read of the messenger of King Mark
coming with a bribe to the hall of King Arthur:

> In either hand he bore
> What dazzled all, and shone far-off as shines
> A field of charlock in the sudden sun
> Between two showers, a cloth of palest gold.

We also have the black and white mustard which, although once treated as a small section of *sinapis,* is now
considered as belonging to the genus *Brassica* of the Cruciferae, plants with flowers of four petals arranged like a
cross.

BLACK MUSTARD (*Brassica nigra*)

This species may be native to England—it is generally
conceded that the white mustard is not—or the Romans
very well might have brought it, since they were so fond
of it. Parkinson in his *Paradisus* (1629) says:

> It hath many rough long divided leaves, of an overworne greene
> colour: the stalke is divided at the toppe with divers branches,
> whereon growe divers pale yellow flowers, in a great length, which
> turne into small long pods, where in is contained blackish seede, in-
> clining to rednesse, of a fiery sharpe taste: the root is tough and
> white running deepe into the ground, with many small fibres at it.

From Parkinson's description, we learn that apparently
the black mustard was the kind used commonly in his time
and he calls it *"sinapi sativum*—Garden Mustard," yet
the roughness of the leaves he describes distinguishes the
white kind.

The plant is an annual growing up to three feet tall.
The leaves are smooth, the lower ones somewhat cut into
rounding lobes, while the upper ones are smaller and un-

cut or entire. The yellow flowers, smaller than those of the white mustard, appear on racemes or "on divers branches in a great length," as Parkinson has it. The seed pods mark the greatest difference from the white variety. Those of the black are erect and smooth while those of the white are horizontal and hairy. The seed pods of the black are about one-half inch long, narrow, smooth, rather flattened in appearance, the lower thick part having four angles and ending in a short knob or beak which contains no seeds. The pods grow point up, straight, close to the stem. In the pod are a dozen or more imperfectly spherical seeds, dark reddish brown and sometimes black, about half the size of those of the white mustard which are the size of the old-fashioned colored glass pinheads. The outside shell of the seed is thin, brittle, and under a magnifying glass shows tiny pits. The whole seeds have no odor. The first taste as you bite into one is bitter but becomes quite aromatically pungent. When the seeds are powdered and soaked in water, the odor is very pungent because of a very pale yellow volatile oil, acid in reaction and so penetrating in effect as to make it a tear gas. Because the sulphur in the oil causes discoloration on metal, spoons or ladles of other material are used in the mustard jar. If the seeds are soaked in water, they become somewhat mucilaginous from the material in cells just underneath the outer shell. A highly complex seed!

If we choose, we may easily raise both black and white mustard in our gardens for the novelty of it, if nothing more. But it would be fun to experiment with the white mustard for a salad herb and with black mustard seed in some of the old time recipes. Any soil will be satisfactory so long as plenty of manure is dug in well. Tusser in his *Five Hundred Points of Good Husbandry* (1573) sowed the seed twice a year, in spring and at Michaelmas. In his "February Husbandry" he says:

> Where banks be amended, and newly up-cast,
> Sow mustard-seed, after a shower be past.

From the spring sowing, the seed will be ripe by the end of summer, when it may be cut down, dried, then the seeds rubbed out of the pods. The only hazard for a good crop of seed is a wet season for mustard likes dry weather.

From early days the uses of mustard have been manifold. The sixth century Greek, Pythagoras, is said to have claimed its worth as an antidote for the bite of a scorpion. The first century Roman, Pliny, had forty remedies with mustard as the chief ingredient. In the nineteenth chapter of his *Natural History,* Pliny says that it "has so pungent a flavour, that it burns like fire, though at the same time it is remarkably wholesome for the body." A cough mixture was prepared by boiling coarsely powdered mustard seed and dried figs in strong ale. Because of the belief in its aphrodisiac properties, mustard was used in love potions.

In later years, great use has been made of black mustard seed in many ways, in industry, medicine, household preparations. The oil is used in soap making, emetics, and many commercial products. Mustard is good for freeing a kettle of cooking odors by putting in it several bruised seeds, adding a little water, shaking the mixture around for a few minutes, then washing out the kettle with boiling water.

However, our interest is in the culinary aspect of mustard. In early Roman days mustard was prepared as a condiment by mixing the pounded seed, which had been soaked in new wine, with enough honey to make a con-

sistency for rolling into tiny balls. The Romans probably
taught the Celts that method of preparing the mustard
and later generations made variations. Often cinnamon
was added; sometimes vinegar instead of wine was used
for soaking the seeds. Parkinson in his *Paradisus* says:
"The seede ground between two stones, fitted for the purpose, and called a Querne, with some good vinegar added
unto it, to make it liquid and running, is that kinde of
Mustard that is usually made of all sorts, to serve as
sauce both for fish and flesh."

John Evelyn in his *Acetaria* (1699) says, "In Italy in
making mustard, they mingle limon and Orange-Peel with
the Seed. How the best is made, see here after"— This
you shall see now. Evelyn, the great connoisseur on salads,
lists 9 essentials to be considered well and carefully if the
perfect salad is to result: Herby ingredients, Oyl, Vinegar,
Salt, Mustard, Pepper, eggs, the Knife, and the salad
bowl! These are his thoughts on mustard:

That the Mustard (another noble Ingredient) be of the best
Tewksberry; or else compos'd of the soundest and weightiest Yorkshire Seed, exquisitely sifted, winnow'd, and freed from the Husks,
a little (not over-much) dry'd by the Fire, temper'd to the consist-
ence of a Pap with Vinegar, in which shavings of the Horse-Radish
have been steep'd: Then cutting an Onion, and putting it into a
small Earthern Gally-Pot, or some thick Glass of that shape; pour
the Mustard over it, and close it very well with a Cork. . . . Note,
that the Seeds are pounded in a Mortar; or bruis'd with a polished
Cannon-Bullet, in a large wooden Bowl-Dish or which is most
preferr'd, ground in a Querne contriv'd for this purpose only.

[James, bring the Cannon-Bullet, I am about to toss a
salad.]

In 1640 Parkinson, in his *Theatrum Botanicum,* de-
plores the decrease in the popularity of mustard sauce.
"Our ancient forefathers, even the better sort, were not

sparing in the use thereof—but now-a-dayes it is seldom used by their successours, being accounted the clownes sauce and therefore not fit for their tables."

Mustard went into a gradual decline in use until the early part of the eighteenth century when one Mrs. Clements of Durham in the north of England is supposed to have originated the idea of grinding the seeds, from which the husks have been removed, into a flour. Whether or not Mrs. Clements was responsible for that bright idea, from that period dated the powdered mustard, more or less as we have it today. George I (1714–27) put his stamp of approval upon the process, and mustard was therefore again restored to its use for "fish or flesh."

Of course there were variations and later additions. Today we find turmeric put into the mustard flour to intensify the yellow color; sometimes the powder is a mixture of black and white seeds, black for the odor and white for the pungency. Starch is added to help preserve the virtue. Somewhat later than Mrs. Clements' time, developed the commercial "prepared mustard." In one kind, known as French mustard, the flour is mixed with salt and vinegar; in another, German mustard, the flour is mixed with Rhine wine, tarragon, vinegar and spices.

White Mustard (*Brassica alba*)

This species is also an annual, resembling the black mustard but smaller, growing only to twelve or eighteen inches in height. The slightly hairy stems are light green, ridged and branched. The leaves are a yellowish-green, hairy on the under side, deeply cut, with the edges lobed, and they grow smaller toward the top of the stem. The pale yellow flowers with four petals are arranged in clusters along the stem. The seed pods are about one and one-half inches long, hairy, and point out almost horizontally on little stalks, away from the stem. The cylindrical pod, ending in a long beak, holds five or six almost spherical seeds with a yellow seed coat which shows tiny pits under a magnifying glass. When the seeds are soaked in water, a mucilaginous mass results, much more so than from the same number of soaked black mustard seeds.

White mustard was much cultivated by the Romans, and the seedlings used as salad herbs, greatly preferred because of the strong flavor to the black variety. The seeds should be planted in rich soil and they germinate very quickly. It has even been rumored that you can grow the salad for dinner while the meat is being roasted.

Nasturtium, *Tropaeolum majus*

The first part of the Latin name means "trophy," because of the resemblance of the leaf to a shield and the flower to a burnished gold helmet. The English name comes from the Latin words for "nose" and "to twist" because of the pungent odor.

Nasturtium, belonging to the cress family, used to be known as Indian cress, and reasonably too, because the leaves and flowers have an odor and taste strongly reminiscent of watercress while the sharp pungency is a characteristic of Eastern seasonings. We find the plant first mentioned on the European continent by the middle of the sixteenth century, and the botanist, Monardes, describes it in 1574. It is thought to have come from South America to France where we read that the famous gardener, De la Quintinye, grew nasturtiums in the royal kitchen garden of Louis XIV. We are not sure when the plant was brought into England. Gerard and Parkinson both mention nasturtiums, and about this time many new plants were being introduced from abroad.

We have all known the old-fashioned spicy refreshing plant from our childhood, and have played house, offering to our dolls sumptuous feasts of the 3-divisioned ridged wrinkled seeds, sometimes one-half inch across. Every gardener either has his pet way to make his nasturtiums grow better than those of his neighbor, or else he moans that he can't grow them at all. So, who am I to tell you the one and only way? I have always had good results by sowing the seed about six inches apart in the open ground after I was reasonably sure there would be no more biting frosts. The soil is light and somewhat sandy and the location sunny. Contrary to most herbs, nasturtiums require everlasting vigilance against aphids which seem to have an affinity for them. I keep the affected leaves picked off, spray the plants with a dry powder or a nicotine solution and often give them a good bath with soapy water.

Dr. Fernie in his *Herbal Simples* (1897) says, "In the warm summer months the flowers have been observed about the time of sunset to give out sparks, as of an electrical kind, which were first noticed by a daughter of Linnaeus" [the botanist]. I have never noticed the phenomena myself.

Sometimes green nasturtium seeds are substituted for capers, which are the pickled buds of the flowers from *Capparis spinosa*. The taste is pleasantly hot, but unlike the characteristic taste of capers. In *The Compleat Housewife* (1728), we find a recipe for pickling nasturtium seeds which may be used as capers. The seeds are soaked three days in cold salted water, stirring once a day. A pickle is made of white wine, shallots, horse radish, salt and pepper, cloves, mace, and coarsely crushed nutmeg.

The salted water is drained off the seeds which are then added to the pickle. The mixture is then put into a bottle and tightly corked.

Another eighteenth century recipe calls for claret, white wine vinegar, cloves, mace and salt. These are boiled up and cooled. Then the pickle is poured over the seeds in an earthenware pot and tightly covered. Either of these recipes could be readily adapted to your own taste for the various ingredients, using the same proportions you do in your favorite pickle recipe.

POPPY, *Papaver somniferum*

This is the opium poppy, an annual not to be confused with the perennial Oriental poppy.

Both varieties grow to a height of three or four feet. The opium poppy has smooth, lobed leaves and white and pinkish crinkly flowers four inches across, while the gray hairy leaves of the Oriental variety are sharply toothed and the vivid red flowers are six inches or more across.

The seed capsule of the opium poppy is a roundish oblong, two inches in length, and about one inch across. Inside are innumerable tiny gunmetal colored seed, rounding or oblong in shape. They remind me of sea shells because of the rough texture, gray color and curving lines. It is estimated that it takes about 900,000 seeds to weigh a pound. Opium is obtained from the shell of the seed capsule after the flower has faded, but the seeds themselves have none of the soporific qualities.

Seeds may be planted in the open ground, will germinate readily and the plants will thrive in a well nourished soil in a sunny place. After the flowers have passed, the capsules should be left on the plant a month longer and then should be broken open and the seeds removed. Then they should be spread out on a heavy cloth to dry.

For centuries the Orientals have made a delicious sweet cake from the seeds mixed with flour and honey. In ancient Greece, those taking part in the great athletic games ate the seeds mixed with wine and honey. Pliny says that poppy seed "parched and mixed with honey used to be served up in the second course at the tables of the ancients; at the present day, too, the country people sprinkle it on the uppermost crust of their bread, making it adhere by means of the yolk of eggs, the undercrust being seasoned with parsley and gith [*nigella sativa*] to heighten the flavor of the flour."

Gerard in 1597 said, "This seed as Galen saith in his booke of the faculties of nourishments, is good to season breade with, but the white is better than the blacke." Many other Elizabethans liked the seeds, too, sprinkled over confectionery as well as in bread. In Europe, particularly in Germany, poppy plants take up a large spot in gardens to provide seed in their famous seed cakes and bread. The most common use now is in different kinds of bread. You may experiment with any kind of ordinary bread dough made from flour in various stages of refinement, whole wheat, cracked or white, and with various crushed seeds mixed in the dough—caraway, coriander, sesame, fennel or poppy. This dough may then be made up into fancy shapes—long narrow finger rolls, crescents, clover-leaf (or three-sectioned biscuit), triangular or diamond—any shape you choose. To insure keeping the shape, be sure to lay the pieces of dough far enough apart in the pan to prevent touching. Then brush over the top of each roll with white of egg and sprinkle poppy seed over that.

Especially good are the rolls made of sweetened dough

with plenty of sesame seed mixed in it. The dough is shaped into small squares, a thick layer of poppy seed toward the center of each and the corners folded over but not quite meeting. Seed cookies are very good. Use the basic sugar cookie recipe given in Chapter X, mix in one tablespoonful of sesame seeds and after cutting the dough into forms, press down one-half teaspoonful of poppy seed on each shape. A filled cookie may be made by rolling out the dough thinly, cutting into small oblongs and spreading each one with a mixture of the seeds of sesame and poppy, ground nut-meats and enough strained honey to hold the mixture together. Then roll up the dough into a cylinder. You might cut the thinly rolled dough into squares with a little of the seed mixture in the center and fold up the corners toward the center.

Although poppy seeds seem to have an affinity for bread and pastry, other foods may be given an unusually delightful nutty taste by the addition of poppy seed. An interesting appetizer may be made by mixing poppy seeds with cream or cottage cheese and spreading it on salted wafers. Seeds of sesame and poppy crushed and stirred into noodles or macaroni add a delicious difference to the usually flat pasty dish when served with meats.

These are but a few possibilities. Experiment with all of these savory seeds in different dishes as your culinary imagination prompts. Cook adventurously, experiment, and increase the number of good dishes to serve to family and guests.

CHAPTER XII

A GARDEN OF VEGETABLE HERBS

I never thought it any disparagement to my best Garden where I make my Soil commonly better than ordinary, to sow, in some of the intermediate Spaces, some of those Reptiles useful in the Kitchen, viz. Carrots, Onions, Parsnips, Spinage, etc. that it may answer its Purpose, a profitable as well as a Pleasant Garden.

—JOHN LAWRENCE, "The Clergyman's Recreation" (1726).

To modern husbands and children, carrots, onions, parsnips and spinach may still be "Reptiles," because they have been told so many times at the dinner table that it was "good for them, so full of vitamins." Don't we all have a distinct dislike for things too patently good for us? But if we gave our family a mixture of carrots and honey for "an old and inveterate cough," as seventeenth century William Coles suggested, then they would protest that carrots are vegetables.

As a child, I can remember drinking steaming bowls of onion soup for bronchitis, and having an onion poultice applied to my aching ear. But boiled onions were also an essential accompaniment for the Sunday roast chicken. The onions grew in a large area, a matter of an acre, but along the flower border was a row of chives with delicate lavender colored flower heads in June. Since chives have a definite medicinal as well as salad value, my grandmother's flower garden would have pleased the

235

clergyman, John Lawrence, who wanted his garden to be "a profitable as well as a pleasant Garden," for hers thus contained food, flowers and medicine.

We find that our seventeenth century ancestors did not consider it incongruous for a vegetable (potherb to

Potatoes of Virginia
from Gerard, 1597.

them) to be also a medicine although it was grown, not in flower garden nor in medicinal plot, but in the "kitchen garden." In the *Countrie Farme* edited by Markham (1616) we may read:

A good hus-wife will have coleworts [cabbages] in her garden at all times, for the relief of her familie: for besides food, she may comfort her people with them in times of sickness.

From ancient times a good many herbs of the field that are used for food have also been a comfort in time of sickness. The two-fold use was no doubt discovered by accident. Perhaps the cook served a dish of leeks to a family in which someone had such a cold that he had lost his voice. By the end of the meal, strange to say, he could squeak his approval of the food. Next day, the left over leeks were served, and he felt even better. At first, of course, the relief was not attributed to the leeks, but after this had occurred time and again throughout a community, leeks were considered, as William Coles said some hundreds of years later, "profitable both for meat and medicine." Similar incidents probably took place in the course of years with other herbs, quite a "vegetable pharmacopoeia" gradually accumulating. Today, a great majority of our important drugs are of vegetable rather than of mineral origin.

Leeks were a substantial food for the poor among ancient Egyptians, as an inscription on a pyramid indicates, and the Israelites in the desert yearned for leeks. From records on the Pyramid of Cheops, built 3700 B.C., radishes, too, were much used. Beans, however, the Egyptians did not eat, but considered sacred.

In Rome also, beans had a religious significance, being thrown into the fire on the altars and on the graves of the departed, because the unpleasant odor was supposed to discourage the approach of unfriendly Manes (spirits of the dead). The Greek Pythagoras, sixth century B.C., advised against eating beans because the black spot was indicative of death, this superstition thus identifying the type of beans common at that time. The Greeks valued vegetables so highly that representations of them were offered to the god Apollo, the radish in gold, the beet in silver, the turnip in lead.

Theophrastus, fourth century B.C., had a good many

ideas both on the virtues and cultivation of vegetable simples. Dandelions he considered unfit for food and very bitter. He wrote:

Both turnip and radish like exposure to winter; for it is supposed that this makes them sweeter and that they are thus made to grow roots rather than leaves.

Theophrastus repeats what "they say" about transplanting celery, that one should hammer into the ground a peg of whatever size he wishes the celery stalk to attain. Also, "They tie up seed of leek and celery in a piece of cloth before sowing and then there is a large crop."

One of the most astonishing customs that prevailed far into the seventeenth century, at least, was advocated by Theophrastus—that the taste of a vegetable could be changed by special treatment of the seed before planting. If the seed of cucumber, for instance, were soaked in milk, you would never dream you were tasting the normal fruit of that seed if someone popped a piece of it into your mouth after you had "shut your eyes and opened your mouth."

For potherbs, Theophrastus mentioned lettuce, onion, cabbage, radish, turnip, beet, cucumber, gourd (squash), leek, celery, garlic, cardoon, mushroom, horseradish, lentil, pea and shallot. Asparagus, he lists among the potherbs to be found wild, as did also the first century Dioscorides, who says, "Asparagus growing in rocky places is a known herb." Only today, as I was writing these words, a letter arrived from New Mexico saying that asparagus grows wild there along the irrigation ditches.

Besides asparagus, Dioscorides mentions in his herbal some forty potherbs, all of course with several medicinal qualities—bean, lentil, turnip, cabbage, radish, beet, cu-

Vegetable Herbs
from Parkinson's, *Paradisus,* 1629.

cumber, garlic, onion, leek, carrot, lettuce, mustard, and many we would not now think of as vegetables nor even medicine, such as rocket, plantain, lupin, flax, sow thistle, although plantain is eaten and the seed of flax is used for poultices.

Cabbage was the most highly esteemed vegetable among the Romans and, according to Pliny and Cato, the only medicine used by their countrymen for six hundred years. It was a panacea for all troubles, headache, sore throat, colic, deafness, ulcers, drunkenness, insomnia, and so on through the whole list of human ills. The radish, originating in China, was popular in Rome as it was in Greece, highly recommended as an "eye opener" by Roman physicians who prescribed it taken raw with bread and salt before the morning ham and eggs. Leeks, so loved by the Israelites, were also in high favor among the Romans, elevated to that estate by Nero who ate them on several consecutive days each month to clear his voice. "If you eat Cummin before you eat Leekes, your breath will not smell afterward of Leeks," says an old book. We hope, for the sake of Nero's friends, that this was an old Roman precaution.

Since the vegetable-medicine garden was of such importance to the Romans, gardeners treated it with the dignity and painstaking care it should receive. What a pleasing sight the garden must have been with plots of onions, cabbages, radishes, beans, turnips, leeks, all edged with sweet, colorful borders of violets and roses.

The Romans introduced into England the custom of cultivating plants in inclosed gardens and in them set those vegetables so prized in their native country. Exactly what varieties they imported cannot be determined, for after the recall of the Legions to Rome, gardening interest died out in England, and only the hardiest plants survived the years of neglect. Most of them, consequently, were re-introduced after the Anglo-Saxon invasion (449 A.D.) by the monks who accompanied and followed Augustine to Kent in the year 597. To the monks goes the credit for the restoration and maintenance of the gardens in England for several centuries during the troublous times of conquest.

Among the very first tasks of the monks in their new home, was the making of a vegetable garden to which certain monks devoted most of their time since it furnished a good share of their food. Moreover, this garden was the source of much of the medicine for the monastery, since most of the potherbs introduced by the monks had real or supposed medicinal qualities. In the Anglo-Saxon translation of the herbal of Apuleius, written in Latin about the fifth century, the virtues of the beet, an early importation, are extolled. The juice was good for snake bites, cancer, inward sores.

For bite of mad dog, take a root of this same wort, pound with coarse salt, lay that to the wound. Against fevers, take a leaf of this same wort; gird it to the fevered patient; soon it will wonderfully put to flight the fever.

From time to time, the monastery gardens were enriched by additional varieties of vegetable herbs as those monks who went on pilgrimages to the continent, or missionary monks from there, proudly brought to the English monastery a few choice roots or a handful of especially fine seeds. In a comparatively few years, among the vegetable herbs thriving in Anglo-Saxon England were bean, cabbage, cucumber, radish, parsnip, gourd, carrot, lettuce, kale. March became known as the sprout kale month.

Of course, there was the universally prized leac (leek).
The leek became a symbol of Wales, the Welsh dedicat-
ing the plant to St. David, and still on that Saint's day
(March first), wearing a leek in their hats. The real origin of the custom is unknown, some claiming that on
St. David's Day (640) the Celts, to which race the
Welsh belong, won a great victory over the Saxons. But
it seems more probable that the wearing of the leek
might have arisen in the fact that around that time, the
first of sprout kale month, gardening began in earnest.
Since the leek was always found in every self-respecting
garden, "leac tun" was one of the Anglo-Saxon names for
the kitchen garden. Garleac, now garlic, which was
thought to be a variety of leek, was also grown, as well
as enneleac. Not until the Norman Conquest did enneleac
assume the French name of onion.

Vegetables played a much larger part in the culinary
life of the early Middle Ages than in later times, especially among the clergy. In the colloquy of the tenth century Archbishop Aelfric, the boy of the dialogue says
that he is not yet old enough to eat meat, but lives on
cabbages, beans, eggs, fish, cheese, butter.

An idea of a typical medieval kitchen garden, either
on the Continent or in England, may be derived from
plans and descriptions of such gardens in monasteries of
the time. On the plan of the Benedictine Monastery at
St. Gall, in the lower right hand corner, is an oblong
shaped garden with, at one end, a tool house and living
quarters for the gardener (*hortulanus*) and his men
(*famuli*). The eighteen narrow rectangular beds are labeled onion, leek, celery, coriander, dill, poppy, radish,
carrot, beet, garlic, shallot, parsley, chervil, lettuce, savory, parsnip, cabbage, corncockle.

Water was given the plants by means of a crude irrigation system, the traditional method which continued through the seventeenth century. The fourth century St. Jerome instructed his gardening monks to "Hoe your ground, set out your cabbages, convey water to them in conduits." In Hyll's *The Gardeners Labyrinth* (1577) is a picture of a gentleman operating a pump for watering his garden to supplement the "great Squirts made of tin." The author says,

> The owner or Gardener, enjoying a Pond with water in his garden ground, or a ditch of water running fast by so that the same be sweet, may with an instrument of wood (named of most men a skiff) sufficiently water all the beds of the Garden, with great ease and expedition.

In 812, the Emperor Charlemagne compiled his famous *Capitulare de Villis Imperiabilis,* a list of about seventy-five herbs to be grown in his gardens. Eighteen of these would also be in our own vegetable plots— melon, cucumber, garden cress, parsley, celery, beet, carrot, parsnip, kohlrabi, cabbage, onion, chives, leek, garlic, radish, bean, endive, chicory.

In early times, the Anglo-Saxons loved feasting and drinking, simple fare being the basis of their banquets, but with the coming of the Danes in the ninth century, eating, drinking and being merry often took on the proportions of a debauch, with long hours spent at table. It is said that Hardekout, last of the Danish kings in England, kept open house, having his tables completely set with food four times each day. The moral of his life may be drawn from the fact that he died from his excesses. One is reminded of the Frankleyn in Chaucer's *Canterbury Tales:*

Withouten bake mete was never his hous,
Of fish and flesh, and that so plenteous
It snewed in his hous of mete and drynke,
Of all deyntees that men coulde thinke:
His table dormant in his halle alway
Stood redy covered all the longe day.

In the latter part of the twelfth century, Alexander Neckham, Abbot of Cirencester, in his *De Naturis Rerum,* wrote of what should be in a nobleman's garden, but the varieties of flowers and potherbs seem to be quite the usual list of even any middle class Englishman of the time. Besides herbs and flowers, he says,

Let there be also beds enriched with onions, leeks, garlic, melons, and scallions; cucumber, poppy, daffodil, and acanthus. Nor let pot herbs be wanting if you can help it, such as beets, herb mercury, orache and the mallow.

We do not know just when the name "vegetable" came into use, potherb or wort being commonly used, so when the German monk, Albertus Magnus, wrote *De Vegetabilibus* in the thirteenth century, he did not mean our word "vegetable" but, rather, "vegetation," including trees, shrubs, plants, and flowers.

The middle class Englishman or Frenchman of the thirteenth century would, according to John de Garlande of Paris in that period, have in his garden these potherbs: borage, mustard, leek, garlic, onion, cibals, scallions— always the onion family. This list, however, we know was somewhat short, after considering the list of potherbs brought from the Continent and enjoyed in England before the Norman Conquest. But still vegetables were not raised in great quantities, nor, as William Hazlitt said, were gardeners familiar with the idea of planting crops at intervals during the season. Consequently, housewives took to salting down the surplus from their one crop of vegetables. We have few records of how these potherbs were prepared for the table, but we suppose, in the words of Gerard they must have been cooked "according to the skill of the cooke and the taste of the eater." The one we consider very slight and the other not very particular, if we gauge them by the recipes that appear in the fourteenth century.

In that period, the fashion of heavy feasting reached a sort of climax with Richard II, the most lavish host of all. As the Danish king Hardekout had done, so did Richard keep open house, gastronomically entertaining about ten thousand persons daily. For such a scale of eating there were, in his service, two thousand cooks and three hundred servitors. Each morning were killed some thirty oxen, three hundred sheep, many fowl, much game, but no mention is made of the number of carrots that had to be scraped, nor the thousands of pounds of spinach to be cleaned.

Of the installation feast of Ralph, Abbot of Canterbury in 1309, at which there were six thousand guests, there still remains a list itemizing the food bought— oxen, hogs, mutton, geese, capons, pullets, pigs, swan, rabbits, partridge, mallards, larks, nine thousand six hundred eggs, spices, but no vegetables. The point here was that vegetables, still used as medicine, had temporarily gone into a decline as food. On the vast menus there were fish, sea-food, meat, poultry, and many "made dishes" fearfully and wonderfully contorted into elaborate forms, gilded and ornamented—but few vegetables. Perhaps there were so many fasting days when meat was forbidden and vegetables had to be eaten, that they came to be considered only as emergency rations and not to be chosen for feasts. But perhaps again, the "skill of the cooke" was so slight as to make the dish of vegetables far from appealing. From reading the few remaining recipes for cooking potherbs in the early days, I would say that little was done to appeal "to the taste of the eater."

Since forks were not introduced to England from Italy until the seventeenth century, a good many of the recorded recipes were soupy things that could be managed with a spoon, or solid enough to be picked up with the fingers. During and after the meal, pages with basins of water and towels came around to the rescue of the guests, our custom of finger bowls on the table at critical points of a dinner being a natural outgrowth of this early practice.

In the *Forme of Cury* (the old form of the word "cookery"), a manuscript compiled about 1390 by the master cooks of Richard II, out of one hundred and ninety-six recipes, not over a dozen and a half contain vegetables as the chief ingredient. One recipe for cabbage is:

Caboches in potage.

Take caboches and quarter hem, and seeth hem in gode [good] broth, with oynonns y mynced, and the whyte of lekes y slyt, and corve smale, and do [add] thereto safronn and salt and force it with powdor douce [allspice].

The following recipe for fried beans sounds harmless enough:

Benes y fryed.

Take benes and seeth hem almost til they bersten [burst]. Take and wryng out the water clene. Do [add] thereto oynons ysode [boiled] and ymynced, and garlic therewith. Frye hem in oile, other [or] in grece; and do thereto powdor-douce, and serve it forth.

Really the amount of onions, garlic and leeks consumed in early days was astonishing. Some people must
have moved in an aura of the odor as, for example, Chaucer's Somnour in the *Canterbury Tales:*

> Wel loved he garleek, oynons, and eek lekes,
> And for to drynken strong wyn, reed as blood.

Perhaps you will like to try these recipes, but I feel as
Gerard did about one for parsnips about which he writes:

> There is a good and pleasant foode or bread made of the rootes
> of Parsneps, as my friend master Plat hath set foorth in his booke
> of experimenes, which I have made no triall of, nor meane to do.

Somehow we never think of vegetables being sold from
the monastery gardens, yet it was the custom for surplus
produce to be thus disposed of. Accounts of the abbey at
Norwich in 1340 lists receipts from sale of beans, garlic,
peas, scallions and leeks. There was also a public market
in early days in London, opposite the Church of St.
Austin near St. Paul's where gardeners of the clergy and
nobility, as well as of middle class citizens, sold their
produce. The market had grown to such proportions that
in 1345, petitioners went to the authorities to have it
stopped since the noise interfered with the church service.
Measures were taken temporarily, but soon again the
market was noisily prospering.

By the fifteenth century, England seemed to have taken
many steps forward in the progress of gardening. There
was even a tiny gardening book, the earliest original English manual on the subject by Ion Gardener, probably a
Kentishman. This book was *The Feate of Gardening,*
comprising one hundred and ninety-six lines of verse
copied about 1440 but written somewhat earlier. It is very

practical in advice and contains none of the superstitions current at that time. It says that garden plots, to bear well, must have fertilizer well dug into them before planting. Onions to be grown for seed must be sown in April or in March and must be staked with ash sticks as they grow tall. Bulbs were to be set with a "dybbyl" and planted three inches deep. Cabbages, then known as wurtes or wortys, and much valued, are discussed by Gardener who was agriculturally advanced enough to suggest that by planting seeds at intervals during the months, a continuous crop of vegetable-herbs could be enjoyed.

In a fifteenth century book of culinary recipes, in a list of "herbys necessary for a gardyn by letter," there are no additional varieties of vegetables than had been grown for years in England. There were coleworts and cabbages, the former with leaves loosely wrapped about, the latter a variety of coleworts—"with leaves wrapped together into a round head or globe, whose head is white of color especially toward winter when it is ripe." Besides these were "betes, cabbage, cyves, kykombres, letuce, mercury, mylons, orage, oynons, radyche, spynache, lekes, perse-nepez, turnepez, karettes."

But though vegetables are mentioned here and there in the fifteenth century, Raphael Holinshed, historian in the reign of Elizabeth, claimed that few vegetables were grown between the reigns of Henry IV (1399–1413) and Henry VIII (1509–1547). It seems to me that a good reason exists for that slump in cultivation of vegetables. During those years occurred the disastrous Hundred Year's War and the War of the Roses, when the strong men were taken into the fighting service. Although the latter war did not affect the towns, since they were not involved in the private fight between nobles and king, it made a great change in the rural districts where farming and gardening were carried on by the very men who were retainers of the Lancastrians and Yorkists and thus bound to fight. After a while the cultivated vegetables no doubt simply reverted to their wild state through lack of proper care. Holinshed claimed that they were "either unknown or supposed as food more meet for hogs and savage beasts to feed upon than mankind."

Then, in Henry VIII's reign, there was a revival of interest in vegetables. Again we hear from Holinshed:

In my time their use is not onely resumed among the poore commons, I meane of melons, pompions, gourds, cucumbers, radishes, skirets, parsnips, carrets, cabbages, navewes, turnips and all kinds of salad herbes, but also feed upon as deintie dishes at the tables of delicate merchants, gentlemen and the nobilitie, who make their provision yearelie for new seeds out of strange countries.

A good many gardeners, perhaps, had a natural pride in British soil and resented importations. Parkinson said:

. . . although our chiefe Gardiners doe still provide their owne seede of divers things from their owne ground, because, as I said, it is of the best kinde, yet you must understand, also, that good share of the same sortes of seeds are brought from beyond the Sea, for that which is gathered in this Land is not sufficient to serve every mans use in the whole Kingdome by many parts; yet still it is true, that our English seede of many things is better than any that commeth from beyond the Seas: as for example, Reddish, Lettice, Carrots, Parsneps, Turneps, Cabbages and Leekes.

Gerard in writing of "madde apples" (possibly eggplant) then eaten in Spain said, "But I rather wish English men to content themselves with the meat and sauce of our owne countrey."

Many vegetables, however, were imported from Holland, and strange to say, not unusual varieties but onions and cabbages, both bringing high prices. Sir Walter Raleigh on one of his privateering wars with the Spaniards around 1585 probably raided one of their vessels containing potatoes which had already been introduced to Europe before that date. The potatoes thus found were taken to Ireland by Raleigh who planted them in his garden near Cork, and hence we have the so-called "Irish potatoes."

A cultivated form of the ancient wild potherb became our asparagus, although in England ignorance in regard to its culture kept back its cultivation for many years. One of the few points suggested in regard to it came from the seventeenth century Worlidge who said the plants should run to seed when green peas and artichokes came in. Fuller said, "Peas were brought in from Holland and were fit for ladies they come so far and cost so dear." However, we know that field peas had been grown in England for some years and a few finer varieties, also.

In the Privy Purse Expenses of Henry VII for May 24, 1496 is a gift or reward of three shillings four pence for a dish of peas, no doubt forced with artificial heat. Hazlitt mentioned the old custom of offering a peck of green peas for sale annually on June first at Covent Garden Market for six pence, as a stipulated obligation.

Leeks, of course, were again much eaten though among the country folk they had never waned in popularity. For March, Tusser mentions them as a customary vegetable along with field peas:

> Now leeks are in season, for pottage ful good,
> And spareth the milch-cow, and purgeth the blood:
> These having with peason, for pottage for Lent,
> Thou spareth both oatmeal and bread to be spent.

The Gardeners Labyrinth: "There be some which use to water their beds with great squirts."

More public markets for fruit and vegetables were now in demand and although most of the market gardens were on the outskirts of London, Henry VIII had a good share of the cottages for poor people in East Smithfield torn down for gardens to supply these markets.

In the sixteenth century vegetables held as firm positions for medicinal herbs as they had in ancient times, and their value was seen in the fact that the dread disease of leprosy was notably decreased with the increase in the use of vegetables. It is interesting to note that the herbalist, William Turner, 1548, in his "Names of herbes in Greeke, Latin, English, Dutch and Frenche wyth the commune names that Herbaries and Apotecaries use" mentioned as medicinal herbs the same ones that Tusser, 1573, listed in his tables of "Seeds and Herbs for the

Kitchen, Herbs and Roots for Sallads and Sauce, Herbs
and Roots to Boil or to Butter." Tusser had still another
table headed, "Necessary Herbs to grow in the Garden
for Physic not rehearsed before," by which it is understood that some plants mentioned previously Tusser recognized as medicinal in value. Both Turner, the herbalist,
and Tusser, the farmer, listed the following: artichoke,
beet, cabbage, carrot, cucumber, kydney bean, lettuce,
leek, onion, radish, skirret, turnip, cress, endive, asparagus, beans, peas, alexanders. All of these except asparagus
were later mentioned by the gardeners Thomas Hyll
(1563) and Richard Gardiner (1597); by the herbalist
Gerard (1597) and by all later gardeners and herbalists
such as the seventeenth century Meager, Culpeper, and
Coles. Strangely enough, Turner did not mention spinach,
included in the books of other herbalists.

By the latter part of the sixteenth century, with the
renaissance of gardening interest after the victory over
the Spanish Armada had made England safe for gardening, along with the many varieties of plants brought into
the country by travelers to the Continent and explorers
to the New World, gardening books in English written by
English gardeners began to appear for the help of the
owner of small grounds and for gardeners on the large
estates then being acquired. Although the Italian influence was great in many ways, and innumerable books on
all sorts of subjects were translated into English before
1600, up to that time none on gardening had been done.
Never was there made an English version of Peter Cre-
scentius' *Opus Ruralium Commodorum,* probably the
most outstanding Italian book on agriculture and gardening. Some works from the Dutch and French were trans-

lated because their style of gardening appealed more to the English than that of the Italian.

An astonishing number of people of the upper class could not read, and most of the lower class were altogether illiterate, so there had been little demand for gardening books. Then, as now, most gardeners learned by the often extravagant method of trial and error.

The first gardening writer after Ion Gardener of the early fourteenth century was Thomas Hyll, a Londoner, who spoke of himself as an unlettered man writing for the unlettered. In his *Brief and Pleasant Treatyse* (1563) and in *The Gardeners Labyrinth* (1577) there are many survivals of ancient beliefs as well as some good ideas of his own, relative to the vegetable garden. Hyll, as well as ancient Theophrastus, mentioned soaking seeds to obtain in the fruit a taste different from normal. He suggested soaking artichoke seeds in rose water, lily juice or oil of bayes, then drying them in the sun so that the fruit would take on the taste of the liquid in which the seeds had been soaked.

In the French *Maison Rustique* (1600) is the same suggestion, and in addition, . . . "oyle of Lavander, or some other sweet and fragrant juice . . . although, that as concerning the former oyles, there be some which are of a contrarie opinion, and doe thinke that the oyle doth spoyle the seed." And well they might think so! It is also advised:

If you would that Artichoke should grow without prickes, you must rub it [the seed] against a stone, and breake the end of the seed which is sharpe: or else put the seed after the manner of a graft in the root of a Lettuce which hath no rinde, and cut in small pieces, in such sort as that everie piece may be grafted with a seed, and so planted.

The marvel of the seed, an age old marvel to everyone, is commented on by the author of *Maison Rustique* in

Spargen·

Asparagus Plant
from the rare German *Herbarius,* 1496.
(Courtesy of Alfred C. Hottes)

contemplating the turnip seed: "It is one of the wonders of nature, that of so small a seed, there should grow so great a fruit, or should sometime weigh thirtie or fortie pound." Apparently they ordered things better in France than in England, or perhaps this was just another turnip story. Boasting of the size of fruit and vegetables is not unknown in modern times.

There is a delightful passage from Leonard Meager's *English Gardener* years later in 1688 that should appeal to every gardener:

If your Plants turn the Ends or Noses upward towards the Air, then they want water the which you are to supply them with discretion, avoiding excess. When they thrive best, they will carry their Ends or Noses close to the ground.

And an easy way, to be sure, of knowing when the plants are thirsty.

The first English gardening book with contents about vegetables alone, is but thirty pages in length. It is *Profitable Instructions for the Manuring, Sowing and Planting of Kitchin Gardens* by Richard Gardiner of Shropshire (probably 1597) but the only extant copy is of the second edition in 1603. It is also the only vegetable gardening book which does not mention the potato, apparently unfamiliar to the author although a plant of it had been grown in Gerard's garden in Holborn, London, in 1596. Gardiner was wonderfully proud of his lettuce but spent most of his literary effort on extolling carrots which, he said, should be grown in large quantities, so that the poor could eat them instead of bread and meat in time of famine. He reproached the English for importing carrots from Holland and said that people should raise them in their gardens and humbly praise God for them.

Admit if it should please God that any City or town should be beseiged with the Enemy, what better provision for the greatest number of people can bee, than every garden to be sufficiently planted with carrots?

And elsewhere Gardiner proceeds "My price of those principall carret seed is after the rate of two shillings the waxe pound, without deceipt."

Lettuce was used in salads in Gerard's time uncooked or boiled in broth, and he mentioned that "it is served in these daies . . . at the beginning of supper and eaten first before any other meat, and eaten after supper it keepeth away drunkenness which commeth by wine."

Spinach was considered valuable for salads and as a potherb during Lent and fasting days, though Gerard's frank opinion was that it "yieldeth little or no nourishment at all." Parkinson said (1629),

Many English that have learned it of the Dutch people, doe stew the herbe in a pot or pipkin without any moisture than its owne, and after the moisture is a trifle pressed from it, they put butter and a little spice unto it and make there with a dish that many delight to eate of.

Modern cooks have rediscovered that ancient Dutch manner of cooking spinach, instead of boiling and boiling it with quarts of water.

Modern gardeners may also rediscover the benefits derived from a plot of vegetable herbs. They have been summarized by William Coles in *The Art of Simpling* (1656):

. . . In a Garden there be Turneps and Carrets which serve for sauce, and if meat be wanting, for that too. Neither doth it afford us Aliment only, but Physic . . . But besides this inestimable profit, there is another not much inferior to it, and that is the wholesome exercise a man may use in it.

CHAPTER XIII

HARVESTING THE HERBS

Good huswives in summer will save their own seeds
Against the next year, as occasion needs:
One seed for another, to make an exchange,
With fellowly neighborhood, seemeth not strange.
—Tusser's "Five Hundred Points of Good Husbandry"

Seed time and harvest! From early primitive days to our modern machine age, that interval between has always been lived with feelings of anxiety and eagerness. What intent watching for the first seedlings in the garden, what extensive exploring of the woods and fields for the tiny new shoots, what careful noting of the growing process week by week! In all ages how many eager wishes and prayers have been carried aloft by summer breezes, with high hopes for a plentiful harvest.

Constantly has man been made to realize his dependence on Nature. For his food, for his medicines, he has always relied on the herbs of the field, which consequently have been jealously watched over, to be protected from blight or from theft by man or beast.

In 800 B.C. in Greece, people were flocking to the temples in the groves sacred to Aesculapius to be cured of myriad diseases. The priests, who were the doctors and also the druggists, were supplied with the necessary healing herbs by "rhizotomoi," root diggers, whose livelihood depended on gathering those medicinal roots and plants. To discourage the uninitiated lay public from encroaching on their business, the root diggers fabricated all sorts of stories about the great dangers attendant upon herb gathering. The roots of the peony, one of the valued drug plants of that time, must be taken only in the dead of night, for if done by day, the collector would be running grave risk of having his eyes plucked out by any observant woodpecker. Gatherers of hellebore would die within a year if an eagle soared near them while they were obtaining the plants.

In those early days of childlike belief in the presence of living spirits presiding over and existing within every plant, there were also naturally the feelings of appreciation to those spirits which so beneficently afforded fruitful harvests to support human needs. As the herbs were gathered for use, the people chanted prayers of praise and gratitude which were transmitted orally from generation to generation. There were many such charms among the people of northern Europe, some of them ancestors of the Anglo-Saxons. Finally those charms took written form in manuscripts laboriously compiled by zealous monks. Since there were many penalties for practicing the pagan rites connected with the gathering of herbs and bark of trees, the monks conscientiously substituted Christian prayers, which often gave an incongruous touch to a charm wholly pagan in spirit.

In one rather long *Nine Herbs Charm* we find extolled the virtues of wormwood, plantain, water-cress, nettle, betony, chamomile, wild apple, thyme and fennel.

> Thyme and Fennel, two exceeding mighty ones,
> These herbs the wise Lord made,
> Holy in the heavens; He let them down,

Harvesting. (Note the paling fence.)
From the famous *Cantica Canticorum,* a Flemish block book
circa. 1430 in the Cracherode Collection.

Placed them, and sent them into the seven worlds
As a cure for all, the poor and the rich
It stands against pain, it dashes against venom,
It is strong against three and thirty,
Against the hand of an enemy and against the hand of the cursèd,
. . . And against the bewitching of my creatures.

We can imagine how closely the ladies of the medieval castles watched their medicinal herb garden for the promise of a good harvest, in those days when doctor or surgeon could not be obtained by a hasty phone call. When her lord and master with a good share of his vassals came back from a hard skirmish with a neighboring baron, the lady with her maids had to be right at hand with healing simples. What great concern for a bumper crop of angelica, mint, wormwood, rosemary, juniper berries, the main ingredients of "aqua vulneria," healing water for wounds.

How the mistress of the eighteenth century manor, miles away from greengrocer or doctor, watched her culinary and physic gardens in hopes of having well filled jars of just the right seasonings for her lord's winter dinners, and full crocks of the needed simples to cure his lameness or possible broken bones after a nasty fall from his mount during the hunting season.

In the period of the great herbalists in England, we find many of them clinging to the vestiges of the early pagan beliefs in the influence of the celestial bodies on herbs, each plant being under the control of one of those bodies which must be in a favorable position at the harvest time of the herb. Culpeper in his *English Physician* (1652) gives this advice about the proper time for harvest:

Let the planet that governs the herb be angular, and the stronger the better; if they can, in herbs of Saturn, let Saturn be in the ascendant; in the herb of Mars, let Mars be in the Mid-heaven, for in those houses they delight; let the Moon apply to them by good aspect, and let her not be in the houses of her enemies.

In his discussion of each herb, Culpeper usually notes the "Government and Virtues." For instance, in treating of angelica, he says:

It is an herb of the Sun in Leo; let it be gathered when he is there, the Moon applying to his good aspect; let it be gathered either in his hour, or in the hour of Jupiter. Let Sol be angular: observe the like in gathering the herbs of other planets and you may happen to do wonders.

What harvest could have been more anticipated with anxious hopeful prayers than that of the first crops planted by the intrepid Pilgrims. That first Thanksgiving was of more significance than we can ever faintly conceive, because of the terrifically adverse conditions under which that harvest came about. Those hardy workers did not have the advantages of those on the English farms they had left, crude though we may have thought that equipment was. These New England settlers had most inadequate tools, little space tilled for raising crops, and those brave Pilgrim mothers had no maid servants to assist in drying and storing the precious herbs that were to help build up the tired bodies of their men folk.

The Indians from early childhood were taught the knowledge and value of herbs, and the lessons of gratitude to be shown to the good spirits presiding over them. Elaborate ritual always accompanied the herb harvests. The herb doctors in gathering the medicinal plants performed a special rite for each plant, singing a chant which ought to be learned and observed by all of us in these days of giving practical thought to conservation:

I will not destroy you but plant your seeds,
Plant them in the hole from which I take you.

Various community enterprises in the past which aimed toward being self-subsisting, grew their own herbs for culinary and medicinal purposes, the Moravian community, for example, at Bethabara, North Carolina, having had a physic garden of ninety-six beds of herbs.

The Shakers were a community that must have been especially grateful for a bounteous harvest, for by 1800 their modest winter supplies of herbs for their own use had developed into a great medicinal herb industry. Dr. Edward Andrews in his "Community Industries of the Shakers" gives a most fascinating account of that industry. The physic garden by 1852 had spread over fifty acres and the community had been purchasing herbs from outside sources. In the main building built for preserving the herbs, the second floor and loft were used for drying. The space was well lighted and airy to provide for the rapid drying of the herbs which were arranged on racks placed through the center of the room. As soon as dried, the herbs were placed in air tight bins ranged against the side walls. During the harvest season, the busy sisters were even busier, for they were assigned to the tasks of gathering the plants, picking them over to detect any decayed leaf or flower, making ointments, cutting labels, cleaning containers and packaging or bottling the various products.

In our own times the harvest of medicinal herbs is eagerly awaited by the natives of certain sections where the plants are found. These people who make their living by selling the herbs to crude drug companies, have been taught the distinguishing features of the herbs desired and just the crucial time to gather them. The plants are

Still-room Cooking
from Evelyn: *French Gardiner,* 1675.

brought to the drug company's drying sheds where they are completely dried, spread in thin layers on racks arranged so that they receive a good circulation of air but no sun to fade out the original green color of the herbs.

But what of our own harvest this year? To be sure, most of us can quickly reach a doctor or the stores where we may now buy some herbs all powdered and packaged. We do not have the anxieties for the harvest for fear the health of our families will suffer. But what about that "nice cup o' tea" of an afternoon in winter before the crackling log fire in the fireplace, not just commonplace China or India tea but a fragrant steaming cup of perhaps lemon balm? Do you remember during hot summer days you would pause by those plants in a tour of the garden and draw the leafy tips through your lightly closed, warm, moist hands? What a fragrance you had learned to know would be released. You, no doubt, did this to the bee-balm, the peppermint, applemint or many another herb which makes a fragrant tea. Some teas will have to be boiled; others just steeped. A handful of the mint leaves in any kind of container not metal, a pint of boiling water poured over the leaves, steep for ten minutes, strain into your pretty thin tea cups in which you have put a little strained honey, if you must have a sweet taste, and there you are! Lemon balm and beebalm (Oswego tea) will not yield their fragrance without boiling in water for about five minutes in an enamel kettle. Don't spoil these delightful teas by adding milk or cream, and mint teas are better without sweetening or lemon.

Some night when you feel shivery up and down your spine from a "cold coming on" or just a "spell of nerves," what a soothing nightcap you will find in a cup of tea made from an infusion of catnip, of marjoram, of sage, or of chamomile. The English drank sage tea altogether before the introduction of China tea, while the Chinese liked the sage infusion so well that the Dutch used to trade one pound of sage for three pounds of China tea in return. Chamomile you may already have enjoyed during a facial treatment at a beauty shop, if you are of the sometime called fairer sex. In case you did not know it, the operator gave you that fragrant tea to relax those tense facial muscles which all the manipulation in the world couldn't do without help from you.

But the culinary herbs you have grown—what changes you can ring with them on those same old dishes and get that different taste your husband has been yearning for ever since he enjoyed the grand meals that his grandmother cooked when he was a boy. When he comes to think of it, she did have an herb garden. Could the sprigs of this and that which she used to pick and throw into the kettle of stew be what made it so good? You show him that it was! What a satisfaction to use the herbs you grew in your own garden and not those depressing looking contents from the packages you can buy now. If you dumped out the contents of a half dozen containers of the commercial brands, you would find the whole mass to look just about alike, regardless of label, and resemble the contents of the vacuum cleaner!

A great part of the joy in growing herbs is the harvest season. All summer you have enjoyed their fragrance in the garden, the basils, thymes, burnet and balms. Now you will have your next treat in gathering and drying the herbs.

Your harvesting will consist of gathering, drying and storing the leaves, flowers, seeds and roots of those herbs you want to preserve for future use. The great bulk of the harvest will be leaves such as parsley, the several varieties of mint, sage, thyme, basil, horehound, marjoram, lemon balm, beebalm, the savories, tarragon, rosemary and chervil. There is a crucial time when the herbs are just ready to be gathered, when they contain the greatest amount of essential oils, those precious oils that furnish the fragrance and taste. Just as the flower buds are ready to blossom out, the plants are richest in oils, some even increasing in amount just at the time of flowering. The seventeenth century Leonard Meager in his *New Art of Gardening* says to gather herbs when the sap is full in the top of them, while Nicholas Culpeper in his *English Physician* (1652) says, "Of leaves, choose only such as are green and full of juice. The leaves of such herbs as run up to seed are not so good when they are in flower as before." In Sir John Hill's *The Family Herbal* (1755) he says,

The time when the entire Plant is in its most full Perfection is when it is in the Bud when the Heads are formed for flowering, but not a single Flower has yet disclosed itself.

If you do not harvest your perennial herbs until late in the season, you will lose not only their flavor but probably the herb as well. You must cut the plants down early enough so they will come up again vigorously before the growing season is over, or the plant may winter kill. One year I just couldn't bear to cut down the luxuriant growth of catnip that formed a beautiful hazy background for the herb garden. I finally brought myself to sacrifice the artistic for practical purposes. The result was disaster. The catnip had lost most of its fragrance, so many of the leaves had to be discarded because of dryness that my tiger cat had to be put on skimpy rations during the next

A Table directing when &c.

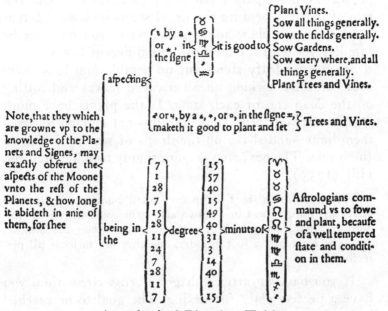

Astrological Planting Table
from *Countrie Farme*, 1616.

winter, and the following spring there was nary a sign of
a catnip plant.

Now that you have taken great pains to grow your
herbs, don't neglect them until it is too late. Nature just
doesn't wait upon any human being's pleasure.

The best time to gather the herbs is on a dry day in
the morning after the dew has disappeared and before
the sun is high enough to volatilize the oils. Cut the plants
of annuals to the ground and of perennials about one-
third of the way down the main stalk and cut off the
tender side branches. If you are a beginner, it is best to

gather but one kind of herb at a time and throughout the process keep it apart from other varieties by some system of labeling because the dried stems look so different from the fresh plant and, furthermore, you may not be familiar yet with the odors of the different. herbs.

Spread the leafy stems out on a table and look them over carefully, picking off all decayed leaves and cutting off the dead end of each stalk. If the plants have much sand or dirt on them, rinse lightly—not enough to make them limp—and shake off the drops of water clinging to the leaves. The next step is quite simply told by Dr. John Hill (1755):

> They are then to be tied up into small bunches, the less the better and hung upon Lines drawn across the room where the windows and doors are to be kept open in good weather; the Bunches are to be Kept half a foot asunder, and they are to hang till perfectly dry.

If you have an attic with good cross circulation, you have a perfect place for drying. The goal to be reached in harvesting herbs is to retain their original color and their essential oils. This will best be accomplished by drying them as quickly as possible by an even heat not strong enough to release the volatile oils. Once the summer heat has warmed an attic, even temperature will be retained for weeks. Thomas Hyll in his *Profitable Art of Gardening* (1568) says to "hang up the herbs in some Garrette or open room and high, being sweete and dry through the Sun's dayley shyning on the place at noone."

There have been schools of thought which recommend drying the herbs in the sun as did Culpeper who says,

> Dry them well in the sun and not in the shade, as the saying of the physicians is, for if the sun draw away the virtues of the herb, it must needs do the like by hay, by the same rule, which the ex-

perience of every country farmer will explode for a notable piece of
nonsense.

But, we are not drying the herbs for the bulk of leafy material, as we do hay, but only for those fragrant oils which
are volatile enough to be carried off by the hot summer
sun so we should take the greatest possible care in drying
the plants.

William Ram in 1606 made a sort of abstract of the

Distilling Oils from the Herbs in Hot Sand
from Baker, 1599.

English translation of the Dutch Rembert Dodoens' *New
Herbal* so that the price of the book would suit slim
pocketbooks. In this "Little Dodoen" we read such practical advice for July as "Keepe close your chamber windows shut all night and open all day in fayre weather,
but shut in wet." In regard to the proper way for drying

herbs, we find a sort of compromise in the sun-shade controversy. "Dry your flowers in the shadow till they be almost dry, and then sunne them well that they mould not, and so also dry your herbes."

I, myself, hold with Leonard Meager who says to "dry them in the shade that the sun draw not out their vertue, but in a clear air and breezy wind that no mustiness may taint them."

Instead of hanging the herbs in bunches, you may strip the good leaves from the stem and spread them out thinly on screens or drying frames such as are described in Chapter XIV for drying rose petals. The cut down plant of short stemmed herbs such as the several varieties of thyme may also be treated in this way. Stir the herbs thoroughly each day so that all the surfaces will be exposed. This may be done in a shady spot out doors but the drying herbs must be taken in at night to avoid dampness retarding the day's progress.

In hot weather this method ought to take about three or four days, while that of hanging the herbs up in bunches will take perhaps a week, but the latter method saves you the daily stirring of the leaves, for you simply let them hang until perfectly dry. This perfect drying is absolutely essential. The slightest dampness will not only cause mold, but the oils will lose their goodness. Culpeper claims that,

Such herbs as are well dried, will keep longer than such that are slack dried. Yet you may know when they are corrupted by their loss of colour or smell or both; and, if they be corrupted, reason will tell you that they must needs corrupt the bodies of those people that take them.

Parsley may be dried by a quick-process method. The leaves stripped from the stems are plunged into boiling salted water for half a minute, strain off the water, spread the leaves on a fine wire mesh and dry in a medium hot oven, just long enough for the leaves to get crisply dry. Mints may be done the same way. An Italian method of preserving basil leaves (curly basil) is to pack them down in a wide mouth crock with a layer of salt between layers of basil. When wanted for use in winter, the salt is shaken from the leaves which are ready then for use as if fresh from the plant.

When you are sure the herbs are dry, "they are then to be taken softly down, without shaking off the Buds of the flowers" and carefully stored. In a passage in the *Flowering of New England,* describing a typical Cambridge home of a well-to-do family in 1815, I read that "on the shelves of the closets lay bundles of mint and catnip, lavender, sweet marjoram, pennyroyal." The fragrance that came out into the room when the closet door was opened must have been delightfully reminiscent of the lovely garden from which the herbs were gathered. However, the oils that were thus dissipated could not be recaptured when those herbs were used in cooking or medicine. To retain the full flavor and fragrance you must store the herbs in containers, preferably glass or pottery, with tightly fitting covers. Paper bags or cardboard boxes are not good because the oils will in time escape through the porous material.

If the herbs are to be kept where the sun strikes them, use opaque jars of china or pottery so the original color of the leaves will not fade. If you keep the yield of your harvest in a dark or shaded place, glass jars are lovely because they will display the herbs so well and show the various greens that you have been so careful to retain in the drying process.

After stripping the leaves from the stems or having gathered them up from the frames, you may first rub them through a sieve to powder them or simply (and better) pack them directly into jars and sieve when used, just as you would your coffee beans or pepper. The herbs to be used for teas should be pressed tightly into jars in full leaf, while the dried parsley which is always used in powdered state might be sieved before storing. Even after you put the herbs into containers, turn them out again every day or two for a week to look for any signs of mold.

Though the drying process is pretty much of a rigid routine, we may express our individuality in the storing of the harvest. Perhaps you have collected attractive little jars that would now be lovely storehouses for your herbs. Labels of your own design with a drawing of your favorite herb would be so distinctively yours. My own labels have a sprig of rosemary down one end and a spray of rue across from it on the other side, thereby representing the favorites of "both of the household."

Don't go picturesque on your family by hanging bundles of herbs from rafters or above the stove. Even in 1568, Thomas Hyll deplored that custom and advised that the container be tightly fastened leathern bags or wooden boxes so the "Hearbes may not lose theyr proper vertue." He went on to say that

the Poticaries in my opinion are verye negligente, which hang uppe the Physicke Hearbes in their open shoppes and warehouses, through which the vertue of these not onlye breath away, but the bags charged and clagged with duste, Copwebs and much other filth.

The flowers of the herbs, such as chamomile and lavender, are dried by cutting off just the heads and spreading them thinly on the screens or racks. The yellow part

Braunschweig and Pupil with Jars of Herbs
from *Ortus Sanitatis*, Paris, 1499.

of the chamomile blossom contains the essential oils that are desired, the rest of the plant not used, although commercially the white petals adulterate the mixture. The time for completely drying the flowers will be much longer than for the leaves, two weeks perhaps.

Some of the herbs you have grown for the seeds, savory seeds, perhaps dill, anise, caraway, fennel, bene (sesame), coriander, cumin. The drying process is the same for all. There is no crucial moment to gather the seeds, but rather when you think they are ripe, no longer green in color but brownish and the stalks dried-looking. Culpeper says, "Let them be full ripe when they are gathered, and forget not the celestial harmony before mentioned." The round coriander seeds are comparatively heavy and drop readily, so watch these and gather as soon as ripe.

Still further to avoid the seeds dropping off, gather them just as soon as the dew is off on a dry day. Have a basket lined with paper or any fine mesh material and cut off the seed umbels directly into the basket. Spread them thinly on heavy cloth like pillow ticking or canvas, and let them dry in a warm airy room for 3 or 4 days. You may dry them on the screens or racks and if you have many seeds, remove to the heavy cloth and beat the umbels gently so as not to bruise the seeds. It is well to do this threshing out of doors where there is breeze enough to blow away a good deal of the chaff. If you do not have many seeds, it will not take long to rub the umbels between the palms of your hands instead of threshing. In this way you will not bruise the seeds at all. Put the seeds into a sieve, fine enough to hold them but coarse enough to pass the small stalks. Spread the cleaned seeds out on your drying screen for a week or 10 days longer, turning them frequently. Store in jars when you are sure the seeds are dry, but watch closely for mold for a week.

You may want to try drying roots if you have enough plants to spare from your garden, roots of lovage, angelica, comfrey, horseradish, sweet flag (*Acorus Calamus*), and Florentine iris. Roots need somewhat more attention than the rest of your harvest because their fleshy nature makes the drying process longer. Culpeper says:

> Of roots choose neither such as are rotten or worm eaten, but proper in their taste, color and smell, such as exceed neither in softness or hardness. The drier time you gather the roots in, the better they are, for they have the less excrementitous moisture in them.

Dig the roots in the fall when the growth has stopped. This will indicate that the plant cells have now been completely filled with plant food. If the roots are taken up before this period, they will shrink to a great degree in the drying process. After the plant part has been cut off, wash and scrub the roots thoroughly, scraping them if necessary to remove the dirt. Split or slice the large roots and spread in thin layers on the drying screens for several weeks but turn the roots frequently. They should be dried in the open air, but the long drying time may be shortened somewhat by the artificial heat of a hot oven if the door is left open so the moisture will be carried off. If desired, the roots may be laid to dry on racks arranged over the stove.

After the work of the harvest is over, you will be entranced by the fresh appearance of your herbs, all stored in neatly labeled jars. When you come to flavor your foods or make your aromatic teas, you will surely agree with our good London friend, Culpeper:

So shall one handful be worth ten of those you buy in Cheapside.

CHAPTER XIV

POTPOURRI FROM THE GARDEN

The early Greeks built their houses so that the living room opened on a garden of herbs that would yield up their essential oils under the gentle insistence of the warm sunshine. The ancients had great faith in the efficacy of breathing sweet odors to preserve the health of mind and body. In those days, when sanitary measures were simply non-existent, foul odors were not only masked but their evil effects somewhat mitigated by strewing the floors with certain herbs from which arose their volatile, health-giving oils as the dried leaves were pressed under foot. What's in a name? We say that "disease germs" are killed by the action of the oils of certain herbs, while the ancients strewed those same herbs—black hellebore (Christmas rose), hyssop, lavender, marjoram—to ward off "evil spirits," to break the spells of "malicious witches and magicians."

Some years ago investigations made in the section of France devoted to flower raising for commercial perfumes, showed that workers in the rooms which were saturated with the essential oils of the flowers were little affected by tuberculosis. Published laboratory reports appear to show that oils from cinnamon, angelica, lavender, thyme and sandalwood kill germs of yellow fever, oils from cinnamon and valerian kill germs of typhoid, while tuberculosis bacilli are said to have succumbed after twenty-three hours of exposure to cinnamon oil, and after twelve hours to lavender and eucalyptus oil. The latter oil is today an important ingredient in the usual prescription for nose drops.

In 1542, Dr. Andrew Borde wrote *The Boke for to Lerne a man to be wyse in buylding of his howse,* really our first book on hygiene. He advises us to keep our houses clean to insure "odyferous saveurs" and not to do the sweeping while the master is still in the house, "for the dust doth putryfy the air, makying it dence." Dr. Borde advised keeping the air pure in plague times by burning juniper, rosemary, bay leaves, and other herbs of woody growth.

The Dutch Erasmus, visiting England at the beginning of the sixteenth century, deplored the terrific stench from the rush strewn floors. It was the custom to throw bones and other scraps from the table to the dogs, whose shaggy coats were none too clean. In time the decaying food, rushes, and other filth caused all manner of disease-breeding vermin. But by the middle of the century, the succulent rushes which decayed so readily were supplanted by the sweet-smelling herbs which dried more quickly and did not rot. At that period another foreign visitor wrote, praising the cleanliness he found in England: "Their chambers and parlours strawed over with swete herbes refreshed me."

Thomas Tusser's *Five Hundred Points of Good Husbandry* (1573) lists twenty-one herbs to be planted for strewing purposes—among them, basil, balm, sweet fennel, germander, hyssop, lavender, lavender cotton (santolina), knotted marjoram, pennyroyal, sage, tansy, and winter savory.

The custom of strewing herbs for sanitary measures was universally practiced, from cottage to hall and church. We find in the record of expenses for the reign of James II, 1685–88, that there was a Royal Herb Strewer who received an annual salary for her services at appointed times. At that monarch's coronation, his progress along 1220 yards of "Blue Broad-cloth" toward that same "King Edward's Chair" about which we have heard so much, was strewn with six bushels of herbs by "The Strewer of Herbs in Ordinary to His Majesty, assisted by six women." This custom of herb strewing long continued, but with certain changes as the original utilitarian purpose of the herbs was lost sight of. At the coronation of George IV (1820) we find among other records of minute detail, that the Herb Strewer and six assistants headed the royal procession and reached the West Gate of the Abbey promptly at ten minutes before eleven. There they stopped, stepped aside and did not enter the Abbey. The whole custom was discontinued by Edward VII who apparently felt, as the elaborate plans for the coronation went forward, that he could do without an Herb Strewer in Ordinary and Six Assistants! With Hamlet he must have complained many times, "I am most dreadfully attended."

However, until quite recently in England at the regular services and at festivals, the church pews have been strewn with herbs and fragrant leaves. From ancient to modern times, herbs have taken a great part in religious rites. According to early beliefs, the smoke from burning aromatic herbs was efficacious in purifying the participants in the rites, in driving away evil spirits, and in pleasing the gods by sending up petitions to them on the smoke which arose in fragrant clouds. A more practical use of the herbs was to pack them into the body of a sacrificial animal so that the unpleasant odor of burning flesh would be masked.

Later, in Charlemagne's time, the benediction of the incense read,

May the Lord bless this incense to the extinction of every noxious smell and kindle it to the odor of its sweetness.

The essayist, Montaigne, of the sixteenth century believed in the aesthetic and practical value of incense in the church, claiming that it had a

Special regard to rejoice, to comfort, to quicken, to rouse, and to purify our senses so that we might be the apter and readier unto our contemplation.

Ancient Athens is said to have been saved from annihilation by the plague through fumigation by burning herbs, and in London during every epidemic, people were ordered to burn aromatic woods and herbs in the streets in front of their houses. Citizens clutched nosegays of sweet herbs and vigorously smelled of them in passing through the crowded streets, while the clergy carried the fragrant little bouquets as they distributed the Maundy money in Westminster Abbey. Nosegays of rue alone, or with other herbs, are still placed on the Justice's bench in English courts, the custom arising in 1750 during an epidemic of jail fever at Newgate, when the sanitary measure was taken of strewing herbs liberally about the building. During plague epidemics, the prices of rue, rosemary, and faggots of other sweet-smelling herbs for burning, became exorbitant, small bundles of rosemary, for instance, selling for eight pence while at other times a whole armful would not bring more than a shilling.

To show how pleasantly the aesthetic and utilitarian functions may work together for the good of body and spirit, we have only to turn back to the early seventeenth century when James I visited the Bodleian Library at Oxford. For that great occasion, the floors of the building were ordered to be thoroughly rubbed with fresh rosemary.

In the old days, the mistress of the house had a full time occupation as guardian of the healths of all those under her care. There was not the neighborhood drug store with show cases before which we stand bewildered by the many brands of cosmetics, patent medicines, moth preventives, hair restoratives, soaps, perfumes, insecticides and patented preparations for practically any household need. There was no physician nor surgeon in those early days, either.

The busy lady—wife, mother, doctor, nurse, druggist and more—studied her still-room book, handed down from mother to daughter as she would eventually hand it down to her own eldest daughter. In passing generations through the simple method of trial and error, recipes and formulas would be deleted from or added to the parchment book. This precious tome treasured practical advice on midwifery, broken limbs, care of animals, distilling oils, making of toilet preparations and pomanders.

The still-room book also contained the secret recipe of that particular family for potpourri, made from baskets of sweet flowers and herbs carefully gathered by the servants under the supervision of their mistress. The resulting fragrant mixtures were put into lovely jars, often priceless heirlooms, and set in wall niches of those ill-ventilated, barn-like rooms where foul odors accumulated and settled down like a pall over the inhabitants. On particularly muggy days, with no wind to carry the smoke and bad odors up to the chimney or to the lantern in the roof, the covers of the potpourri jars would be removed and the mixture stirred to its depths. Then our lady would be rewarded by the exquisite perfume, growing more fragrant as months passed.

It seems to me a shame that we have almost forgotten the art of those old-fashioned potpourris. One day recently in discussing with a druggist a few of my fortysome recipes, come upon here and there, I asked him whether the ingredients called for in the older recipes could be easily obtained. What a shock to hear him say that he hadn't had a call for them in twenty-five years! Do let's revive potpourris. They are so fragrantly reminiscent of our summer garden when the raw dampness of winter days is upon us. To open the jar and stir it up as the logs in the fireplace blaze and crackle will make you feel cozy, at peace with the world, and a bit luxurious.

Do you remember the Reverend Septimus in *Edwin Drood?* His mother loved to give him horrible medicines from the herb closet on the upper staircase landing. Dickens said the closet was a long, narrow, white-washed cell where bunches of dried leaves hung from rusty hooks in the ceiling and were spread out upon the shelves. The good man submitted graciously to please his mother and

would quietly swallow what was given him, merely taking a corrective dip of hands and face into the great bowl of dried rose-leaves, and into the other great bowl of dried lavender.

If you have even one rose bush and some other flowers and herbs, enough to make a bulk of one quart of petals, you have the makings of a potpourri. But remember that the blossoming time of some of the roses is short and you must gather the petals when the roses are ready. You may be fortunate enough to have so many varieties that there will be blooms from June to October. The later petals you may add to the earlier ones and considerably increase the bulk by the end of summer.

Roses to be used for potpourri should be the most fragrant ones. First in choice is the old cabbage or Provence rose (*Rosa centifolia*), large and, true to its name, has at least a hundred petals of a rich pink hue. The Red Provence is an old favorite, very large, very fragrant, and a deep crimson in color. Next in choice is the Damask rose (*Rosa damascena*), the Damas officinalis with rose colored petals, at least eighteen in number. Third in preference is the French rose commonly called the Apothecaries' Rose (*Rosa gallica*), the true ancestor of all other French roses.

We may have a rose bowl or rose jar which will contain no other flowers than roses. Or we may prefer a true potpourri with many other kinds of sweet smelling flowers or leaves mixed with the rose petals. There are two ways of preserving the flowers—by the "dry" or by the "moist" method. In the first method, we dry the petals thoroughly and then add any sweet smelling leaves and petals we choose, a spice mixture and a fixative like orris powder. The result will be a delicate elusive odor and practically the original color of the flowers. The "moist" method is the old-time one of first partially drying the petals, then "curing" them by the addition of salt, making what is called the "stock" before adding the other ingredients. From this latter process came the name, pot pourri, literally and unpleasantly enough, "rotten jar," from the French verb *pourrir,* to rot. This method will result in a stronger perfume, but the color will be lost because of the bleaching action of the preservative, usually salt.

Whichever method we use, the preliminary drying is done in the quickest way possible, to keep the petals from molding. Gather the roses on a dry day after two or three days of fair weather, before the sun is so high that it has drawn out much of the essential oils. Choose freshly opened flowers, not those almost ready to fall and with most of their fragrance and vitality gone. After you have gathered the flowers, pull the petals off and separate them from each other. You may spread the petals out thinly on a table covered with sheets of newspaper, brown paper, or tissue paper, the last being most absorbent and consequently the best. A much better way is to make a drying frame, so the air will circulate all about the petals, underneath them particularly. If you have a curtain frame, stretch lengths of cheesecloth on it or, put two chairs back to back about a yard or so apart and fasten the corners of the cheesecloth to the tops of the chairs. Keep the cloth stretched out as much as possible so the petals will keep somewhat apart from each other and dry more quickly. If you don't have much space, don't try to dry so many that they will have to be crowded in a thick layer on the cloth. Window screens placed in an elevated horizontal position will make good drying frames if covered with cheesecloth or tissue paper, to prevent the small bits of flowers falling through the mesh.

In some recipes we are told to dry the petals in the sun but, to keep all the precious oils, it would be much better to set up the drying frame in a warm shady place where you can get good circulation of air, as an attic with windows at opposite ends. Cover the petals with a length of cheesecloth propped up over them, so they will not blow off in those sudden little gusts of wind that come even on a hot day.

If you are going to use the dry method for your pot-pourri, leave the petals on the frame for about ten days, but do not let them get damp or you will have to continue for several days longer. In one recipe I read that the petals should be "chip dry." In the old days artificial heat was employed for part of the process. In the *Receipt Book* of one John Nott (1723) he advised picking the roses before they are fully opened, pulling the petals off and laying them on boards in a room where

the Heat of the Sun may not come at them; when they are pretty dry, let a large Still be made warm, and lay them on the Top of it till they are crisp, but let them not lie so long as to change their colour. Then spread them thin; and when they are thoroughly dry'd, press them down in an Earthen Pan, and keep close covered.

In another recipe we are instructed to lay a half inch layer of petals on a sieve and put in an oven till the top part is dry, then stir thoroughly. Repeat till all the petals are quite dry. Then we are to put them into a narrow mouthed earthen pot leaded within which the "Refiners of gold and silver call Hookers." The pot is to be corked tightly and hung in a chimney near a medium fire. If we "feare their relenting," we are advised to take the petals out about Candlemas and dry them again on a sieve.

The main point to observe in the dry method is to be sure the petals are absolutely dry; then mix about two ounces of orris root powder or of violet powder with two quarts of petals. To insure still further the dryness of the petals, stir the petals and powder with a wooden spoon in a large pan, every other day for another three weeks. If the pan is exposed to the sun, cover it with a paper. If the color of the flowers is still bright at the end of the drying period, a crystal bowl would be a lovely container in which to store the potpourri permanently.

Some use a sort of dry-moist method. Spread the petals out to dry for seven or eight days, then put into a large crock, alternating one-half inch layers of salt and petals. Let the jar stand for three days, cover at night to prevent dampness, and stir thoroughly each morning. Then pour out the mixture and shake the salt from the petals. You will be surprised how damp the salt is though you may have thought the petals "chip dry" before you put them in the jar with the salt. Then return the petals to the jar, stirring in thoroughly three ounces of mixed spices to two quarts of petals. Cover tightly for six weeks, then mix in two ounces of orris root powder, a few drops of the essential oils of other flowers you like, and any thoroughly dried sweet scented leaves. In this method, however, most of the color of the flowers will be lost because of the action of the salt. The usual potpourri jars or rose bowls are of some opaque substance like china or porcelain, so the preserving of the natural color of the flowers is not important.

In the moist method, as in the dry method, the petals are pulled from the flowers, separated from each other and spread out to dry but, in this method, for only one or two days, or until they are leathery in appearance and have lost about half their original bulk. Have ready a large, wide mouth, straight sided jar with a tightly fitting cover. It should be sufficiently large so that it will be but two-thirds full when you have put into it all the petals you are going to use. Having a straight sided jar will make it easier to stir the contents thoroughly and will allow for a weight almost large enough to cover the petals.

Into this jar place a half inch layer of petals and cover

with a sprinkling of salt, about one handful to three of petals. The recipes usually call for a mixture of "bay salt" and table salt, about half and half proportion. Salt obtained from deposits is made by running a stream of water on the salt rocks, then boiling down the brine, from which crystals form. Bay salt is the coarsest grade, containing about ten per cent impurities; table salt, a finer grade. Be sure the table salt is not iodized. Coarsely ground salt petre or crushed bath salt may be used as part of the salt mixture.

Each day that you gather the petals, spread them out thinly, let them dry for a day or two and then, after thoroughly stirring with a wooden spoon the petals already in the jar, add the newer ones to them with a sprinkling of salt as before. With a wooden potato masher, press down the mass and put a weight on top. Continue until you have all the petals you are going to use. If a sort of broth rises, stir the mixture thoroughly, and when that action has stopped, leave the jar for ten days. By that time a cake will have formed which may be taken out, broken into bits, and will then be ready to be mixed with the other ingredients and placed in the permanent potpourri jar.

Next must be added a fixative, a material to absorb and help retain the fragrance of the essential oils which are so volatile. There are two classes of fixatives, those of animal origin and those of a vegetable nature, the latter much less expensive, more easily obtainable, and most often used now-a-days except in commercial products. The fixatives from animal sources are castoreum, civet and ambergris. Castoreum is a peculiar, bitter, orange brown substance with a strong penetrating odor, found in sacs in the body of the beaver. Civet is a yellowish brown substance with the consistency of butter, found in a sac in the body of the true civet cat. Before dilution, it has a musky offensive odor, but when very small portions are mixed with another substance, an agreeable odor results. Ambergris, a substance like wax, and in color white, ash gray, yellow, black, or often variegated like marble, is a secretion in the alimentary canal of the sperm whale.

Of the fixatives of vegetable nature, the most common are gum benzoin, storax, calamus powder, orris root powder, and violet powder. Benzoin, which you will find written in the old time recipes in the corrupt form of "benjamin," is a resin from the benzoin tree (*Styrax Benzoin*), a tree of Malacca, Java, and Sumatra, and perhaps obtained from other species of the styrax family. The hard resin must be finely ground before using for your potpourri. Storax, also to be used in fine powdered form, is a balsam now usually obtained from the bark of the tree called *Liquidamber orientalis*. It is a brown, honey-like liquid which hardens on standing. Storax in the old days was, and still is to some extent, obtained from the tree, *Styrax officinalis,* and is used in a tincture of benzoin compound. In an old potpourri recipe, I found that for the fixative "both storaxes" were called for, meaning the resin from the two trees, *Styrax Benzoin* and *Styrax officinalis.*

Calamus powder is made from the root of the sweet flag, *Acorus Calamus.* Orris root is the root of the Florentine iris and is used in the powdered form when used as a fixative. Violet powder is simply powdered orris root scented with oil of violet. There is no definite proportion of fixative to petals, but one ounce of fixative to two quarts of petals is a good ratio.

The next ingredient to be added is a spice mixture,

equal proportions of crushed nutmegs, cloves, cinnamon, mace and allspice, about one heaping tablespoonful to one quart of petals. Many other fragrances may be added at this time, a few drops of essential oils, perhaps, of patchouli, bergamot, rose geranium, bitter almond, orange flowers, eucalyptus, rosemary, etc. It is risky to introduce too many oils and essences because of the reaction they have upon one another, one counteracting or changing the effect of another. Some potpourri experts strongly advise against the addition of oils or of pouring over the mixture extracts of perfumes or cologne which you will find recommended in some recipes.

Sometimes fragrant additions are made with one-half ounce each of crushed anise, coriander and cardamom seeds; shavings of cedar and sandalwood; sliced dried roots of angelica and orris (iris) root, one-half ounce finely crushed tonka or vanilla beans. A most delightful fragrance results from the addition of orange, lemon and tangerine skins cut into strips with the pith carefully removed. It is even better if these strips are stuck full of whole cloves. Grains of musk may be added with restraint, but only a few. Musk is a substance obtained from the body of the musk deer and has a most powerful and to many people, unpleasant odor.

Fragrant petals other than roses, and sweet-scented leaves if not too succulent and hard to dry, may also be added but must be thoroughly dried. Lavender flowers are lovely, but do not add more than a handful or the potpourri will be pungent. After a thorough mixing of the contents, the making of the potpourri will be completed. The cover of the jar is then sealed and the jar allowed to stand for six weeks before opening. Six months or a year afterwards, the contents will be more fragrant than when freshly made.

The foregoing process is the routine usually followed. Many variations may be made so long as the main procedure is maintained—ten days of curing the half dried petals before mixing with fixative and spices, then six weeks of standing in the tightly closed jar. In one recipe alcohol, instead of salt, is used as a preservative. A few drops of geranium oil and glycerine are rolled about the bottom of the empty jar, then four cupfuls of partially dried petals are put in, and four drops of geranium oil and one teaspoonful of alcohol are added. This procedure is followed with every four cupfuls of the petals. The mixture is thoroughly stirred every morning and covered at night. After the last petals have been added, stir in the spice mixture, two drops of glycerine, four of geranium oil, and one tablespoonful of alcohol. Stir this mixture frequently until there is no further danger of molding.

Recently I saw one of the most delightful potpourri jars imaginable. The square container was of smooth glass with the wide mouth stopper of cut crystal. Pansies and one red hollyhock had been carefully pressed and the colors were still bright. A few drops of transparent glue had fastened the hollyhock on the bottom of the jar and the pansies on the side. The potpourri mixture, made by the moist method, had then been added and since it was a beige color, made a neutral background setting off the pressed flowers.

A potpourri made of herb flowers and leaves without any roses is a delightful mixture. It is simply your herb garden concentrated into a bowl which, when uncovered and stirred up on a bleak wintry day, brings back the fragrant hours of last summer. You need add nothing but a little powdered gum benzoin, and perhaps little slices of dried orris root, the Florentine iris which you no doubt have grown in your own garden. You may like a little of a spice mixture but not enough to detract from the fragrance of your herbs. Herbs that I have used are leaves of pineapple sage, basil, apple mint, orange mint (but any of the mints sparingly), garden sage, sweetbrier, Oswego tea, lemon verbena; the tips of rosemary, lavender cotton, knotted marjoram, sweet mugwort, southernwood, lemon thyme, sweet woodruff, lavender; seeds of anise, coriander, fennel. For color, as well as odor, I add the pink petals of the clove carnations, those fragrant old-fashioned flowers which the seventeenth century gardener, William Lawson, so loved and which were known then as clove gilliflowers.

Few flowers except lavender and rose have any fragrance when dried. Jasmine, violet, and mignonette, for instance, lose theirs. But the petals of the colorful flowers may be dried so as to retain their bright hues, and kept in crystal jars. Your imagination will lead you to develop many motifs—a national color scheme, perhaps. A red, white and blue combination I made was of the red petals of Oswego tea and of red geranium, the white phlox and bachelor buttons, and the blue bachelor buttons or cornflower. You might have a spectrum potpourri of *red* Oswego tea, yarrow, hollyhock, peony, geranium; *orange* tansy, calendula, nasturtium, safflower, elecampane; *yellow* yarrow, hollyhock, mullein, cowslip, foxglove; *green* leaves; *blue* bachelor buttons, borage, aconite, widow's tears, hyssop, larkspur, flax, rosemary; *violet* pennyroyal, peppermint, wild bergamot, autumn crocus, violets, knotted marjoram.

A pleasant diversion may be found in drying buds or flowers whole, keeping their original color. In the *Toilet of Flora* of the eighteenth century, I found a rule simple enough to be workable:

Take fine white Sand, wash it repeatedly, till it contains not the least earth or salt, then dry it for use. When thoroughly dry, fill a glass or stone jar half full of Sand in which stick the Flowers in their natural situation, and afterwards cover them gently with the same, about the eighth part of an inch above the Flower. Place the glass jar in the sun or, if in winter time, in a room where a constant fire is kept till the Flower is perfectly dried. Then Remove the Sand with the utmost precaution and clean the Leaves with a feather brush.

Instead of drying rosebuds in sand, I bury them in granulated sugar, set them in the sun for about a month. Not only are the rosebuds dried with the original color preserved but the sugar is delightfully perfumed with rose. I have followed the same process with sweet leaved geraniums, particularly the rose and peppermint varieties. I put an inch layer of sugar in a bowl, then a layer of leaves not touching each other, and alternate the layers till I have as much sugar as I want perfumed.

A suggestion that Sir Hugh Plat (1594) makes is to dry the leaves of herbs in the same way as he suggested for drying rose petals, so that you may study them.

This secret is very requisite for a good simplifier, because he may dry the leaf of any herb in this manner; and lay it being dry, in his herbal with the simple which it representeth, whereby he may easily learn to know the names of all simples which he desireth.

From the time the first roses come in June until the last one has bloomed in autumn, you may gather petals for a fragrant potpourri that you will delight in for many a long winter. You will agree with John Parkinson, who loved his flowers so much:

Many herbes and flowers with their fragrant sweet smels doe comfort, and as it were revive the spirits and perfume the whole house.

CHAPTER XV

POMANDERS

I have sold all my trumpery; not a counterfeit stone, not a ribbon, glass, pomander, brooch, table book, ballad, knife, tape, glove, shoe-tie, horn-ring, to keep my pack from fasting.
—"Winter's Tale," iv, 4: 587

The pomander might have seemed a trumpery to that rogue, Autolycus, who sold his wares among the crowd at fairs as a blind for his more gainful calling of picking pockets. But to his Elizabethan contemporaries, pomanders were far from trumperies. They performed the multifold services of ornament, cure for insomnia, perfume for counteracting the many evil odors at home and abroad, and much-valued antiseptic agents during plague epidemics or at any time or place where crowds gathered.

In our modern practical age in which science is seldom taken sugar coated, we prosaically have moth balls and very-hard-to-pronounce preparations for protecting winter clothes and blankets. In the old days, our ancestors scattered spicy potpourri and laid tips of lavender, rosemary and southernwood among the quilts and paisley shawls which today are still fragrantly lovely when we bring them forth, and quite as whole as if vile smelling moth preparations had been used.

To protect ourselves from germs when we go into the subway rush, theatres, shopping districts, offices, there is

an infinite number of nationally advertised gargles, loz-
enges, inhalers, all scientifically antiseptic and no nonsense. Herbs feature largely in those preparations—
peppermint, thyme, lavender, and sage—but it is the
laboratory formula that is emphasized in advertising.

Today when contagious diseases are in our homes, or
when stale odors have permeated the house, there is a
great variety of commercially packaged preparations with
which to fumigate the rooms which then become clinically
antiseptic and the air filled with chemical vapors. In early
days, when odors within castle or cottage became too
much for the occupants, floors were strewn with herbs—
hyssop, basil, lavender, tansy, balm, the mints—and the
huge bowls of potpourri were uncovered and stirred, so
that a wholesome fragrance drifted out into the air.

From ancient times, before sanitary measures were
taken to protect entire communities, when dirt, evil odors,
and disease were accepted naturally as a necessary evil,
individuals took what simple measures they could to cover
up the odors of the crowded streets, and in an elementary
way, to have about them antiseptic preparations. In those
"good old days" doctors greatly advocated continually
smelling of aromatic herbs in places where disease was
rampant, or where the odors simply screamed imminent
infection. Bunches of rue and rosemary were commonly
carried and sniffed at by even the poor man on the street
in order to live above the "foul and filthy air." Sprigs of
herbs were placed on the judge's bench and in the pris-
oner's dock to ward off jail fever. Priests and laymen
alike buried their noses in herbal nosegays during ceremonies where the none too careful crowds gathered, as at
the distribution of the Maundy money at Westminster
Abbey.

The popular favorite, however, which served the double purposes of ornament and use with those having plump purses was the pomander. The name applied both to the ball, usually the size of a nutmeg and made of perfumes and fragrant fixatives, and later to the receptacle for the ball. The English word, pomander, came in early days from France where it was called *pomme d'ambre* or *poume de aumbre,* as we find in the old inventories of jewels. The word was derived from "pomme" because of the shape of an apple into which the ingredients were formed, and from "ambergris," which was usually one of the fixatives for the perfumes. But similar balls and cases were used long before the name pomander came to be applied to them. The receptacles, made variously of gold, silver, ivory, wood or crystal, were often hung from chains about the neck or from the girdle at the waist, not only to envelop the wearer in an aura of perfume, but also to please the nose when crowds were too pressing and to protect when danger of infection was great.

In Isaiah III: 19, we find the prophet declaring that among other punishments that would visit the haughty daughters of Zion, the Lord would take away "the chains and the bracelets and the mufflers." If we may believe authoritative commentators, these chains terminated at one end in costly pomander cases.

The constituents of those fragrant pomander balls were amazing in variety from the simplest to the most costly, almost prohibitive now in price or practically impossible to obtain. Probably the ingredient that most astonishes us was very often used as a base or foundation to form the bulk of the pomander—just plain earth or sometimes very good garden mold. The seventeenth century poet, Michael Drayton, in the *Quest of Cynthia* says,

> As when she from the water came,
> Where first she touched the mould,
> In balls the people made the same
> For pomander and sold.

We note how common was the custom of wearing a pomander for antiseptic measures, in Drayton's further mention of moss from the inside of wells being worn as "pomander against infectious damps." Sometimes, however, fine white wax was the base into which the perfumes were worked.

Among the ingredients believed then, and in many cases today, to have germicidal qualities, we find lavender, usually in the form of "Oyle of Spike" which Matthioli, a sixteenth century commentator on the first writer of herbals, the first century Dioscorides, claimed was efficacious against disease, especially so when used with cinnamon. A locality where sweet bay (laurel) grew abundantly was considered practically insurance for the inhabitants against disease. In the *Natural History* of Pliny we find that the "leaves of the Delphic Laurel (*laurus nobilis*) bruised and applied to the nostrils from time to time are a preservative against contagion in pestilence." Naturally then, we find bay leaves used in these health-inducing pomanders.

From extensive laboratory tests made some years ago in France, it was reported that certain essential oils have properties fatal to disease bacteria. Among these oils were cinnamon, clove, sandal, cedar, lemon and jasmine, all commonly found in pomander balls. Mace and nutmeg were also used, the latter often mounted whole in silver and elaborately ornamented with precious stones and

pearls. Small amounts of camphire, probably the camphor
of today, certainly must have had its antiseptic effect
when used as ingredient. Does that recall to any of you
the distinct odor of camphor in a hot school room on a
cold winter's day when you were a child? How many children wore little red flannel bags of camphor about their
necks so they wouldn't get colds?

Flowers themselves were little used because so few
keep their scent when they have lost their freshness. We
do find one or two recipes calling for Damask rose buds
but they were, for the most part, to give a foundation for
the other ingredients. Occasionally we find the oil of a
flower, as "30 drops of Lilly Convally," our lily of the
valley (*Convallaria majalis*). The sweet waters of rose,
jasmine and orange flower served to keep the ingredients
moist. We do find a few fruits, the shredded rind of
orange, lemon and quince and the juice of lemons. In
place of flower scents, there were fragrant substances
with names most enchantingly connotative, or mysterious
words that are fascinatingly uncommunicative. There
was the precious spikenard, not from our American spikenard (*Aralia racemosa*), but from the Indian nard, a
shrub (*Nardostachys Jatamansi*) of the valerian family.
This was one of the most permanent aromatic ingredients in the costly unguents used in ancient times. The
ointment made from spikenard cost about $50. a pound,
or 300 denarii in Roman money. The recipes also call for
the betel nut, red sanders, lignum aloes, a resinous East
Indian wood; castus, root of a fragrant annual herb indigenous to Kashmir; gumdragon or tragacanth, a gum
from the oriental plant, *astragalus gummifer,* an herb of
the pea family.

Then there was labdanum, a great favorite with the

makers of pomanders as it was with the Orientals. It is a sort of bitter resin of the cistus shrub, or rock rose, widely distributed in the Mediterranean countries, and is gathered by the amazingly simple method of scraping it from the beards of goats allowed to browse on the shrub or from whips used to beat the foliage.

The lovely scents of these perfumes, often very costly, were retained in the pomander balls by the use of fixatives also fragrant and usually expensive. When we consider that four or five fixatives were used, we can see that pomander balls and their precious cases were not found among the possessions of the poor classes, who were quite content with smelling of fresh sweet herbs. The fixatives most generally used were benjamin from the benzoin tree, styrax benzoin; storax from the tree, *styrax officinalis;* liquid storax from the bark of the tree, *Liquidamber orientalis;* ambergris, civet, musk. Besides those fixatives was the less expensive calamus powder, sometimes perfumed with oil of violet or of rose.

In reading many old recipes with the idea of formulating one that would be workable nowadays, I found each one a rule by itself and that rule would quickly drive to despair anyone who is a slave to precise instructions. It was not so bad that no two recipes contained the same ingredients, but in no one were there consistent statements about proportions or process. Too often we are to take a little of this and somewhat of that. The composer of the recipe always presupposed that the maker of the pomander ball had a sort of sixth sense about the whole affair and had been endowed with the quality of judgment adapted to handling what seems to us an odd assortment of ingredients. A composite recipe would, I am afraid, result in a kind of pomander nightmare, but if

you had been living in those casual days you would have
found the instructions crystal clear.

In measuring our fixatives and perfumes, we would use
musk and civet with a light hand, just as little or as much
as will go on the point of a knife, while we might take
anywhere from one dram to a half pound of benjamin.
Of the other resinous perfumes we would use from one
dram to one half ounce, or perhaps one or two penny-
worths of each. These ingredients, with other sweet smelling substances, oils and spices, then had to be reduced to
a paste of a consistency to roll into a firm ball. Gumdragon steeped in a "pretty quantity" of rose water for
24 hours or so, was usually the solvent. The ingredients
were put into a heated mortar, the gumdragon added and
all ground together with a hot pestle. Sometimes the
process was hastened by boiling the mass in somewhat
of rose water. Now was the time your good judgment
worked overtime. If the paste was "too limber," you
added some powder of roses, perhaps a thimbleful, and
incorporated the ingredients all together, or if too stiff
you added, possibly, "not half an ounce" of orange
flower, or rose water or lemon juice.

Then came into play your individuality as well as your
alertness. While it was still hot, you were to "rowle up
the paste suddenly," first moistening your hands with oil
of jasmine, with rose or orange flower water, or with civet,
to keep the ball smooth, to give it a gloss and to add
more fragrance. You could mold the material "in any
fashion you please, of such a bignesse as you will," often
the size of a nutmeg. The balls were then dried "betwixt
2 papers" and in the shadow.

In some recipes we are directed to weigh the paste into
equal amounts, roll each portion into beads while they

are still hot and wet, "make holes through them with a bodkin" and string them. The pomander balls were often strung on chains long enough to encircle the waist. We read of Queen Elizabeth's great delight in a "gyrdle of pomanders" presented by a courtier who must have felt fortunate to have struck the fancy of the capricious queen.

When you were very young, did you ever try to make a perfumed necklace of flowers which you had hopefully boiled up and then down to a thick pasty mass? When I read these pomander recipes, I think of my own attempts at flower beads. At that time there was a great fad of violet, rose, jasmine and other flower scented bead necklaces, supposed to have evolved from fresh flowers. What had been done, could be repeated. So I tried making flower beads, with no knowledge of fixatives, gums or chemistry but with complete faith in advertising. The beads failed to "jell" and far from being dainty rose and violet colored balls of sweet perfume, the poor worn out worried flowers were dirty in color and distinctly unpleasant in odor. One of my early disillusionments about what we see in print!

Two old recipes for pomander balls I particularly like because of the naive directions. One is from William Ram's *Little Dodoen* (1606):

Take Labdanum one ounce, Benjamin and Storax of each two drams, Damaske powder finely searced [sieved], one Dram, Cloves and Mace of each a little, a Nutmeg and a little Camphire, Muske and Civet a little. First heate your morter and pestle with coales, then make them verie cleane and put in your labdanum, heate it till it waxe softe, put to it two or three drops of oyl of spike, and so labour them a while: then put in all the rest finely in powder, and worke them till all be incorporated, then take it out, anoynting your hands with Civet, roll it up and with a Bodkin pierce a hole thorow it.

The other recipe is from seventeenth century Gervase Markham's *English House-Wife:*

To make Pomanders, take two penny-worth of Labdanum, two penny-worth of Storax liquid, one penny-worth of calamus Aromaticus, as much Balm, half a quarter of a pound of fine wax, of Cloves and Mace two penny-worth, of liquid Aloes three penny-worth and Mace two penny-worth and of Musk four grains: beat all these exceedingly together, till they come to a perfect substance, then mould it in any fashion you please, and dry it.

Pomander balls included ingredients not only germicidal but sometimes sleep-producing in their effect. One recipe calls for opium, mandrake, juice of hemlock, henbane seed and winelees "to which must be added musk that by the scent it make provoke him that smells unto it. Make a ball as big as a man may grasp in his hand; by often smelling to this it will cause him to shut his eyes and fall asleep." Just as simple as that—no doctor's prescription, no counting of sheep jumping in endless procession over fences. A mere inhaling of the soporific herbs did the trick in the sixteenth century, according to this procedure.

There were other types of interesting pomanders. One was the musk ball, with no other scent combination. There were balls of various drugs for curing fevers, the amount for each dose scraped from the ball. Then there were scented pomanders made more costly by adding powdered gold and finely crushed precious stones, rubies, pearls, sapphire and topaz.

For these pomander balls of great price, there were cases of costly material with elaborate ornament. In inventories of jewels and household effects or in portraits, we find that these were made usually to hang from a chain about the neck or from a girdle at the waist, but often had a flat base so they could stand on a table. The simplest type of case was of wood, silver mounted, or of metal, globular or oval in shape, about two and three-quarters inches in diameter, with a split across the center, the parts hinged together and fastened by a clasp. The case was perforated to allow the escape of the perfume, and the surfaces between were tooled. These were used in England before the elaborate pomanders were introduced from the continent in the early sixteenth century, when the name began to be applied to the case itself, which did not always inclose a solid ball of perfumed antiseptics, but sometimes contained a mixture of spices alone, or various perfumes. We read in J. H. Short-house's *John Inglesant* that "he himself carried a pomander of silver in the shape of an apple, stuffed with spices, which sent out a curious faint perfume through small holes."

Cardinal Wolsey, as related in Cavendish's *Life of Wolsey,* held "in his hand a very fayre orrynge, whereof the mete, or substance within, was taken out and fylled uppe agayne with the part of a sponge wherein was vyne-gar and other confecsions agaynst the pestylente ayers; to which he most commonly smelt unto, passing among the prease [priests] or ells when he was pestered with many sewters." Perhaps it was inclosed in a pomander case of true English origin or perhaps the ingredients within mummified the orange skin.

One particularly good example of the English type of case is made of hollowed out wood, mounted in silver, of about the size of an orange. Engraved on the outside

are circles of various sizes. Around the five larger circles
are inscribed these five lines:

"O man, consider thou must goe"
"When this short and brittle life do end"
"To everlasting Joy or Payne and Woe"
"Passe well the time which God to thee do lend"
"With a pure heart delight His Word to heare."

A lovely gold pomander, globular and elaborately
wrought and chased, two inches in diameter and weigh-
ing about two and one half ounces, now rests in the British Museum. This treasure, dating from the sixteenth
century, so rare to come upon these days, was brought
up on the anchor of a barge man years ago, on the Sur-
rey side of the Thames.

There are three silver pomanders in the Metropolitan
Museum of Art in New York City. One, shown in Fig. 1,
is of seventeenth century Dutch design. It looks like a
miniature oval shaped sap bucket, above two and one
half inches high and one and one half inches across the
long axis at the top, and narrows to an inch at the bottom. In the medallion, left foreground, see the hunter
with his gun and dog approaching the gate on his way
home to the hut beneath the tree at the right, with a
windmill in the background. The tool work of conventional flowers in the medallion on the top and around the
body of the case, is beautifully done.

A development in the sixteenth century of the early
pomander case, was a type made up of sections or loculi,
like a horse chestnut burr, from two to eight in number,
so that various scents and spices could be inclosed in the
case but kept separate. Each could be separately turned
down, resembling a hollow segment of orange with a
slide along the ridge, which opened to allow the escape of

Fig. 1. A Dutch Pomander.   Fig. 2. A French Pomander.
(Courtesy of the Metropolitan Museum of Art)

the precious perfume, the name of which was indicated on the side. The straight inner sides and the curved outer wall of each segment was often elaborately ornamented. On the outside panels of one case containing four loculi, there are portraits of Henry VIII, and his children, Edward VI, Mary, and Elizabeth.

In one sixteenth century German pomander, globular in shape, of gilt metal with figures in relief ornamenting the eight panels, we find the slides engraved with the names of the perfumes, Canel (cinnamon); Rosmarin (rosemary); Shlag (germander); Ruten (rue); Rosen (rose); Lavendel (lavender); Citron (citron); and one blank, apparently for the owner's temporary favorite.

In some instances the segment coverings may be turned down, like the sections of a chestnut burr, and reveal the loculi which remain stationary. In Fig. 2, a seventeenth century French pomander shows eight shells open, revealing but four perfume loculi. Instead of slides we have the covers hinged at the right, with a lip at the left to open the entire top of the loculus. When the case is closed, the bell shaped top fits down over the points. The base of the pomander can be seen between the two front shells, showing that this pomander not only could be worn on a chain through the ring above the cap, but it could also stand by itself.

In Shakespeare's *Henry IV*, Part 1, 1–3, we find Hotspur, angrily scorning the lord who "made me mad to see him shine so brisk" after the battle, with the dead and dying carried off by exhausted soldiers.

> He was perfumed like a milliner;
> And 'twixt his finger and his thumb he held
> A pouncet-box, which ever and anon
> He gave his nose, and took't away again.

Pouncet-box is an archaic word for the pomander, which we can see was used by the fop to conceal the stench of the battlefield.

> And as the soldiers bore dead bodies by,
> He call'd them untaught knaves, unmannerly,
> To bring a slovenly, unhandsome corse
> Betwixt the wind and his nobility.

By the time of Charles II (1630–1685) there had begun the trend toward the use of liquid scents, by what seems a compromise in that both were inclosed in the same case, separate sections opening out for the solid perfume while the base was hollow, with perforations, and inclosing a piece of sponge to be saturated with aromatic vinegars which were beginning their very popular vogue. Another variety was somewhat like a vase with a sponge in the perforated body part and a small loculus at the foot for musk.

These pomanders later became tests of ingenuity for the designer. One type was cylindrical with separate loculi for perfume, with a whistle, perhaps, at one end and a perforated ball for vinegar at the other. Another was spherical with four detachable loculi for perfume, and in the interior was a syringe for liquid perfume. Still a different type was really a marvel! This was made up of five parts: a thimble covered a winder for embroidery silks, fitting around a small loculus for musk; all this screwed on a receptacle for aromatic vinegar; on the other end was a needle case. The whole contraption rests on a base which is a personal seal. Need we go on? Fantastic shapes and ingenious arrangements continued in the making of pomanders which lost something in loveliness of line and true beauty of workmanship.

By the end of the seventeenth century the idea of the sponge soaked in aromatic vinegars had become extremely popular. Many an aching brow had been bathed in the vinegars, which owed their refreshing qualities to the acetic acid which dissolved the fragrant perfumes and also had an antiseptic effect. This was made use of greatly by doctors and probably by many others. The heads of walking sticks were mounted with a perforated hollow silver globe in which was a sponge soaked in the antiseptic vinegars. While at the bedside of a patient with a contagious disease, the doctor would "smell unto it" as did Cardinal Wolsey of his "fayre orrynge." Sometimes in these silver balls were simply crushed fresh herbs.

The aromatic vinegars are really more refreshing

than toilet waters with the perfumes distilled in alcohol. Many of the old recipes could be followed and used with positive pleasure. We find in the *Toilet of Flora* of the eighteenth century, a recipe calling for a handful each of rosemary, wormwood, lavender and mint to be put into a jar with a gallon of strong vinegar, kept near a fire for four days, strained, an ounce of powdered camphor added and then bottled for use. These vinegars were so highly regarded as disinfectants that the "Vinegar of the Four Thieves," supposed to have been used by villains who robbed the houses of those stricken with the plague, without contracting the disease themselves, was in general use not only for washing face and hands to prevent infection, but also for sprinkling about the living quarters and over clothes. The ingredients consisted of Beach and Roman wormwood, rosemary, sage, mint, rue, lavender flowers, calamus powder, cinnamon, cloves, nutmeg, and garlic. These were put into a crock, red wine vinegar poured over, left in the sun for several weeks and distilled off, filtered, camphor added, and then it was bottled for use.

The vinaigrettes of our forebears, I am sure, come naturally to our minds as we think of aromatic vinegars and pomander cases containing sponges saturated with them. I have a tiny oblong vinaigrette of gold and silver with a ring at the top so it could be worn on a chain. On its face are engraved two Biblical references, Song 1 : 12, and St. John 12 : 3 :

While the King sitteth at his table, my spikenard sendeth forth the smell thereof; and

Then took Mary a pound of ointment of spikenard, very costly, and anointed the feet of Jesus and wiped his feet with her hair, and the house was filled with the odour of the ointment.

But instead of the precious spikenard, this old vinaigrette contained an aromatic vinegar held by a tiny sponge which still lies under an oblong perforated gold inner cover. As I hold this treasure in my hand, I think of the old Victorian days when ladies had the vapors and were very subject to fainting spells because, prosaically enough, their tight lacings would not permit of a long breath when they were startled, and not as we romantically would like to imagine, because they were emotionally overcome. However, that is a very dull thought, and we can more pleasantly look back on those fragrant days of lavender and old lace, of gentle ladies, lovely as Dresden dolls, who wore the vinaigrettes just in case "the latest novel proved too moving," perhaps, or the embroidery silks they were using could not be matched. Today we have our practical smelling salts which, just the other day, I saw a lovely lady deeply sniffing as she was enduring the tortures of being permanently waved.

In the early days it was the custom to give New Year's gifts, pomanders being a favorite offering. We have a record of Henry VIII's gift to his daughter, Mary. "Firste, ij long girdles of goldesmythes wrke wt pomander at thende." Few people could afford the costly ingredients for the pomander balls, the cases themselves, or the perfumes of the elaborate sectional cases. So there grew up the custom of using a real orange and sticking it with whole cloves. The pomander ball was thus sweetly and spicily achieved, and had the same benefits of the more expensive balls. In Ben Jonson's *Christmas Masque,* we find an allusion to that custom in, "He has an orange and Rosemary, but not a clove to stick in it."

Clove stuck oranges have grown very popular among

my household and guests, so that at Christmas time during my free moments, I am always found quietly sticking one clove after another into an orange. It is a process that tests one's patience for it cannot be hurried, but it is a facinating, fragrant task and the result most satisfying. We keep a few orange "pomanders" in a dish at the foot of the stairs and, after many years, the spicy orange scent greets us strongly as we come down, particularly on a damp muggy morning. As gifts, you will find them lovely.

Take a small orange with thin skin which must be perfect, a box of whole cloves, about two and one half hours of your time, and you will have achieved a result admired by all. If you want the orange especially pretty, use only the whole cloves—those with heads still on. Cover the whole fruit with cloves, first piercing the hole in the skin with a darning needle or pointed meat skewer, sticking them close enough so that the prongs of the cusp holding the fruit just touch. As the orange dries, it will shrink and when completely cured, no part of the skin will show. Be careful not to stick the cloves down a straight line or hold the orange too tightly, or the skin will split. Small splits will heal, however, in a few days. As the orange cures, it will grow lighter because the juice gradually seeps out and the pulp dries. For many centuries the great preservatives have been spices, so the cloves will prevent decay as the drying goes on.

For variety in odor, powdered cinnamon or nutmeg, or a combination of both with powdered cloves, may be sifted over the orange when still freshly stuck with cloves, and will cling to the juice adhering to the skin between the stems. If you do not like the powdery effect on the top of the cloves, simply wipe the ball over with a damp cloth. In about ten days the orange will be dried out enough to handle without its splitting.

The finished pomanders may be used in several ways besides heaping them in bowls for table decoration. You may pierce them through with non-corroding wire looped into a tiny circle at each end, put a long ribbon through one of the loops of each orange and hang several together in a cluster, from the bracket of a bridge lamp perhaps. A gift to please can be made by padding a coat form and hanging a pomander from the middle by a ribbon. Cloves have long been used, not only as preservatives against decay but also against moths. The coat hanger with pomander, slipped into cloth coat, suit or dress, will lend a pleasing odor to the clothes and protect them well from moths.

As I was preparing an orange pomander one evening, it occurred to me that limes and lemons would also make fragrant variety. I tried them with excellent results, both drying much sooner than the oranges because so much more juice seeps out during the process of sticking in the cloves. The combination of lime, lemon and orange, varying in size and fragrance, makes a most attractive table decoration. At Christmas time one year, I made a table centerpiece with a base of evergreens, then piling on them the citrus pomanders, brightened up by small colored Christmas tree ball ornaments, with here and there a tip of pine with a small cone on it.

Though you may not attempt making a pomander ball, old style, you will find that the oranges stuck with cloves will, as the *Toilet of Flora* puts it, "give perfect satisfaction to the most delicate judge."

CHAPTER XVI

SWEET BAGS AND FRAGRANCIES

Many herbes and flowers with their fragrant sweet smels doe comfort, and as it were revive the spirits and perfume the whole house.

—JOHN PARKINSON (1629)

The herbs you harvest to use in cooking and in home remedies have, by this time, been perfuming your whole kitchen as they seasoned many a delicious dish or gave their bracing aroma to fragrant cups of tea for drooping spirits! What about all those other uses for which our forbears cherished the aromatic herbs and many of us moderns now grow them? Pillows, lotions, incense, germicides, insecticides, perfumed ink, furniture polish,—these are but a few. What lovelier offerings could we make than those filled with the aromatic fragrance from our herb gardens, gifts that can be made without the elaborate equipment of the old-time still-rooms.

For centuries, all races and nations have shared Parkinson's faith in the virtues of "fragrant sweet smels." In early days, people delighted in aromatic woods and plants simply because the fragrance "revived their spirits." In later centuries, scientists coldly explained that this delight was really due to the curative effects of which the primitives had been instinctively but unscientifically aware.

Babylonians and Assyrians, 3000 years ago, believed

that burning those aromatic plants which have odors disliked by evil spirits, would restore sick people to health
by clearing the air of demons which they thought caused
disease. Later evolved the custom, among Greeks and Romans as well as among the Orientals, of offering fragrant
odors that would please their deities and the spirits of the
dead. These odors were wafted on the breezes to them
from burning incense or from fragrant plants and flowers
made into wreaths placed on statues and graves. The
ancient Mexicans attached so much importance to "sweet
smels" that, with elaborate ceremony, four times a day,
aromatic incense was burned in the temples as a propiti-
atory offering to their gods.

Sweet fragrance, however, surrounded not only ob-
servance of religious rites but also celebrations of a
secular nature. At the great athletic games, the King of
Syria commanded that all the spectators be anointed with
perfumes. In Egypt during festivals, incense was burned
in the streets so the poor might enjoy the fragrant odors
which poverty had denied them. At Egyptian banquets,
the heads of the guests were anointed with sweet unguents and the floors and tables were strewn with petals.
Cleopatra had her banquet floors covered almost knee
deep with roses, the flower which the Arabians and Persians also particularly liked for strewing. The Greeks and
Romans placed fragrant chaplets on the heads of ban-
queting guests and set perfumed boxes about the halls.
Those attending banquets of the Nahuas, a race of ancient Mexicans, were given reeds filled with aromatic
herbs which were burned to diffuse fragrance about the
hall, as we burn bayberry candles. Many were the other
uses for herbs—for embalming, for bathing, and in foods
and sweetmeats. Seldom was anything but the aromatic

herbs used, which were purifying, preservative in nature
and refreshingly fragrant.

As we look down through the centuries, we continue to
find abundant uses for "sweet smels." Some advanced
minds were beginning to realize the real value of herbs
as antiseptics, germicides and restoratives, while others
still loved them simply because the fragrance was a pleas-
urable experience which they did not analyze. The sixteenth century essayist, Michel de Montaigne, was cog-
nizant of the virtue of herbs:

Physicians might in my opinion draw more use and good from
odours than they do. For myself, I have often perceived that according unto their strength and quality, they change and alter and move
my spirits and make strange effects in me.

In these days we can do much with herbs to freshen the
air of the sick room, and to make the long days and nights
of the patient somewhat easier. Pliny recommended hanging pennyroyal in bed rooms because he thought it conducive to health. Nowadays scientists tell us that in the
flowering tops of all varieties of the mint family, including pennyroyal, are present tiny particles of camphor,
used so universally as a restorative. Years ago, the Japanese prized mint so highly as a refreshing odor that they
crowded the leaves into hollow, perforated metal balls,
pomander cases, and wore them on chains from their girdles.

Just as we bathe aching foreheads with eau de cologne,
so the nurses of Tudor times put the bruised fresh leaves
of bergamot, mint and lavender on the brows of their
patients. For nervous headaches, the nurses would give
herbal snuffs of basil alone, or a combination of rosemary, betony, marjoram and lavender. Now eucalyptol,
a powerful antiseptic, has been discovered to be present

in sage, rosemary and lavender. Long ago, open bowls of dried lavender flowers were used to disinfect sick rooms while rosemary, called "incensier" in old France, where it was often burned instead of the more costly incense, is still used in French hospitals for fumigation. Other herbs may be used as purifying incense in an open pan if you do not have a fireplace in the sick room. The dried leafy tops of lavender, sage, rosemary or southernwood may be crumbled into a little heap and burned. The leaves of southernwood are so fine that when dry they may be ground into a fine powder. I keep this powder in a shallow jar and when I want to burn it, I plunge a sort of cone-shaped tweezer of metal into the powder, squeeze it tightly and open it carefully on my incense burner. The little mound of powder fragrance burns with a pleasing lemony odor.

Insomnia is not a modern affliction due to Wall Street or to bridge debts, but is as ancient as aching bodies or troubled minds and spirits. Some of the simplest means have been taken to insure sound sleep by the use of fragrant herbs. The Malays fill pillow and mattress with an East Indian mint which yields an essential oil from which patchouli perfume is made. Cleopatra, on the other hand, had her mattress filled with rose petals. Sleeping on pillows filled with aromatic herbs was considered an especially good means of producing sleep and rejoicing the soul. In Ram's *Little Dodoen* (1606) we find:

Take drie rose leaves keep them in a glasse which will keep them sweet and then take powder of mynte, powder of cloves in a grosse powder, and putte the same to the Rose leves thanne putte all these togyther in a bagge and Take that to bedde with you and it wyll cause you to sleepe and it is goode to smelle unto at other tymes.

Hop pillows, so popular with George III, are mentioned in the *American Household Adviser* (1875) as
good for insomnia. Nowadays they are used not only to
prevent sleeplessness but also to make sleep easier for
sufferers from asthma, which appears to be aggravated
by dust from feathers used in ordinary pillows.

Just as those little pillows filled with fir, balsam pine,
and sweet grass are such acceptable gifts after summers
spent in the mountains, so Christmas gifts of pillows filled
with herbs from your garden will "revive the spirits" of
any recipient, sick or well. Most people have definite preferences which will determine the choice of herbs. One of
my friends loathes the scent of lemon but likes spicy
odors. So I reserve my lemon verbena, lemon thyme,
lemon balm, costmary and southernwood for another
friend and use the clove-like basil, the "nutmeggish" rosemary and the indefinable spicy marjoram.

Both lavender and southernwood, so strongly aromatic, each in its own distinctive way, make delightfully
refreshing pillows, but each should be used alone or else
with a very light hand if in combination. Pillows are especially invigorating in effect if filled with the mints, including bergamot, because of the traces of camphor and in
peppermint, the presence of menthol.

The sweet leaved pelargoniums with such varied odors
make fragrant pillows—rose, skeleton leaf and Lady
Plymouth, both the latter also rose but with a whiff of
mint; Schottesham Pet or filbert scent, Pretty Polly like
almonds, Oak Leaf reminiscent of walnuts, Clorinda
something like eucalyptus oil; Nutmeg, Peppermint, Coconut, Applescented—all definitely of these odors. Then
for those who like lemon odors are the lemon (*P. limo-*

neum), finger bowl or Italian (*P. crispum*), Prince of Orange (*P. citriodorum*), balm (*P. melissimum*).

In the old days people dealt with insomnia quite firmly. Besides the soporific pillows there were herbs to be taken internally and applied externally. In ancient Egypt, there was a famous perfume called Kyphi with ingredients varying with its maker. Plutarch tells us of one containing 16 ingredients, including cardamon, juniper, saffron and dock. He claims that its aromatic substances "lull to sleep, allay anxieties and brighten the dreams." Perhaps this perfume was applied on the upper lip under the nose as many people today apply perfumes of soporific effect.

The seventeenth century herbalist, Nicholas Culpeper, advises heating rose petals with mint and applying them to the forehead to "cause rest and sleep." In Askham's Herbal (1550) we find a sleep inducing remedy for the sleepless one in soaking the feet to the ankles in an infusion of violets and binding the bruised petals on the forehead and he will "slepe well by the grace of God." Sir John Hill (1755) gives this recipe:

Clip 4 ounces of southernwood leaves fine and beat them in a mortar with 6 ounces of loaf sugar till the whole is like paste. Three times a day take the bignesse of a nutmeg of this. It is pleasant and one thing is it in particular, it is a composer and always disposes persons to sleep.

Fragrant baths have always been popular, the refreshingly aromatic herb odors always preferred in olden days. Thyme was much used, that herb which became a symbol of courage and bravery because of the energy acquired from its use in the bath. Thyme baths are still a favorite not only for relaxing tired muscles of perfectly healthy people but for relieving nervous ailments, skin diseases and

Distilling Herbs for Fragrant Waters
from Baker, 1599.

poor circulation. Parkinson said that "mintes are often-times used in Baths with Balm and other herbs as a help to comfort and strengthen the nerves and sinews," the "other" herbs being thyme, lavender and rosemary.

Herbs were introduced into the bath by means of the liquor in which they had been steeped. In the *Toilet of Flora,* we are directed to take 4 handfuls each of penny-royal, sage, rosemary, 3 handfuls of angelica, 4 ounces of juniper, boil in water and strain off the liquor for the bath. We find more elaborate recipes for the making of the herbal preparation containing fixatives, like amber-gris and musk, to hold the perfume. One recipe calls for several herbs, including roses, orange flowers, jasmine, bay, rosemary, lavender, and pennyroyal. We are to take "a sufficient quantity," boil them in water, adding 6 drops of oil of Spike (lavender), 5 grains of musk, and 3 grains of ambergris.

A very simple method of making our bath aromatic is to tie a handful of the herbs we prefer in a four or five inch square of cheesecloth and drop them into the hot bath water or into a quart of boiling water fifteen minutes before the bath water is drawn, and pour the infusion into the tub. Very pleasing gifts may be made by laying a dozen or so herb bags of various combinations and of preferred odors, carefully labeled in an attractive box. The most refreshing odors will be most appealing, a combination of thyme and any of the mints; thyme; peppermint; sage; rosemary; pennyroyal; chamomile; lavender.

We sometimes consider ourselves very modern with our expensive cosmetic preparations, but usually the preparations cost very little to prepare, the packaging and advertising tempting us to buy. From the ancient times to the modern, people have indulged in luxurious, scented baths, followed by rubdowns of fragrant oils or lotions. The Beau Brummels of ancient Greece went so far in their use of perfume that special scents were preferred for each part of the body. Antiphanes, a foreigner coming to live in Athens in the fourth century B.C. wrote that the typical dandy of his day after a very elaborate bath rubbed his jaws and breasts with oil of palm, his arms with juice of mints, his forehead and hair with essence of marjoram, and his neck and knees with extract of ground thyme. Gerard, living in London in the sixteenth century, claimed that the oil of jasmine is "good to be anointed after baths, in those bodies that have a need to be suppled and warmed."

A fragrant rubbing alcohol was made in early days by infusing herbs in wine for several days, then straining off the liquid for use. A most acceptable gift today would be small bottles filled with rubbing lotions of various scents, the more bracing the better. Buy a large bottle of rubbing alcohol, pour into small wide mouth jars over the herbs which have been placed, about a handful to a pint of alcohol. Let the jars stand for about two weeks, with an occasional good shaking. Then strain off the liquid and pour into the lotion bottles which have been labeled with the name of the herb which is used. The most refreshing herbs I have found used in this way are lavender leaves and flowers, rosemary, lemon balm, and the mints, all giving a beautiful shade of green to the liquid.

Hair rinses have always been used for the fragrance or color they impart to the hair. In early days, rosemary tips were simmered for an hour in rain or artificially softened water, then the liquid strained off and bottled for use. In most beauty parlors here and abroad, chamomile rinses are given to preserve the golden tints of the hair. The liquid is obtained in the same way as for rosemary using, however, only the flower heads of the chamomile.

Sweet bags for scenting clothes and linen were universally used in Tudor days by rich and poor, the material for the bags of the wealthy made of taffeta or soft silk and for fixatives, the costly ambergris, musk and civet. The poorer classes used cheaper cloth and spices instead of expensive fixatives, but the bulk of the ingredients was the same fragrant herbs, grown in the gardens of cottage and hall.

The mixtures for the sweet bags are made on the same principle as those for potpourris, both containing fixatives and spices to hold the scent of the dried leaves and flowers. The pungent herbs are more often used and in greater bulk in the sweet bags, and the ingredients to be ground are really crushed, made into a "grosse powder," as the Elizabethans termed it. Just about any combination and proportion of herbs were used, but about one heaping tablespoonful of spices and one-half ounce of fixative to one quart of herbs, was the usual rule for the final mixture.

The popular herbs used for the sweet bags were, first of all, petals of roses, the crushed seeds of coriander, anise and caraway, leaves of sweet marjoram, basil, rosemary, thyme, flowers and leaves of lavender. The spices were cinnamon, cloves, mace and nutmeg. The fixatives, besides musk, civet and ambergris, were tiny pieces of orris root, and coarsely ground benjamin (*Styrax Benzoin*) and storax (*Styrax officinalis*). Other ingredients were frequently introduced into the mixture to give a pleasing variation—coarsely crushed dried peel of lemon and orange, finely cut up vanilla pods, thin shavings of a stick of juniper, of sanders (sandalwood), of rhodium, (rosewood) and of lignum aloes. Gerard says that seeds of nigella "serveth well among other sweets to put into sweet waters, bagges and odoriferous pouders." In recent years, much use is made of the many varieties of sweet leaved pelargoniums unknown in early days.

In making up mixtures for sweet bags, we may have one predominating odor depending on personal preference, or upon the use to which the bag will be put—to scent little pillows, cushions or sachets for linen and clothes. The fourteenth century French King, Charles VI, liked his cushions filled with lavender flowers. The fifteenth century English King, Edward IV, liked his linen perfumed with a combination of anise and iris. In the *Toilet of Flora* we find a bag with the emphasis on roses. The little four-inch wide bag was to be made of thin Persian linen and filled with a mixture of rose petals dried in the shade, cloves beaten to a "gros powder" and mace scraped. In the seventeenth century Gervase Markham's *English Housewife,* we find a more pungent rose mixture:

Take of Orris four ounces, of Gallaminis one ounce, of Citis half an ounce, of Rose leaves dryed two handfuls, of dryed marjerom one handful, of Spike [lavender] one handful, Cloves one ounce, Benjamin and Rax of each two ounces, of white Sanders and yellow of each one ounce, beat all these into a gross powder, then put to it of musk a dram, of Civet half a dram and of Ambergreece half a dram, then put them into a Taffety Bag and use it.

You may prefer a blend of odors instead of one predominating one like lavender or southernwood which overwhelm any others with which they are put. From experience you will learn which herbs have the stronger scents and treat them accordingly. The Greeks preferred a blend of odors, no one prominent. The routine by which this was obtained was to mix a variety of crushed perfumed ingredients and shut them up in a box for several days. Then the ingredient of predominating odor was reduced in amount or taken out all together in the next trial combination. This was done over and over until no one odor was distinguishable. The final mixture was put into bags to perfume clothes.

Many are the uses for sweet bags and pads. They give a refreshing odor if hung over the bed posts in a sick

room or over the arms or back of an invalid's chair. Very
lovely gifts may be made, appealing to the recipients in
choice of scents, favorite colors and kind of material, and
size and shape most useful. In an old recipe we find that
after you have made little bags of taffeta "of what bignesse you will," you should make a mixture of musk,
ambergris and civet, and rub along the length of the
seams to fill in the holes made by the stitching. We also
read that it would be a good idea to sew ribbon on the
seams, too. The comment is made that although musk
and ambergris are the best to put into bags for fixatives,
cloves, cinnamon and mace may be substituted to lessen
the expense.

Small bags of very thin silk filled with these fragrant
mixtures, attached by a length of one and one-half inch
wide ribbon and hung from the hook of a coat hanger
would be appreciated by anyone, particularly if the recipient's preference in odors is considered. An extra touch
could be added by wrapping padding cotton evenly about
the hanger, sprinkling therein some of the herb mixture,
and covering with the silk used in the bags and tufting
with narrower ribbon of the same shade as that on the
bag.

A lovely fragrant foundation for bureau drawers may
be made by cutting two pieces of cheesecloth or fine net
a half inch larger than the size of the drawer. Then cut
two pieces of thin cotton padding a bit smaller than the
drawer. Lay one piece flat on a table, sprinkle over it a
generous layer of the desired scented mixture of herbs,
lay the other piece of cotton over it, baste all around the
edges and make tackings of thread through the two pads.
Of the net make a bag open at one end and carefully place
the scented padding in it. Sew up the end and tuft with

contrasting or harmonizing ribbon through several places to hold the pad firmly. The edges may be featherstitched or bound with ribbon to match that of the tufts.

Mrs. Milton J. Hassan of Newtown, Ohio, makes sachets the size of postage stamps, of herbs and a few balsam needles and sends them with Christmas cards. She also finds "powder puff muslin" ideal for little pillow-bags, the variety of floral designs offered allowing the pattern to suggest the contents. One piece with gray predominating was used for an herb mixture emphasizing lavender. Another, lemon yellow and brick red, was used for a mixture of geranium, lemon verbena and lemon balm.

Miss Margaret MacKenzie of Newtown, Connecticut (is there anything in the name Newtown that makes for inspired herb ideas?) buys small, inexpensive chiffon handkerchiefs, puts in a handful of herbs, and ties them up with matching or contrasting colors. A favorite mixture is lavender flowers, rose geranium leaves, petals of Rugosa roses, and a little lemon verbena.

To lay between piles of linen, I prefer flat pads to the fat little bags which make a high pile a bit precarious. I make envelopes of organdy, about four by five inches in size, fill with just enough herb mixture to make a plump pad, but not over-stuffed, then tuft in four places with narrow contrasting or harmonizing ribbon. With matching silk I featherstitch the ends, primarily to cover the sewing on the end left open for filling. I like pads of lavender flowers and leaves in lavender organdy envelopes, tufted with a deeper shade of ribbon. Other herbs I like for the pads are mixtures of rose geranium and a little bit of lavender or sometimes of rosemary; lemon verbena with finger bowl pelargoniums; lemon thyme and lemon verbena; costmary and skeleton leaf pelargonium.

My twenty-pound tiger cat, Orphie Whiffendorfer (just Orphie in hot weather), trails me about the garden all summer and assumes the responsibility of overseer of the harvest by practically living in the drying room, particularly watchful that his own pet herb, catnip, is being taken care of properly. While I am making sweet bags and pads, he sits up opposite to me and superintends that process. Just as grandmother made the last of the batter into a gingerbread man for me, so I fill the last pad with catnip. Orphie carries it to his master's desk and lays it over a grille covering the radiator. There he takes his afternoon naps and any attempt to move the pad only makes Master Whiffendorfer very unhappy.

For sweet bags, lavender has been the popular scent in England ever since it began to be cultivated there commercially back in the sixteenth century. Ike Walton once said to a fellow traveler, "Let's go to that house, for the linen looks white and smells of lavender and I long to be in a pair of sheets that smell so." Sometimes the lovely dried sprays of rosemary, lavender, costmary, or sweet woodruff were laid between the piles of linen or on the beds themselves. Parkinson in his *Paradisus* speaks of combining costmary and lavender. Costmary flower sprays were:

Tyed up with small bundels of Lavender toppes, these being put in the middle of them, to lye upon the toppes of bed, presses, etc. for the sweet sent and savour it casteth.

Moths have always "liked nice things," not a modern taste at all, only now we make more to-do about them than our ancestors, who took them in their stride. Our grandmothers dealt with moths quite effectively and with more respect to the nose than we do now. As a little girl,

I can remember the sweet scented days I spent in the attic with grandmother while she put away the winter clothes, not a quick camphorous episode, but sweet scented hours. I was allowed to carry up the basket full of fragrant bags and pads which I held out one by one to be laid among the clothes which moths would be loath to attack because of their dislike of such clean, spicy, fragrant odors. When we had finished the task, grandmother would open a certain old trunk with curving top and such a heavenly blend of fragrant odors rushed forth to greet my nose, which in my earliest trips to the attic didn't come much above the opened treasures. Then grandmother would "go through the things just to see whether they were all right." A matter of fact statement, to be sure, but I thought there was a sort of breathless eagerness, strange for the pursuit of a dull moth. What beautiful laces she took gently out, shawls, dresses with voluminous skirts, nightgowns with long sleeves and high necks, furs. Many of them had lovely stories that grandmother would repeat to me as she had before. One day when the trunk was finally closed, I asked grandmother if she had found any moths. She looked blankly at me, "What? Oh—no—let's go down stairs now. No, there weren't any moths." Afterwards, I wisely thought it all out. She hadn't been looking for moths but simply letting old memories come out of the sweet-smelling trunk.

One day in turning over the pages of my much cherished *Godey's Lady's Book,* I came across, in the May, 1864 issue, these directions for perfuming clothes:

Cloves, in coarse powder, one ounce; cassia, one ounce; lavender flowers, one ounce; lemon peel, one ounce. Mix and put them into little bags, and place them where the clothes are kept, or wrap the clothes round them. They will keep off insects.

The ancient Greeks and Romans used to keep their robes in chests of perfumed woods for protection and for the perfume which still lingered when the garments were worn, while Elizabethans sewed slices of fragrant Florentine iris root into their clothes.

Besides filling bags and pads with spices and herbs, the crushed herbs mixed with freshly crushed cloves may be scattered among clothes and furs. Laying in the dried tops of some herbs is also effective, the tips of santolina (lavender cotton), rosemary, southernwood, yellow melilot (sweet clover), thyme, wormwood, mint, tansy, lavender, also flower heads of the lavender, and dried and sliced roots of valerian and sweet flag. Choose what combination you will and mix about two tablespoonfuls of crushed spices to a scant pound of herbs. Southernwood used to be so universally used in France that it was called "Garde robe," its modern name "citronelle" coming from the distinct odor of lemon which it has.

Culpeper has a good word to say for wormwood: "This herb, wormwood, being laid among cloaths will make a moth scorn to meddle with cloathes as much as a lion scorns to meddle with a mouse or an eagle with a fly." Any spray of wormwood certainly ought not to throw Culpeper down after such high praise! In Banckes' *Herbal* (1525) you are directed to "take the flowers of rosemary and put them in thy chest among thy clothes or among thy Bookes and Moths shall not destroy them."

During the harvesting season I save the stems and branches after I have stripped off the dried leaves. I tie them up into little fagots and keep them near the fireplace for dropping into the flames some cold, blustery day when a cup of tea and a few minutes just to relax and chat with friends are most welcome. We make quite a game of guessing which herb fagot was thrown on the fire: thyme, savory, hyssop, basil, marjoram, lemon verbena, catnip. Orphie always guesses right on the last one. His head goes up and his nose goes searching out his favorite odor.

Sometimes we throw the herbs, particularly southernwood, on the fire to take away traces of stale tobacco or of cooking. Coarsely broken up pieces of Florentine iris with a faint violet odor, give off a delicate fragrance when scattered over the fire. I also dry the skins of citrus fruit, break them up and keep them in a bowl near the fire to throw on as a fragrant variation.

Starch was brought into England in Tudor times from Holland, and Mistress Dinghen taught the art of making and using it to anyone who would pay her five pounds. This became very popular in those days of ruffs rising to a height of three feet at the back of the neck. Not only were frames needed but a stiffening of the ruff itself.

Starch was often colored to suit the wearer of the ruff. Then came the use of perfume in starch. This was done by boiling petals of roses, flower heads of lavender, leaves of fragrant herbs, in water until a concentrated liquid resulted. Then a little musk and ambergris were added to hold the scent and the mixture allowed to stand overnight. This was added to a thick starch solution and when used would "make your linnen to smell most pleasantly."

William Langham in the *Garden of Health* (1579) gives us another method for perfuming clothes and suggests the use of lavender. "Boyle it in water and wett thy shirt in it and dry it again and weare it." Nowadays fragrant waters, or a few drops of perfume, are added to the water with which clothes are sprinkled before ironing.

Parkinson tells us that ferns made into balls were often used instead of soaps. The ferns were burned until they "became blewish, which being then layd by will dissolve into powder of itself like unto lime." A few balls dissolved in water were considered excellent for a basket of clothes.

You will find that many of these old-fashioned uses of herbs still have their useful points. It is fun to experiment with the preparations which need only your herbs and ordinary kitchen equipment. Elaborate concoctions made in the old still-rooms are fascinating to make and you will be more than pleased with the good results and especially you will agree with Thomas Tusser's angle on home preparations:

> What cost to good husband, is any of this?
> Good household provision only it is:
> Of other the like, I do leave out a many,
> That costeth the husbandman never a penny.

CHAPTER XVII

A LIST OF NOTEWORTHY HERBS

Thus have I lined out a Garden to our Countrey House wives, and given them Rules for common hearbes.—The skill and paines of weeding the Garden with weeding knives of fingers, I refer to themselves, and their maides, willing them to take the opportunitie of a showere of rain; withall, I advise the Mistresse either to be present herselfe, or to teach her maids to know hearbs from weeds.
—WILLIAM LAWSON (1617)

Basil, savory and thyme for cooking; boneset, horehound and peppermint for ills of the flesh; lavender, rosemary and southernwood for the nose and also for the sensibilities of moths; these and a dozen other varieties of herbs constituted my grandmother's herb garden, separated by a rose covered fence from the rest of the space devoted to vegetables and flowers. That there might be more herbs than grew in that sweet scented garden, I never dreamed.

Later, in reading much of Elizabethan literature, I came upon fascinating old gardening books and herbals which dealt with hundreds of herbs that had been used as commonly as my grandmother had used her score or more. The naive descriptions of the plants, the discussion of their habits and peculiarities, the stories of their use and virtues—these all enchanted me. "Curiouser and curiouser," I thought. And now each year as I add a few more with which I would like to become acquainted, I learn of many others equally charming. The fields are full of the wild greens and potherbs so precious to our forbears, and the woods still hold the ferns that were prized for medicine and for soap making. Any attempt to merely list "all the herbs there are," as I am frequently asked to do, would be a hopeless task. The following list of slightly over two hundred herbs are easily obtained and readily grown almost anywhere in the United States. I have grown all of them repeatedly and for the most part from seed sown out of doors. All are perennial unless otherwise noted and each has some particular quality, use or history, that makes it a worthwhile companion in the best of gardens.

Space permits little more than a bare list but with the botanical (Latin) name, full description of almost any one of the listed plants is readily obtained in standard botanical works of reference available in public and college libraries.

ACONITE. *Aconitum Napellus*. Monkshood. Tall dark violet-blue flowers. Needs shade. Roots poisonous.

ALKANET. *Anchusa officinalis*. Dyer's bugloss. Gentian blue flowers. Red dye from root used. Will bloom for weeks.

Anchusa italica. Dropmore variety. Turquoise blue clusters.

ALLIUM. *A. Schoenoprasum*. Chives. Small lilac flower heads, a lovely edging in the spring.

karataviense. French garlic. Large lilac flower heads in July. Stems coarse and inclined to break off.

AMBROSIA. *Chenopodium Botrys*. Jerusalem oak. Fragrant annual with small leaves shaped like oak leaves.

ANGELICA. *Angelica archangelica*. Biennial. Perennial if flower heads are cut off.

ANISE. *Pimpinella Anisum*. Annual.

ARTEMISIA. *A. albula*. Silver King. Grayish white delicate branches. Everlasting. Confused with *A. gnaphaloides*.

A. Abrotanum. Southernwood. Old man Lad's love. Pungent lemony thread-like leaves.

A. Absinthium. Wormwood. Grayish, finely cut, fragrant leaves. Use a spray with roast goose.

A. Dracunculus var. sativus. French tarragon. Long narrow leaves, anise taste.

A. frigida (Fringed). Delicate silvery foliage. Lovely background for color.

A. lactiflora. Hawthorn-scented; White mugwort. Tall, fragrant. Tiny white flower panicles.

A. pontica. Roman wormwood; Crusader's herb. Silvery, finely cut foliage. Pleasing.

A. Purshiana. Cudweed. Striking whitish woolly leaves.

A. stelleriana. Beach wormwood; Dusty miller; Old woman. Abundant along Cape Cod. Yellowish flower heads.

A. vulgaris. Mugwort. Tall. Grayish effect.

A. annua. Ambrosia. Annual. Fragrant. Self sows.

BALM. *Melissa officinalis.* Bee plant; Lemon balm. Dark green leaves, yellowish white flower whorls.

BASIL. *Ocimum basilicum.* Sweet basil. Spicy yellow green leaves. Annual. Culinary.

O. minimum. Dwarf bush. Either green or purple, a miniature lovely sweet basil for edgings. Annual.

O. crispum. Italian basil. Large crinkly leaves. Annual.

O. sanctum. Sacred basil. Pungently fragrant. Annual.

BENE. *Sesamum orientale.* Sesame. Seeds used. Ali Baba's brother forgot the word. Annual.

BERGAMOT. *Monarda didyma.* Oswego tea; Bee balm. Tall. Red flowers.

M. fistulosa. Wild bergamot. Lavender flowers.

M. fistulosa var. alba. White.

BETONY. *Stachys betonica* or *Betonica officinalis.* A medicinal herb from early Saxon times in high esteem.

Stachys grandiflora superba or *Betonica superba rosea.* Woundwort. Showy purplish spikes in July.

BORAGE. *Borago officinalis.* Annual.

BUGLE WEED. *Ajuga genevensis.* Gentian blue flower heads. Unlike *A. reptans,* does not creep. Neat, compact.

BURNET. *Sanguisorba minor.* Hardy. Other varieties are *S. of-*

ficinalis; S. canadensis; S. spinosa; S. tenuifolia; S. obtusata. S. canadensis is the wild kind.

BUTTER & EGGS. *Linaria vulgaris.* Resembles snapdragon. In England the toad flax is called eggs and bacon, monkey flower. Many popular names. Used medicinally. Laxative.

CALAMINT. *Calamintha alpina.* Fragrant ground cover. Evergreen.

    C. officinalis or *C. montana.* Mountain balm. Whorls of lilac flowers all up the stem.

CALENDULA. *Calendula officinalis.* Pot marigold. Annual. Flowers used to color butter.

CAMPHOR PLANT. *Achillea Ageratum.* Maudeline. Resembles young costmary but leaves more pointed with sharp scalloped edges. Distinct odor of camphor.

CARAWAY. *Carum Carvi.* Biennial.

CELANDINE. *Chelidonium Majus.* Bright yellow flowers all season. Bright orange acrid juice dyes your fingers.

CHAMOMILE. *Matricaria Chamomilla.* German. Cut and rolled for fragrant paths. Coarser foliage, richer green. Annual.

    Anthemis nobilis. Roman or true chamomile. Flowers used in teas, hair washes. Used to be smoked for asthma. Annual. Dies out if not cut back.

CHERVIL. *Anthriscus Cerefolium.* Biennial. Needs a cool spot and shade of other plants. Temperamental.

CHICORY. *Cichorium Intybus.* Blue dandelion; Succory. Lovely next to tansy. An Italian species used like asparagus.

SWEET CICELY. *Myrrhis odorata.* Myrrh. Not the Biblical myrrh. Finely cut, fernlike, anise-scented leaves.

    Osmorhiza brevistylis. American sweet cicely. Found growing wild in rich moist woods. Flat coarser leaf.

COLTSFOOT. *Tussilago Farfara.* Son before father. Flower passes before leaves appear. Bright yellow blossom earlier than crocus and similar. Coltsfoot candy for coughs.

COMFREY. *Symphytum officinale.* Bruisewort. Huge leaves. White or reddish flowers. Needs shade. Likes moisture.

CORIANDER. *Coriandrum sativum.* Named from Greek koros (bug) from odor of green plant. Annual.

COSTMARY. *Chrysanthemum Balsamita* or *Tanacetum Bal-*

samita. Mint geranium; Bible leaf; Sweet Mary. Large sprawling leaves, rounding scalloped edges, minty odor.

AUTUMN CROCUS. *Colchium autumnale.* Naked lady. Lavender flowers shoot up, one after the other, stark and alone.

CUMIN. *Cuminum Cyminum.* Scraggly, hard to raise unless seeds are fresh. Used in Kümmel. Seeds in cheese. Annual.

DANDELION. *Taraxacum officinale.* Good spring tonic.

DILL. *Anethum graveolens.* Annual. Tall.

ELECAMPANE. *Inula Helenium.* Horseheal. Huge leaves like an elephant's ears. Tall stalk, large bright yellow flowers.

ENGLISH DAISY. *Bellis perennis.* Leaves used for poultices.

FENNEL. *Foeniculum vulgare.* Wild or bitter fennel (also sweet fennel).

F. vulgare var. dulce. Florence; Finocchio. Annual.

F. vulgare var. piperitum carosella. Raw stems as appetizer.

FEVERFEW. *Chrysanthemum Parthenium.* Lovely flowering medicinal herb. Pungent odor resembles chrysanthemums.

FLAG. *Iris versicolor.* Blue flag. Confused with sweet flag.

Acorus Calamus. Sweet flag. Root dried as fixative.

FLAX. *Linum usitatissimum.* Delicate light blue flowers from early summer to late fall. Petals drop by noon.

FLEABANE. *Erigeron elatior.* Purplish daisy-like flowers.

FORGET-ME-NOT. *Myosotis scorpioides.* Used in lung troubles.

FOXGLOVE. *Digitalis purpurea.* Digitalis. Heart medicine.

FRAXINELLA. *Dictamnus alba.* Gas plant. Not to be confused with dittany. Causes skin irritation, painful to some people. Gives off traces of an inflammable gas.

Dictamnus rubra. Gas plant. Rosy red flowers.

FUMITORY. *Fumaria officinalis.* "Earth smoke." Annual.

GERMANDER. *Teucrium Chamaedrys.* Erect variety. Lovely shiny dark green leaves and rose colored flowers.

GOOD KING HENRY. *Chenopodium bonus-henricus.* Arrow shaped leaves, tiny white flowers on spikes. Used as spinach in olden days.

HELIOTROPE. *Heliotropium peruvianum.* Cherry pie. Turns from east to west with the sun. Tender.

HENBANE. *Hyoscyamus niger.* Annual of the potato family. Hard to raise because of the potato beetle.

HOLLYHOCK. *Althaea rosea.* Medicinal herb from early days. Used as a dye for volumetric analysis paper.

HOLY THISTLE. *Carduus benedictus.* Early plague remedy. Annual.

HONESTY. *Lunaria annua.* Poor man's shilling; Silver dollar; Satin flower. Broad oval seed pods. Slipping off outer parchment covering leaves lovely satiny oval. Biennial.

HOREHOUND. *Marrubium vulgare.* Woolly grayish leaves used in teas and well-known candy.

HOUSELEEK. *Sempervivum tectorum.* Hen and chickens. Popular early medicinal herb with much lore.

HYSSOP. *Hyssopus officinalis.* Not the Biblical hyssop. Fine low hedge often used for mazes. Lovely purple flowers.

 H. officinalis var. ruber. Pink hedge hyssop. Often pink flowers appear in the midst of a purple haze. There is also a lovely white hyssop which blooms much later here.

LARKSPUR. *Delphinium Consolida.* Self sows. Lovely blue and white flowers. Plant against orange calendulas.

LAVENDER. *Lavandula spica var. Munstead.* Dwarf. Large very sweet vivid deep-lavender flowers.

 L. atropurpurea nana. Dwarf French. Neat bushes, narrow leaves, bluish flowers.

 L. spica or *spicata.* Spike. More pungent than *L. vera* and much used for its oil.

 L. vera or *officinalis.* Sweet lavender. Best oil.

 L. pinnata. Fringy grayish leaves.

 L. dentata. Narrow dark green leaves with small regular scalloped edges. Lovely plant.

 L. pedunculata. Dark purple flowers.

LILY OF THE VALLEY. *Convallaria majalis.* Medicinal. Used even now for cardiac troubles in remedies.

LOVAGE. *Levisticum officinale.* Tall handsome plant for a shady border. Resembles celery. Stalks blanched and used. Do not confuse with Sea lovage or Scotch parsley (*Ligusticum scoticum*).

LUNGWORT. *Pulmonaria officinalis.* Low growing, mottled leaves, distinctive shape. Flowers deep pink then purple.

MALLOW. *Althaea officinalis.* Marsh mallow. Early medicinal herb used now for colds. Rose colored flowers. Tall.

MARJORAM. *Origanum onites.* Pot marjoram. Beautiful plant enlarging itself each year by layering. Leaves like sweet marjoram. Small pinkish lilac flowers swarming with bees.

O. *majorana.* Sweet or Knotted. Annual slow to germinate. Many uses for food, medicine, fragrance.

O. *Dictamnus.* Dittany of Crete. Recently brought to America. Mentioned in Virgil's *Aeneid.*

MAYAPPLE. *Podophyllum peltatum.* Large white flower followed by soft waxy yellow apple.

MINT. *Mentha citrata.* Orange or Bergamot mint; French bergamot.

M. *spicata var. crispata.* Curly. Crinkly, heavily veined broad leaves.

M. *piperita var. officinalis.* White peppermint. Finest oil.

M. *piperita var. vulgaris.* Black or English peppermint.

M. *gentilis.* American or golden applemint. Loveliest mild fragrant odor. Low spreading plant with vivid green leaves streaked with golden yellow.

M. *rotundifolia var. variegata.* Silver or striped applemint. Rough gray green leaves, whitish lines.

M. *Pulegium.* Pennyroyal, pudding grass, English pennyroyal. Prostrate habits, leaves small dark roundish.

Hedeoma pulegioides. American pennyroyal. Upright plant. Narrow light green fragile leaves.

M. *Requieni.* Corsican. Crème de menthe. Tender. Tiny roundish vivid green leaves strongly pungent.

M. *rotundifolia.* Woolly mint. Lovely soft woolly roundish leaves about one inch broad.

M. *aquatica.* Water mint. Strong pungent. Found along the shores of lakes.

M. *sylvestris.* English horsemint. Tall handsome plant with coarse gray-green leaves.

M. *spicata.* Garden mint; Spearmint; Lamb mint.

Monardella villosa. Southern Oregon mint. Delicately scented, small leaved low growing variety.

MULLEIN. *Verbascum Thapsus.* Great mullein; Our Lady's Flannel. Tall stout stalk topped by a thick spike of tiny yellow flowers. In early days was dipped in fat to burn at ceremonials. Gray green flannel leaves.

V. Blattaria. Moth mullein. Slender delicate single stalks with flat yellow flowers set close to stem.

MULLEIN PINK. *Lychnis coronaria.* Rose Campion. Stems and leaves greenish gray. Single cerise flowers.

MUSK. *Mimulus moschatus.* Small low growing plant, now without scent. Nobody knows why.

MYRTLE. *Vinca minor.* Periwinkle. Shiny waxy leaves with flat single flowers. Ground cover.

Myrtus angustifolia minor. Erect myrtle. Like a miniature tree with narrow shiny leaves.

NASTURTIUM. *Tropaeolum majus* and *T. minus.* Subject to aphids unless sprayed and leaves picked. Known in the 17th century as Lark's heels and Indian cress. Seeds used. Annual.

NEPETA. *Nepeta cataria.* Catnip. Cut back in July. Pale lavender flowers, white hairs on leaves give grayish effect.

N. mussini. Many small lavender blue flowers. Edging for bare lower stalks of taller plants.

N. macrantha. Larger variety than the *mussini.*

NETTLE. *Lamium maculatum album.* Dead nettle. A lovely old-fashioned medicinal herb. Small white flower, rough coarse leaves with white streaks.

L. maculatum purpureum. A purple flowered variety.

NICOTIANA. *Nicotiana alata.* Annual. White flowered variety very fragrant at night. Red is scentless. A clump is very attractive.

OREGON TEA. *Micromeria Douglasii.* Yerba buena. Fragrant leaves much used in mild tea. Leaves slightly hairy.

PANSY. *Viola tricolor.* Popular as a medicinal herb in olden times. Cut central heart out to promote blooms.

PARSLEY. *Petroselinum hortense filicinum.* Biennial small fernlike much cut leaves.

P. hortense crispum. Vivid green crinkly leaves.

PRIMROSE. *Primula vulgaris.* Long narrow rough textured leaves. Lovely single loose lemon yellow flower clusters.

PYRETHRUM. *Pyrethrum cinerariaefolium.* Insect powder flowers. Profuse blooms resembling daisies. Pungent chrysanthemum odor. Dried flowers basis of many insect powders and sprays.

RAMPION. *Campanula Rapunculus.* Tall erect stems. Delicate lavender bells.

RHUBARB. *Rheum Rhaponticum.* From earliest times a medicinal herb.

ROSE. *Rosa gallica.* Apothecaries' rose. Still used medicinally for its astringent qualities.

R. rubiginosa. Sweet Brier; Eglantine. Tiny prickly stems and shiny dark green leaves, beautifully fragrant after a shower.

ROSEMARY. *Rosmarinus officinalis.* Woody shrub, beautiful narrow dark green leaves. Tiny bright blue flowers. Spicy nutmeg odor. Warm balsam taste.

RUE. *Ruta graveolus.* Herb o' Grace. Easy from seed. Lovely bluish green lacy leaves. Yellow blossoms. Foliage can be trimmed into a graceful hedge.

SAFFLOWER. *Carthamus tinctorius.* American saffron. The true saffron—*Crocus sativus*—is a bulb. The safflower comes from seed and is used similarly. Orange flower heads have spiny bracts.

SAGE. *Salvia Sclarea.* Clary. 3 or 4 feet tall. Usually flowers are mauve, some varieties yellow or white. Suffocatingly camphorous odor.

S. officinalis. Garden sage. Salviol oil in leaves prevents evil effect of excessive grease. Hence its use in stuffing.

S. rutilans. Pineapple sage. Quick growing woody much branching bush. Wonderfully fragrant of pineapple when bruised. Tender.

ST. JOHN'S WORT. *Hypericum perforatum.* Small leaves containing transparent oil sacs seem to be full of pin pricks. Tiny bright yellow flowers.

SANTOLINA. *Santolina Chamaecyparissus.* Lovely decorative grayish bushy plant looking like coral. Pungent.

S. pinnata. Green santolina. Rich green branching plant with more base stems, smaller coral effect. Flower heads are small pungent lemon colored balls.

SATUREIA. *Satureia croatica.* Evergreen. Showy purple flowers.

S. hortensis. Summer savory. Slender woody branches. White blossoms give appearance of snow. Annual.

S. montana. Winter savory. Quite woody low plant. Slow growing. Leaves stiff and spiny. Does not blend so well in food as the *hortensis.*

SEA HOLLY. *Eryngium amethystinum.* Purplish gray stalks, thistle shaped flower heads. Decorative though scraggly.

SENNA. *Cassia marilandica.* Wild senna. Tropical looking tall bush. Leaves turn completely over and fold tight at night.

SKIRRET. *Sium sisarum.* Salad or potherb. Roots were boiled and eaten with butter.

SNAKE ROOT. *Cimicifuga racemosa.* An old medical herb.

SORREL. *Rumex Acetosella.* Small acid tasting leaves.
   R. scutatus. French sorrel. Larger, more succulent, not so sour.

SPIDERWORT. *Tradescantia virginiana.* A showy lavender spidery flower head of weird arrangement.

SQUILLS. *Scilla sibirica.* Bulb blossoming early with small blue flowers in racemes. From ancient times medicinal.

TANSY. *Tanacetum vulgare.* Tall handsome plant with fern-like leaves. Flower heads are massed orange blossoms.

THORNAPPLE. *Datura Stramonium.* Jimson weed. Large trumpet shaped white flowers. Plant smells like potato. Annual.

THOROUGHWORT. *Eupatorium perfoliatum.* Boneset. Stems appear to pierce the leaf. Old fashioned herb for fever.

THYME. *Thymus azoricus.* A mat of softly bristling tiny tubes.
   T. citriodorus. Lemon thyme. Mound of bright green leaves with lovely lemon odor. Self layering.
   T. citriodorus var. argenteus. Silver. Green leaves variegated with pale greenish white.
   T. corsicum. Same as *mentha requieni.*
   T. herba-barona. Caraway thyme. Spreads beautifully to cover a large area. Purplish flower.
   T. jankae. Dark purple flowers.
   T. nitidus. Erect little bush, pinkish flowers.
   T. nummularius. Creeping prostrate variety.
   T. serpyllum. Mountain thyme; Mother of Thyme. Lilac flowers in spring on creeping mats.
   T. serpyllum var. album. White creeping thyme.
   T. serpyllum var. aureus. Mounds of green variegated with golden yellow. Lovely.
   T. serpyllum var. coccineum. Crimson creeping.

T. serpyllum var. lanuginosus. Woolly. Tiny gray green hairy leaves. A rock garden treasure.

T. serpyllum splendens. Bushy. Red flowers.

T. vulgaris var. narrow leaved. French. Erect low gray bush.

T. vulgaris var. broad leaved. English. Erect green.

T. vulgaris var. German winter. Low scraggly bush. Very dark leaves.

TURTLE HEAD. *Chelone Lyoni.* Pink.

VALERIAN. *Valeriana officinalis.* Garden heliotrope.

VERBENA. *Aloysia citriodora.* Lemon verbena. Tender.

VERONICA. *Veronica longifolia subsessilis.* Speedwell. An old medicinal herb. Deep blue flower spikes.

V. incana. Long narrow soft gray leaves. Racemes of lovely blue flowers.

VIOLET. *Viola odorata.* An ancient medicinal and culinary herb.

WOAD. *Isatis tinctoria.* Tall plant with bluish green arrow shaped leaves and small yellow flowers.

WOODRUFF. *Asperula odorata.* Sweet woodruff; Waldmeister. A lovely ground cover, star-like leaves. Sweet scented.

YARROW. *Achillea Millefolium var. rubrum.* Not so coarse as the common white. Red flower heads, each tiny flower has white eye.

A. ptarmica. Sneezewort. Wild variety.

CHAPTER XVIII

TABLES

1. Herbs for fragrance
2. Culinary herbs for foliage
3. Culinary herbs for savory seeds
4. Herbs of legendary or historic interest
5. Stately herbs
6. Colorful herbs
7. Doctrine of signatures
8. Herb teas
9. Language of the herbs
10. The importance of herbs (chart)

TABLE 1

HERBS FOR FRAGRANCE

Except for the flowery heads of lavender and of ambrosia, the fragrance comes from the volatile oil in the leaves. To appreciate fully the scent, the leaves must be bruised in the hands and the warmth will start the flow of oil. All of these are good for potpourri, except possibly Corsican mint which is very strong. Lavender should be used sparingly except where that scent is desired. This is true also of lemon verbena and southernwood. All these herbs are perennial except ambrosia, an annual. All should have sun but several, as noted, are happy in shady places.

HERB	Height Inches	Type of Odor	Best Soil	Remarks
Ambrosia	24	Intensely fragrant	Ordinary loam	Reseeds itself easily
Camphor plant	36	Definitely camphorish	Poor	Divide every third year
Sweet Cicely	48	Reminiscent of anise	Rich loam under trees	Do not move plants until well established
Lavender	12-36	Varieties vary greatly	Light, dry chalky, sandy	Should be somewhat protected in a sunny spot
Corsican mint	Flat mat	Crème de menthe	Moist shady	Not hardy
Rosemary	48*	Piny	Chalky	Must be taken indoors in winter
Santolina	24	Oily pungency	Sandy	Gray resembles coral. Green vivid with pungent lemon colored balls
Southernwood	48	Somewhat lemony	Sandy dry, poor	Becomes a shrub
Lemon verbena	36	Deliciously lemon	Moderately rich	Must be taken indoors in winter
Sweet woodruff	6-8	New mown hay	Moist preferred	Good ground cover under trees

* Tradition has it that rosemary never grows higher than the height of Christ on earth.

TABLE 2

CULINARY HERBS FOR FOLIAGE

Just as the flower buds are ready to open, the volatile oils increase to their greatest amount. At that time cut tops and tender stems, on a dry morning after dew has gone and before sun is high enough to volatilize the oils. Keep each variety separate. Except chervil, applemint, and tarragon, all need sun. Those marked (A) are annuals and parsley (B) is a biennial. All others are perennials.

HERB	Height Inches	How used	Best soil	Remarks
Sweet basil (A)	12	Tomato & cheese dishes. Soups, stews.	Rich, light dry	Smells and tastes like sweet pepper.
Chervil (A)	10	Fresh in salad. Dried in meat loaf.	Ordinary	Resembles parsley. Needs broken shade of taller plants.
Chives	12	In soft cheese, vegetable cocktails, salads.	Light	Always used fresh. Lovely edging in late spring.
Sweet marjoram (A)	10	Meat loaf. Vegetable cocktails.	Sandy	Perennial in warm climates. More delicate than the hardy pot marjoram.
Golden applemint	12	Fruit cup, jelly.	Moist Limy	Mild odor and taste.
Parsley (B)	10	Powdered over soups. Fresh as garnish.	Ordinary somewhat moist	Makes a pretty edging for culinary plot.
Sage	18	Sausage. Stuffings.	Ordinary	Renew every 3rd year—gets woody.
Summer savory (A)	12	With green beans, stuffing, cocktails, meat.	Rich, light, dry	Grand herb. Small flowers resemble snow in summer.
French tarragon	24	Vinegar. Egg or chicken dishes, vegetable cocktails.	Light	Must be obtained as plants. Needs shade of taller plants.
Garden thyme	9	Meat loaf, stuffings, cocktails.	Lime or chalk. Dry	Spreads rapidly. Thin each spring.

TABLE 3

CULINARY HERBS FOR SAVORY SEEDS

Don't transplant any seedlings in this group. All are umbelliferae with delicate roots except nasturtium which has fine spreading roots, and sesame which is so sure and easy of germination that it may be sowed thickly and thinned out. Harvest seed heads as soon as ripe or they will fall and reseed. Use tender tips of thinned out dill, finely cut, in salads and on broiled chops; likewise tips of fennel in cream or cottage cheese. Caraway is biennial, sweet fennel is perennial. All others are annuals. All require sun. Coriander (annual) and caraway (biennial) are sometimes planted together to leave a ground cover when coriander is harvested.

HERB	Height Inches	How Used	Best Soil	Remarks
Anise	18	Soup, teas, liqueur, pastry, apple sauce	Warm, light	Slow growing. Use fresh seed. Keep weeded.
Caraway	18-24	Same as anise and in cheese	Dry, clayey, rich	First year forms rosette of carrot-like leaves.
Coriander	24	Pastry, liqueur, sausage, potpourri	Warm, dry, light	Self sows if heavy seed is not promptly harvested when ripe.
Cumin	12	Cheese, soup, pastry, liqueurs	Light fertile	Sow fresh seed in warm, sunny, protected spot.
Dill	36	Pickles, soup, pastry, spiced beets	Moist sandy	Must be staked for protection.
Sweet fennel	60	Sauerkraut, soup, pastry	Lime or chalk	Plants need staking.
Nasturtium	12	Mustard pickles, salads	Sandy	Sow at 3 week intervals until July.
Sesame	24-36	Confections, pastry	Light warm	Sturdy stems need no staking.

TABLE 4

HERBS OF LEGENDARY OR HISTORIC INTEREST

Most of the herbs, unlike our garden flowers, have been known and used for thousands of years. All those listed here are perennial except Holy Thistle, which is annual. Except for costmary and houseleek, all prefer sun.

HERB	Height Inches	Best Soil	Remarks
Alkanet	18	Deep but not damp	Red dye from root used to color lipsalve of court ladies, concealing real color.
Costmary	36	Average dry	Called Bible leaf, because of early use as a fragrant marker between pages.
Dittany	12	Light, sandy, enriched by leaf mold	Flowers resemble small pinkish hops. Roundish woolly leaves. Mentioned in Virgil's *Aeneid* as a healing herb.
Good King Henry	12	Poor	Liked by Heinrich, household goblin who played tricks and helped who played tricks and helped servants.
Rampion	36	Ordinary	Formerly a potherb. Old belief that its presence causes quarrels among children. Grimm's tale tells of its theft from magician.
Houseleek	3	Dry	Early belief that the plants on roofs of houses were safeguarded from bad luck and lightning.
Mugwort	42	Ordinary	Pilgrims wore it in shoes to prevent fatigue.
Saffron	6	Rich, light sandy	Separate bulbs each year. Set bulbs in August. Henry VIII so fond of it in his food, he forbade use of it by court ladies for hair dye. Came to England in a Crusader's staff.
Holy Thistle	36	Ordinary	Valued in early times as plague remedy.
Woad	36	Good loam	Blue juice from leaves long used in cloth dye.

TABLE 5

STATELY HERBS

Some are medicinal and some are culinary herbs. None are annual. Angelica, mullein and clary sage may be biennial. Angelica becomes perennial if flower heads are cut off before seed forms. All are very tall, at least 4 ft., and mostly 5 to 6 or even 7 ft. Hollyhock, of course, may go up 12 to 15 ft. All like sun, but aconite, angelica, lovage, marshmallow, snakeroot like shade, too.

HERB	Color of Flower	Part Used	Best Soil	Remarks
Aconite	Dark violet-blue	All parts. Root is poisonous	Average rich moist	Takes a year or so to become adjusted. Don't move it.
Angelica	Greenish-white	All parts, even the seed	Rich, moist	Place in a different spot every 3rd year. Cut off flowers.
Elecampane	Orange	Roots	Clayey moist	Huge leaves.
Wild Fennel	Yellow	Leaves Seed	Limy dryish	Smells and tastes like anise.
Hollyhock	Pink, red, yellow, white	Flowers	Rich, well prepared	Old medicinal herb.
Lovage	Greenish-yellow	Roots	Moist, rich sandy	Likes shelter, shade. Leaves taste like celery.
Marshmallow	Rose	Root	Moist loose	Protect young plants. Tends to winter kill.
Snakeroot	White	Parts below ground	Moist rich, leaf mold	Must be in one spot several years before the full display.
Mullein	Yellow	All parts except stalk	Poor	Greeks cut lamp wicks from leaves. Romans dipped heads in fat for torches.
Clary sage	Pink & blue	Seeds in drink. Leaves in tea	Average	Leaves used to be fried in batter & served with orange juice.

TABLE 6

COLORFUL HERBS

Contrary to the belief among many gardeners, the herbs are not drab. They have not been hot-housed and forced, to provide showy blossoms almost devoid of fragrance, with the exception of calendula (pot marigold) and larkspur. One has only to compare the originals of these plants with any resulting varieties to appreciate the simple beauty, the sturdiness, and the friendliness of the original plant. Others are colorful, too, and have, in addition, a decorative, restful foliage which you will appreciate. All are perennial unless marked (A) annual. All like sun except as noted.

HERB	Height Inches	Color	Time of Flowering	Best Soil	Remarks
Bergamot	36	Red, white, lilac	July to Sept.	Ordinary, sun or shade	Divide every 3rd year. Cut back in fall.
Borage (A)	24	Open pink and turn to blue	July & August	Poor loose	Leaves have cucumber taste. Used in iced beverages.
Calendula (A)	12	Orange	July to Sept.	Sandy	Adulterant for saffron.
Chicory	48	Light blue	July to Sept.	Poor	Flowers close by midday
Flax	18	Light blue	July to Sept.	Light sandy	Petals scattered by late morning.
Hyssop	18	Purplish blue and pink	July & August	Warm, light. Sun or shade	Crushed leaves have strong pungent odor.
Larkspur	24	Blue, white, and rose	June to Sept.	Ordinary	Dainty flowers and lacy leaves.
Rue	24	Yellow flower heads	June to August	Limy	Beautiful edging. Back with French marigolds.
Safflower (A)	18	Orange heads like dandelion	August	Fine mellow	Don't transplant. Cultivate until buds appear.
Tansy	60	Orange buttons	July to Sept.	Medium heavy	At Easter, leaves flavored a pudding.

TABLE 7

DOCTRINE OF SIGNATURES

No phase of gardening is so entrancing as the old belief in the Doctrine of Signatures first given most fully in *The Art of Simpling* by William Coles, 1656. It has been alluded to in all the old herbals and gardening books, and modern science has shown that however fantastic the basis ascribed to the belief may be, it is often correct in its results. The herbs in this table provide a study of the belief. All are perennial except canterbury bells (B), a biennial. Except wood sorrel, all like sun though prunella isn't fussy.

HERB	Height Inches	Part Showing Signature	Best Soil	Remarks
Canterbury bells (B)	30	Flower	Light	Corolla resembles throat. Used for bronchitis.
Celandine	36	Root	Ordinary	Root in white wine turns bilious yellow. Used in yellow jaundice.
Prunella	12	Flower	Poor	Corolla like throat. Cure for mouth and throat. Bruised for "green wounds."
Garlic	12	Stalk	Ordinary	Hollow stalk. Used for windpipe cures.
Lungwort	12	Leaf	Ordinary	Leaves shaped like lungs. Chest diseases.
Eyebright	8	Flower	Ordinary	Spot of yellow with dark center like pupil. Whole flower like bloodshot eye. Used in eye troubles.
St. John's Wort	36	Leaf	Poor	Apparent perforations like skin pores. Used for cuts, etc.
Saxifrage	8	Bulblets	Ordinary	Used to break up gallstones, as plants split rocks.
Viper's Bugloss	18	Seed, stem, leaf	Poor, coarse	Seed like snake's head, stem and leaf spotted. Used for snake bites.
Wood sorrel	12	Leaf	Moist	Heart shaped leaf. Cure in cardiac troubles.

TABLE 8

HERB TEAS

In general, herb teas are made just as you would make any tea. Either the fresh or the dried herb may be used, the leafy tips being preferred except, as in the case of chamomile, when the flower head contains the essential elements. Normally a tablespoonful of the herb is steeped in a pint of boiling water for ten minutes or so, using a non-metallic teapot, and then the liquid strained off. Lemon balm and bergamot require a little boiling to start the oils. Add nothing except possibly honey for sweetening or a slice of lemon. All of the herbs listed are perennial and all like sun, although lemon balm and Oregon tea do well in broken shade and peppermint will stand shade.

HERB	Height Inches	Part Used	Best Soil	Remarks
Balm, lemon	18	Leaves and tips	Poor, warm friable	Weedy in fertile soil. Pinch out tips.
Boneset	48	Leaves and tips	Rich, moist	Light mulch in winter.
Catnip	48	Tender leafy stems	Medium dry Avoid lime	Most fragrant in sun.
Chamomile	18	Flowers	Rather dry— ordinary	German chamomile grows all season.
Feverfew	24	Tender leafy stems	Ordinary	Spreads unless thinned out.
Oregon tea	18	Leaves	Moist—sun or shade	Yerba Buena—
Pennyroyal	10-12	Whole stem	Moist	2 varieties. American upright. English prostrate.
Peppermint	36	Leaves and tips	Ordinary— some moisture	2 varieties. Black English. White American.
Thyme, Lemon	Low mound	Whole stem	Ordinary	Inclined to layer itself and spread.
Yarrow	36	Whole stem & flower head	Ordinary	Divide every third year. Spicily aromatic flavor.

TABLE 9

LANGUAGE OF THE HERBS

Angelica—inspiration
Balm—sympathy
Basil—hatred, love
Betony—surprise
Borage—courage
Bugloss, Dyer's—falsehood
Burnet—merry heart
Chamomile—patience, humility
Chicory—frugality
Coltsfoot—maternal care
Coriander—hidden merit
Cumin—fidelity, avarice
Dandelion—oracle
Elder—compassion
Fennel—flattery
Flax—appreciation
Forget-me-not—true love
Foxglove—sincerity, adulation
Fumitory—hatred
Heliotrope—eternal love
Henbane—defect
Hollyhock—ambition
Horehound—health
Houseleek—vivacity
Hyssop—sacrifice
Larkspur—fickleness
Laurel (sweet bay)—glory
Lavender—silence, mistrust
Lily—purity
Lily of the valley—return of happiness
Marigold—grief, cruelty in love
Marjoram—happiness
Marshmallow—beneficence
Mint—wisdom

Mugwort—weary traveler
Nasturtium—patriotism
Nettle—slander, cruelty
Pansy—sad thoughts
Parsley—festivity, death
Pennyroyal—flee away
Pimpernel—assignation
Pink, clove—resignation
Poppy—oblivion
Rose—love
Rose, centifolia—grace
Rose, musk—capricious beauty
Rose, white—silence
Rose, yellow—infidelity
Rosemary—remembrance
Rue—repentance, purification
Saffron, crocus—mirth
Sage—immortality
St. John's Wort—animosity
Sorrel—parental affection
Southernwood—constancy
Speedwell (veronica)—fidelity
Spiderwort—transient love
Stonecrop—tranquillity
Sunflower—false riches
Tansy—hostile thoughts
Thistle—austerity
Thrift—sympathy
Thyme—activity, bravery
Valerian—readiness
Verbena—delicacy of feeling
Violet, blue—loyalty
Violet, white—innocence
Wormwood—absence, displeasure

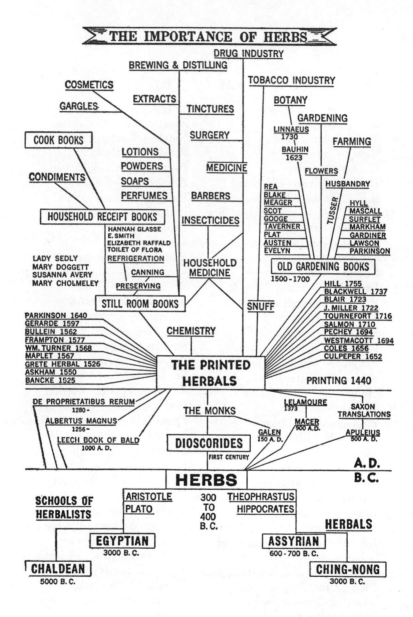

THE IMPORTANCE OF HERBS

INDEX TO BOOKS AND AUTHORS

Chapters XVII and XVIII are not indexed here as they are alphabetical.

INDEX OF HERBS

Chapters XVII and XVIII are not indexed here as they are alphabetical.

355

INDEX TO SUBJECT MATTER

Chapters XVII and XVIII are not indexed here as they are alphabetical.

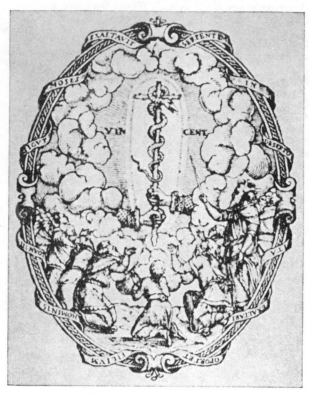

John III: 14
from Matthioli, 1565.

A CATALOGUE OF SELECTED DOVER BOOKS
IN ALL FIELDS OF INTEREST

A CATALOGUE OF SELECTED DOVER BOOKS
IN ALL FIELDS OF INTEREST

AMERICA'S OLD MASTERS, James T. Flexner. Four men emerged unexpectedly from provincial 18th century America to leadership in European art: Benjamin West, J. S. Copley, C. R. Peale, Gilbert Stuart. Brilliant coverage of lives and contributions. Revised, 1967 edition. 69 plates. 365pp. of text.

21806-6 Paperbound $3.00

FIRST FLOWERS OF OUR WILDERNESS: AMERICAN PAINTING, THE COLONIAL PERIOD, James T. Flexner. Painters, and regional painting traditions from earliest Colonial times up to the emergence of Copley, West and Peale Sr., Foster, Gustavus Hesselius, Feke, John Smibert and many anonymous painters in the primitive manner. Engaging presentation, with 162 illustrations. xxii + 368pp.

22180-6 Paperbound $3.50

THE LIGHT OF DISTANT SKIES: AMERICAN PAINTING, 1760-1835, James T. Flexner. The great generation of early American painters goes to Europe to learn and to teach: West, Copley, Gilbert Stuart and others. Allston, Trumbull, Morse; also contemporary American painters—primitives, derivatives, academics—who remained in America. 102 illustrations. xiii + 306pp.

22179-2 Paperbound $3.50

A HISTORY OF THE RISE AND PROGRESS OF THE ARTS OF DESIGN IN THE UNITED STATES, William Dunlap. Much the richest mine of information on early American painters, sculptors, architects, engravers, miniaturists, etc. The only source of information for scores of artists, the major primary source for many others. Unabridged reprint of rare original 1834 edition, with new introduction by James T. Flexner, and 394 new illustrations. Edited by Rita Weiss. 6⅝ x 9⅝.

21695-0, 21696-9, 21697-7 Three volumes, Paperbound $13.50

EPOCHS OF CHINESE AND JAPANESE ART, Ernest F. Fenollosa. From primitive Chinese art to the 20th century, thorough history, explanation of every important art period and form, including Japanese woodcuts; main stress on China and Japan, but Tibet, Korea also included. Still unexcelled for its detailed, rich coverage of cultural background, aesthetic elements, diffusion studies, particularly of the historical period. 2nd, 1913 edition. 242 illustrations. lii + 439pp. of text.

20364-6, 20365-4 Two volumes, Paperbound $6.00

THE GENTLE ART OF MAKING ENEMIES, James A. M. Whistler. Greatest wit of his day deflates Oscar Wilde, Ruskin, Swinburne; strikes back at inane critics, exhibitions, art journalism; aesthetics of impressionist revolution in most striking form. Highly readable classic by great painter. Reproduction of edition designed by Whistler. Introduction by Alfred Werner. xxxvi + 334pp.

21875-9 Paperbound $2.50

CATALOGUE OF DOVER BOOKS

VISUAL ILLUSIONS: THEIR CAUSES, CHARACTERISTICS, AND APPLICATIONS, Matthew Luckiesh. Thorough description and discussion of optical illusion, geometric and perspective, particularly; size and shape distortions, illusions of color, of motion; natural illusions; use of illusion in art and magic, industry, etc. Most useful today with op art, also for classical art. Scores of effects illustrated. Introduction by William H. Ittleson. 100 illustrations. xxi + 252pp.
21530-X Paperbound $2.00

A HANDBOOK OF ANATOMY FOR ART STUDENTS, Arthur Thomson. Thorough, virtually exhaustive coverage of skeletal structure, musculature, etc. Full text, supplemented by anatomical diagrams and drawings and by photographs of undraped figures. Unique in its comparison of male and female forms, pointing out differences of contour, texture, form. 211 figures, 40 drawings, 86 photographs. xx + 459pp. 5⅜ x 8⅜.
21163-0 Paperbound $3.50

150 MASTERPIECES OF DRAWING, Selected by Anthony Toney. Full page reproductions of drawings from the early 16th to the end of the 18th century, all beautifully reproduced: Rembrandt, Michelangelo, Dürer, Fragonard, Urs, Graf, Wouwerman, many others. First-rate browsing book, model book for artists. xviii + 150pp. 8⅜ x 11¼.
21032-4 Paperbound $2.50

THE LATER WORK OF AUBREY BEARDSLEY, Aubrey Beardsley. Exotic, erotic, ironic masterpieces in full maturity: Comedy Ballet, Venus and Tannhauser, Pierrot, Lysistrata, Rape of the Lock, Savoy material, Ali Baba, Volpone, etc. This material revolutionized the art world, and is still powerful, fresh, brilliant. With *The Early Work,* all Beardsley's finest work. 174 plates, 2 in color. xiv + 176pp. 8⅛ x 11.
21817-1 Paperbound $3.00

DRAWINGS OF REMBRANDT, Rembrandt van Rijn. Complete reproduction of fabulously rare edition by Lippmann and Hofstede de Groot, completely reedited, updated, improved by Prof. Seymour Slive, Fogg Museum. Portraits, Biblical sketches, landscapes, Oriental types, nudes, episodes from classical mythology—All Rembrandt's fertile genius. Also selection of drawings by his pupils and followers. "Stunning volumes," *Saturday Review.* 550 illustrations. lxxviii + 552pp. 9⅛ x 12¼.
21485-0, 21486-9 Two volumes, Paperbound $10.00

THE DISASTERS OF WAR, Francisco Goya. One of the masterpieces of Western civilization—83 etchings that record Goya's shattering, bitter reaction to the Napoleonic war that swept through Spain after the insurrection of 1808 and to war in general. Reprint of the first edition, with three additional plates from Boston's Museum of Fine Arts. All plates facsimile size. Introduction by Philip Hofer, Fogg Museum. v + 97pp. 9⅜ x 8¼
21872-4 Paperbound $2.00

GRAPHIC WORKS OF ODILON REDON. Largest collection of Redon's graphic works ever assembled: 172 lithographs, 28 etchings and engravings, 9 drawings. These include some of his most famous works. All the plates from *Odilon Redon: oeuvre graphique complet,* plus additional plates. New introduction and caption translations by Alfred Werner. 209 illustrations. xxvii + 209pp. 9⅛ x 12¼.
21966-8 Paperbound $4.00

DESIGN BY ACCIDENT; A BOOK OF "ACCIDENTAL EFFECTS" FOR ARTISTS AND DESIGNERS, James F. O'Brien. Create your own unique, striking, imaginative effects by "controlled accident" interaction of materials: paints and lacquers, oil and water based paints, splatter, crackling materials, shatter, similar items. Everything you do will be different; first book on this limitless art, so useful to both fine artist and commercial artist. Full instructions. 192 plates showing "accidents," 8 in color. viii + 215pp. 8⅜ x 11¼. 21942-9 Paperbound $3.50

THE BOOK OF SIGNS, Rudolf Koch. Famed German type designer draws 493 beautiful symbols: religious, mystical, alchemical, imperial, property marks, runes, etc. Remarkable fusion of traditional and modern. Good for suggestions of timelessness, smartness, modernity. Text. vi + 104pp. 6⅛ x 9¼. 20162-7 Paperbound $1.25

HISTORY OF INDIAN AND INDONESIAN ART, Ananda K. Coomaraswamy. An unabridged republication of one of the finest books by a great scholar in Eastern art. Rich in descriptive material, history, social backgrounds; Sunga reliefs, Rajput paintings, Gupta temples, Burmese frescoes, textiles, jewelry, sculpture, etc. 400 photos. viii + 423pp. 6⅜ x 9¾. 21436-2 Paperbound $5.00

PRIMITIVE ART, Franz Boas. America's foremost anthropologist surveys textiles, ceramics, woodcarving, basketry, metalwork, etc.; patterns, technology, creation of symbols, style origins. All areas of world, but very full on Northwest Coast Indians. More than 350 illustrations of baskets, boxes, totem poles, weapons, etc. 378 pp. 20025-6 Paperbound $3.00

THE GENTLEMAN AND CABINET MAKER'S DIRECTOR, Thomas Chippendale. Full reprint (third edition, 1762) of most influential furniture book of all time, by master cabinetmaker. 200 plates, illustrating chairs, sofas, mirrors, tables, cabinets, plus 24 photographs of surviving pieces. Biographical introduction by N. Bienenstock. vi + 249pp. 9⅞ x 12¾. 21601-2 Paperbound $4.00

AMERICAN ANTIQUE FURNITURE, Edgar G. Miller, Jr. The basic coverage of all American furniture before 1840. Individual chapters cover type of furniture—clocks, tables, sideboards, etc.—chronologically, with inexhaustible wealth of data. More than 2100 photographs, all identified, commented on. Essential to all early American collectors. Introduction by H. E. Keyes. vi + 1106pp. 7⅞ x 10¾. 21599-7, 21600-4 Two volumes, Paperbound $11.00

PENNSYLVANIA DUTCH AMERICAN FOLK ART, Henry J. Kauffman. 279 photos, 28 drawings of tulipware, Fraktur script, painted tinware, toys, flowered furniture, quilts, samplers, hex signs, house interiors, etc. Full descriptive text. Excellent for tourist, rewarding for designer, collector. Map. 146pp. 7⅞ x 10¾. 21205-X Paperbound $2.50

EARLY NEW ENGLAND GRAVESTONE RUBBINGS, Edmund V. Gillon, Jr. 43 photographs, 226 carefully reproduced rubbings show heavily symbolic, sometimes macabre early gravestones, up to early 19th century. Remarkable early American primitive art, occasionally strikingly beautiful; always powerful. Text. xxvi + 207pp. 8⅜ x 11¼. 21380-3 Paperbound $3.50

ALPHABETS AND ORNAMENTS, Ernst Lehner. Well-known pictorial source for decorative alphabets, script examples, cartouches, frames, decorative title pages, calligraphic initials, borders, similar material. 14th to 19th century, mostly European. Useful in almost any graphic arts designing, varied styles. 750 illustrations. 256pp. 7 x 10. 21905-4 Paperbound $4.00

PAINTING: A CREATIVE APPROACH, Norman Colquhoun. For the beginner simple guide provides an instructive approach to painting: major stumbling blocks for beginner; overcoming them, technical points; paints and pigments; oil painting; watercolor and other media and color. New section on "plastic" paints. Glossary. Formerly *Paint Your Own Pictures*. 221pp. 22000-1 Paperbound $1.75

THE ENJOYMENT AND USE OF COLOR, Walter Sargent. Explanation of the relations between colors themselves and between colors in nature and art, including hundreds of little-known facts about color values, intensities, effects of high and low illumination, complementary colors. Many practical hints for painters, references to great masters. 7 color plates, 29 illustrations. x + 274pp.
20944-X Paperbound $2.75

THE NOTEBOOKS OF LEONARDO DA VINCI, compiled and edited by Jean Paul Richter. 1566 extracts from original manuscripts reveal the full range of Leonardo's versatile genius: all his writings on painting, sculpture, architecture, anatomy, astronomy, geography, topography, physiology, mining, music, etc., in both Italian and English, with 186 plates of manuscript pages and more than 500 additional drawings. Includes studies for the Last Supper, the lost Sforza monument, and other works. Total of xlvii + 866pp. 7⅞ x 10¾.
22572-0, 22573-9 Two volumes, Paperbound $10.00

MONTGOMERY WARD CATALOGUE OF 1895. Tea gowns, yards of flannel and pillow-case lace, stereoscopes, books of gospel hymns, the New Improved Singer Sewing Machine, side saddles, milk skimmers, straight-edged razors, high-button shoes, spittoons, and on and on . . . listing some 25,000 items, practically all illustrated. Essential to the shoppers of the 1890's, it is our truest record of the spirit of the period. Unaltered reprint of Issue No. 57, Spring and Summer 1895. Introduction by Boris Emmet. Innumerable illustrations. xiii + 624pp. 8½ x 11⅝.
22377-9 Paperbound $6.95

THE CRYSTAL PALACE EXHIBITION ILLUSTRATED CATALOGUE (LONDON, 1851). One of the wonders of the modern world—the Crystal Palace Exhibition in which all the nations of the civilized world exhibited their achievements in the arts and sciences—presented in an equally important illustrated catalogue. More than 1700 items pictured with accompanying text—ceramics, textiles, cast-iron work, carpets, pianos, sleds, razors, wall-papers, billiard tables, beehives, silverware and hundreds of other artifacts—represent the focal point of Victorian culture in the Western World. Probably the largest collection of Victorian decorative art ever assembled— indispensable for antiquarians and designers. Unabridged republication of the Art-Journal Catalogue of the Great Exhibition of 1851, with all terminal essays. New introduction by John Gloag, F.S.A. xxxiv + 426pp. 9 x 12.
22503-8 Paperbound $4.50

A HISTORY OF COSTUME, Carl Köhler. Definitive history, based on surviving pieces of clothing primarily, and paintings, statues, etc. secondarily. Highly readable text, supplemented by 594 illustrations of costumes of the ancient Mediterranean peoples, Greece and Rome, the Teutonic prehistoric period; costumes of the Middle Ages, Renaissance, Baroque, 18th and 19th centuries. Clear, measured patterns are provided for many clothing articles. Approach is practical throughout. Enlarged by Emma von Sichart. 464pp.   21030-8 Paperbound $3.50

ORIENTAL RUGS, ANTIQUE AND MODERN, Walter A. Hawley. A complete and authoritative treatise on the Oriental rug—where they are made, by whom and how, designs and symbols, characteristics in detail of the six major groups, how to distinguish them and how to buy them. Detailed technical data is provided on periods, weaves, warps, wefts, textures, sides, ends and knots, although no technical background is required for an understanding. 11 color plates, 80 halftones, 4 maps. vi + 320pp. 6⅛ x 9⅛.   22366-3 Paperbound $5.00

TEN BOOKS ON ARCHITECTURE, Vitruvius. By any standards the most important book on architecture ever written. Early Roman discussion of aesthetics of building, construction methods, orders, sites, and every other aspect of architecture has inspired, instructed architecture for about 2,000 years. Stands behind Palladio, Michelangelo, Bramante, Wren, countless others. Definitive Morris H. Morgan translation. 68 illustrations. xii + 331pp.   20645-9 Paperbound $3.00

THE FOUR BOOKS OF ARCHITECTURE, Andrea Palladio. Translated into every major Western European language in the two centuries following its publication in 1570, this has been one of the most influential books in the history of architecture. Complete reprint of the 1738 Isaac Ware edition. New introduction by Adolf Placzek, Columbia Univ. 216 plates. xxii + 110pp. of text. 9½ x 12¾.
21308-0 Clothbound $10.00

STICKS AND STONES: A STUDY OF AMERICAN ARCHITECTURE AND CIVILIZATION, Lewis Mumford.One of the great classics of American cultural history. American architecture from the medieval-inspired earliest forms to the early 20th century; evolution of structure and style, and reciprocal influences on environment. 21 photographic illustrations. 238pp.   20202-X Paperbound $2.00

THE AMERICAN BUILDER'S COMPANION, Asher Benjamin. The most widely used early 19th century architectural style and source book, for colonial up into Greek Revival periods. Extensive development of geometry of carpentering, construction of sashes, frames, doors, stairs; plans and elevations of domestic and other buildings. Hundreds of thousands of houses were built according to this book, now invaluable to historians, architects, restorers, etc. 1827 edition. 59 plates. 114pp. 7⅞ x 10¾.
22236-5 Paperbound $3.50

DUTCH HOUSES IN THE HUDSON VALLEY BEFORE 1776, Helen Wilkinson Reynolds. The standard survey of the Dutch colonial house and outbuildings, with constructional features, decoration, and local history associated with individual homesteads. Introduction by Franklin D. Roosevelt. Map. 150 illustrations. 469pp. 6⅝ x 9¼.   21469-9 Paperbound $4.00

THE ARCHITECTURE OF COUNTRY HOUSES, Andrew J. Downing. Together with Vaux's *Villas and Cottages* this is the basic book for Hudson River Gothic architecture of the middle Victorian period. Full, sound discussions of general aspects of housing, architecture, style, decoration, furnishing, together with scores of detailed house plans, illustrations of specific buildings, accompanied by full text. Perhaps the most influential single American architectural book. 1850 edition. Introduction by J. Stewart Johnson. 321 figures, 34 architectural designs. xvi + 560pp.
22003-6 Paperbound $4.00

LOST EXAMPLES OF COLONIAL ARCHITECTURE, John Mead Howells. Full-page photographs of buildings that have disappeared or been so altered as to be denatured, including many designed by major early American architects. 245 plates. xvii + 248pp. 7⅞ x 10¾. 21143-6 Paperbound $3.50

DOMESTIC ARCHITECTURE OF THE AMERICAN COLONIES AND OF THE EARLY REPUBLIC, Fiske Kimball. Foremost architect and restorer of Williamsburg and Monticello covers nearly 200 homes between 1620-1825. Architectural details, construction, style features, special fixtures, floor plans, etc. Generally considered finest work in its area. 219 illustrations of houses, doorways, windows, capital mantels. xx + 314pp. 7⅞ x 10¾. 21743-4 Paperbound $4.00

EARLY AMERICAN ROOMS: 1650-1858, edited by Russell Hawes Kettell. Tour of 12 rooms, each representative of a different era in American history and each furnished, decorated, designed and occupied in the style of the era. 72 plans and elevations, 8-page color section, etc., show fabrics, wall papers, arrangements, etc. Full descriptive text. xvii + 200pp. of text. 8⅜ x 11¼.
21633-0 Paperbound $5.00

THE FITZWILLIAM VIRGINAL BOOK, edited by J. Fuller Maitland and W. B. Squire. Full modern printing of famous early 17th-century ms. volume of 300 works by Morley, Byrd, Bull, Gibbons, etc. For piano or other modern keyboard instrument; easy to read format. xxxvi + 938pp. 8⅜ x 11.
21068-5, 21069-3 Two volumes, Paperbound $10.00

KEYBOARD MUSIC, Johann Sebastian Bach. Bach Gesellschaft edition. A rich selection of Bach's masterpieces for the harpsichord: the six English Suites, six French Suites, the six Partitas (Clavierübung part I), the Goldberg Variations (Clavierübung part IV), the fifteen Two-Part Inventions and the fifteen Three-Part Sinfonias. Clearly reproduced on large sheets with ample margins; eminently playable. vi + 312pp. 8⅛ x 11. 22360-4 Paperbound $5.00

THE MUSIC OF BACH: AN INTRODUCTION, Charles Sanford Terry. A fine, nontechnical introduction to Bach's music, both instrumental and vocal. Covers organ music, chamber music, passion music, other types. Analyzes themes, developments, innovations. x + 114pp. 21075-8 Paperbound $1.25

BEETHOVEN AND HIS NINE SYMPHONIES, Sir George Grove. Noted British musicologist provides best history, analysis, commentary on symphonies. Very thorough, rigorously accurate; necessary to both advanced student and amateur music lover. 436 musical passages. vii + 407 pp. 20334-4 Paperbound $2.75

CATALOGUE OF DOVER BOOKS

JOHANN SEBASTIAN BACH, Philipp Spitta. One of the great classics of musicology, this definitive analysis of Bach's music (and life) has never been surpassed. Lucid, nontechnical analyses of hundreds of pieces (30 pages devoted to St. Matthew Passion, 26 to B Minor Mass). Also includes major analysis of 18th-century music. 450 musical examples. 40-page musical supplement. Total of xx + 1799pp.
(EUK) 22278-0, 22279-9 Two volumes, Clothbound $17.50

MOZART AND HIS PIANO CONCERTOS, Cuthbert Girdlestone. The only full-length study of an important area of Mozart's creativity. Provides detailed analyses of all 23 concertos, traces inspirational sources. 417 musical examples. Second edition. 509pp.　21271-8 Paperbound $3.50

THE PERFECT WAGNERITE: A COMMENTARY ON THE NIBLUNG'S RING, George Bernard Shaw. Brilliant and still relevant criticism in remarkable essays on Wagner's Ring cycle, Shaw's ideas on political and social ideology behind the plots, role of Leitmotifs, vocal requisites, etc. Prefaces. xxi + 136pp.
(USO) 21707-8 Paperbound $1.50

DON GIOVANNI, W. A. Mozart. Complete libretto, modern English translation; biographies of composer and librettist; accounts of early performances and critical reaction. Lavishly illustrated. All the material you need to understand and appreciate this great work. Dover Opera Guide and Libretto Series; translated and introduced by Ellen Bleiler. 92 illustrations. 209pp.
21134-7 Paperbound $2.00

HIGH FIDELITY SYSTEMS: A LAYMAN'S GUIDE, Roy F. Allison. All the basic information you need for setting up your own audio system: high fidelity and stereo record players, tape records, F.M. Connections, adjusting tone arm, cartridge, checking needle alignment, positioning speakers, phasing speakers, adjusting hums, trouble-shooting, maintenance, and similar topics. Enlarged 1965 edition. More than 50 charts, diagrams, photos. iv + 91pp.　21514-8 Paperbound $1.25

REPRODUCTION OF SOUND, Edgar Villchur. Thorough coverage for laymen of high fidelity systems, reproducing systems in general, needles, amplifiers, preamps, loudspeakers, feedback, explaining physical background. "A rare talent for making technicalities vividly comprehensible," R. Darrell, *High Fidelity*. 69 figures. iv + 92pp.　21515-6 Paperbound $1.25

HEAR ME TALKIN' TO YA: THE STORY OF JAZZ AS TOLD BY THE MEN WHO MADE IT, Nat Shapiro and Nat Hentoff. Louis Armstrong, Fats Waller, Jo Jones, Clarence Williams, Billy Holiday, Duke Ellington, Jelly Roll Morton and dozens of other jazz greats tell how it was in Chicago's South Side, New Orleans, depression Harlem and the modern West Coast as jazz was born and grew. xvi + 429pp.
21726-4 Paperbound $2.50

FABLES OF AESOP, translated by Sir Roger L'Estrange. A reproduction of the very rare 1931 Paris edition; a selection of the most interesting fables, together with 50 imaginative drawings by Alexander Calder. v + 128pp. 6½x9¼.
21780-9 Paperbound $1.50

AGAINST THE GRAIN (A REBOURS), Joris K. Huysmans. Filled with weird images, evidences of a bizarre imagination, exotic experiments with hallucinatory drugs, rich tastes and smells and the diversions of its sybarite hero Duc Jean des Esseintes, this classic novel pushed 19th-century literary decadence to its limits. Full unabridged edition. Do not confuse this with abridged editions generally sold. Introduction by Havelock Ellis. xlix + 206pp. 22190-3 Paperbound $2.00

VARIORUM SHAKESPEARE: HAMLET. Edited by Horace H. Furness; a landmark of American scholarship. Exhaustive footnotes and appendices treat all doubtful words and phrases, as well as suggested critical emendations throughout the play's history. First volume contains editor's own text, collated with all Quartos and Folios. Second volume contains full first Quarto, translations of Shakespeare's sources (Belleforest, and Saxo Grammaticus), Der Bestrafte Brudermord, and many essays on critical and historical points of interest by major authorities of past and present. Includes details of staging and costuming over the years. By far the best edition available for serious students of Shakespeare. Total of xx + 905pp. 21004-9, 21005-7, 2 volumes, Paperbound $7.00

A LIFE OF WILLIAM SHAKESPEARE, Sir Sidney Lee. This is the standard life of Shakespeare, summarizing everything known about Shakespeare and his plays. Incredibly rich in material, broad in coverage, clear and judicious, it has served thousands as the best introduction to Shakespeare. 1931 edition. 9 plates. xxix + 792pp. (USO) 21967-4 Paperbound $3.75

MASTERS OF THE DRAMA, John Gassner. Most comprehensive history of the drama in print, covering every tradition from Greeks to modern Europe and America, including India, Far East, etc. Covers more than 800 dramatists, 2000 plays, with biographical material, plot summaries, theatre history, criticism, etc. "Best of its kind in English," *New Republic*. 77 illustrations. xxii + 890pp. 20100-7 Clothbound $8.50

THE EVOLUTION OF THE ENGLISH LANGUAGE, George McKnight. The growth of English, from the 14th century to the present. Unusual, non-technical account presents basic information in very interesting form: sound shifts, change in grammar and syntax, vocabulary growth, similar topics. Abundantly illustrated with quotations. Formerly *Modern English in the Making*. xii + 590pp. 21932-1 Paperbound $3.50

AN ETYMOLOGICAL DICTIONARY OF MODERN ENGLISH, Ernest Weekley. Fullest, richest work of its sort, by foremost British lexicographer. Detailed word histories, including many colloquial and archaic words; extensive quotations. Do not confuse this with the Concise Etymological Dictionary, which is much abridged. Total of xxvii + 830pp. 6½ x 9¼. 21873-2, 21874-0 Two volumes, Paperbound $6.00

FLATLAND: A ROMANCE OF MANY DIMENSIONS, E. A. Abbott. Classic of science-fiction explores ramifications of life in a two-dimensional world, and what happens when a three-dimensional being intrudes. Amusing reading, but also useful as introduction to thought about hyperspace. Introduction by Banesh Hoffmann. 16 illustrations. xx + 103pp. 20001-9 Paperbound $1.00

POEMS OF ANNE BRADSTREET, edited with an introduction by Robert Hutchinson. A new selection of poems by America's first poet and perhaps the first significant woman poet in the English language. 48 poems display her development in works of considerable variety—love poems, domestic poems, religious meditations, formal elegies, "quaternions," etc. Notes, bibliography. viii + 222pp.
22160-1 Paperbound $2.50

THREE GOTHIC NOVELS: THE CASTLE OF OTRANTO BY HORACE WALPOLE; VATHEK BY WILLIAM BECKFORD; THE VAMPYRE BY JOHN POLIDORI, WITH FRAGMENT OF A NOVEL BY LORD BYRON, edited by E. F. Bleiler. The first Gothic novel, by Walpole; the finest Oriental tale in English, by Beckford; powerful Romantic supernatural story in versions by Polidori and Byron. All extremely important in history of literature; all still exciting, packed with supernatural thrills, ghosts, haunted castles, magic, etc. xl + 291pp.
21232-7 Paperbound $2.50

THE BEST TALES OF HOFFMANN, E. T. A. Hoffmann. 10 of Hoffmann's most important stories, in modern re-editings of standard translations: Nutcracker and the King of Mice, Signor Formica, Automata, The Sandman, Rath Krespel, The Golden Flowerpot, Master Martin the Cooper, The Mines of Falun, The King's Betrothed, A New Year's Eve Adventure. 7 illustrations by Hoffmann. Edited by E. F. Bleiler. xxxix + 419pp.   21793-0 Paperbound $3.00

GHOST AND HORROR STORIES OF AMBROSE BIERCE, Ambrose Bierce. 23 strikingly modern stories of the horrors latent in the human mind: The Eyes of the Panther, The Damned Thing, An Occurrence at Owl Creek Bridge, An Inhabitant of Carcosa, etc., plus the dream-essay, Visions of the Night. Edited by E. F. Bleiler. xxii + 199pp.   20767-6 Paperbound $1.50

BEST GHOST STORIES OF J. S. LeFANU, J. Sheridan LeFanu. Finest stories by Victorian master often considered greatest supernatural writer of all. Carmilla, Green Tea, The Haunted Baronet, The Familiar, and 12 others. Most never before available in the U. S. A. Edited by E. F. Bleiler. 8 illustrations from Victorian publications. xvii + 467pp.   20415-4 Paperbound $3.00

MATHEMATICAL FOUNDATIONS OF INFORMATION THEORY, A. I. Khinchin. Comprehensive introduction to work of Shannon, McMillan, Feinstein and Khinchin, placing these investigations on a rigorous mathematical basis. Covers entropy concept in probability theory, uniqueness theorem, Shannon's inequality, ergodic sources, the E property, martingale concept, noise, Feinstein's fundamental lemma, Shanon's first and second theorems. Translated by R. A. Silverman and M. D. Friedman. iii + 120pp.   60434-9 Paperbound $1.75

SEVEN SCIENCE FICTION NOVELS, H. G. Wells. The standard collection of the great novels. Complete, unabridged. *First Men in the Moon, Island of Dr. Moreau, War of the Worlds, Food of the Gods, Invisible Man, Time Machine, In the Days of the Comet.* Not only science fiction fans, but every educated person owes it to himself to read these novels. 1015pp.   (USO) 20264-X Clothbound $5.00

LAST AND FIRST MEN AND STAR MAKER, TWO SCIENCE FICTION NOVELS, Olaf Stapledon. Greatest future histories in science fiction. In the first, human intelligence is the "hero," through strange paths of evolution, interplanetary invasions, incredible technologies, near extinctions and reemergences. Star Maker describes the quest of a band of star rovers for intelligence itself, through time and space: weird inhuman civilizations, crustacean minds, symbiotic worlds, etc. Complete, unabridged. v + 438pp. (USO) 21962-3 Paperbound $2.50

THREE PROPHETIC NOVELS, H. G. WELLS. Stages of a consistently planned future for mankind. *When the Sleeper Wakes,* and *A Story of the Days to Come,* anticipate *Brave New World* and *1984,* in the 21st Century; *The Time Machine,* only complete version in print, shows farther future and the end of mankind. All show Wells's greatest gifts as storyteller and novelist. Edited by E. F. Bleiler. x + 335pp. (USO) 20605-X Paperbound $2.50

THE DEVIL'S DICTIONARY, Ambrose Bierce. America's own Oscar Wilde— Ambrose Bierce—offers his barbed iconoclastic wisdom in over 1,000 definitions hailed by H. L. Mencken as "some of the most gorgeous witticisms in the English language." 145pp. 20487-1 Paperbound $1.25

MAX AND MORITZ, Wilhelm Busch. Great children's classic, father of comic strip, of two bad boys, Max and Moritz. Also Ker and Plunk (Plisch und Plumm), Cat and Mouse, Deceitful Henry, Ice-Peter, The Boy and the Pipe, and five other pieces. Original German, with English translation. Edited by H. Arthur Klein; translations by various hands and H. Arthur Klein. vi + 216pp. 20181-3 Paperbound $2.00

PIGS IS PIGS AND OTHER FAVORITES, Ellis Parker Butler. The title story is one of the best humor short stories, as Mike Flannery obfuscates biology and English. Also included, That Pup of Murchison's, The Great American Pie Company, and Perkins of Portland. 14 illustrations. v + 109pp. 21532-6 Paperbound $1.25

THE PETERKIN PAPERS, Lucretia P. Hale. It takes genius to be as stupidly mad as the Peterkins, as they decide to become wise, celebrate the "Fourth," keep a cow, and otherwise strain the resources of the Lady from Philadelphia. Basic book of American humor. 153 illustrations. 219pp. 20794-3 Paperbound $1.50

PERRAULT'S FAIRY TALES, translated by A. E. Johnson and S. R. Littlewood, with 34 full-page illustrations by Gustave Doré. All the original Perrault stories— Cinderella, Sleeping Beauty, Bluebeard, Little Red Riding Hood, Puss in Boots, Tom Thumb, etc.—with their witty verse morals and the magnificent illustrations of Doré. One of the five or six great books of European fairy tales. viii + 117pp. 8⅛ x 11. 22311-6 Paperbound $2.00

OLD HUNGARIAN FAIRY TALES, Baroness Orczy. Favorites translated and adapted by author of the *Scarlet Pimpernel.* Eight fairy tales include "The Suitors of Princess Fire-Fly," "The Twin Hunchbacks," "Mr. Cuttlefish's Love Story," and "The Enchanted Cat." This little volume of magic and adventure will captivate children as it has for generations. 90 drawings by Montagu Barstow. 96pp. 22293-4 Paperbound $1.95

THE RED FAIRY BOOK, Andrew Lang. Lang's color fairy books have long been children's favorites. This volume includes Rapunzel, Jack and the Bean-stalk and 35 other stories, familiar and unfamiliar. 4 plates, 93 illustrations x + 367pp.
21673-X Paperbound $2.50

THE BLUE FAIRY BOOK, Andrew Lang. Lang's tales come from all countries and all times. Here are 37 tales from Grimm, the Arabian Nights, Greek Mythology, and other fascinating sources. 8 plates, 130 illustrations. xi + 390pp.
21437-0 Paperbound $2.50

HOUSEHOLD STORIES BY THE BROTHERS GRIMM. Classic English-language edition of the well-known tales — Rumpelstiltskin, Snow White, Hansel and Gretel, The Twelve Brothers, Faithful John, Rapunzel, Tom Thumb (52 stories in all). Translated into simple, straightforward English by Lucy Crane. Ornamented with headpieces, vignettes, elaborate decorative initials and a dozen full-page illustrations by Walter Crane. x + 269pp.
21080-4 Paperbound $2.00

THE MERRY ADVENTURES OF ROBIN HOOD, Howard Pyle. The finest modern versions of the traditional ballads and tales about the great English outlaw. Howard Pyle's complete prose version, with every word, every illustration of the first edition. Do not confuse this facsimile of the original (1883) with modern editions that change text or illustrations. 23 plates plus many page decorations. xxii + 296pp.
22043-5 Paperbound $2.50

THE STORY OF KING ARTHUR AND HIS KNIGHTS, Howard Pyle. The finest children's version of the life of King Arthur; brilliantly retold by Pyle, with 48 of his most imaginative illustrations. xviii + 313pp. 6⅛ x 9¼.
21445-1 Paperbound $2.50

THE WONDERFUL WIZARD OF OZ, L. Frank Baum. America's finest children's book in facsimile of first edition with all Denslow illustrations in full color. The edition a child should have. Introduction by Martin Gardner. 23 color plates, scores of drawings. iv + 267pp.
20691-2 Paperbound $2.50

THE MARVELOUS LAND OF OZ, L. Frank Baum. The second Oz book, every bit as imaginative as the Wizard. The hero is a boy named Tip, but the Scarecrow and the Tin Woodman are back, as is the Oz magic. 16 color plates, 120 drawings by John R. Neill. 287pp.
20692-0 Paperbound $2.50

THE MAGICAL MONARCH OF MO, L. Frank Baum. Remarkable adventures in a land even stranger than Oz. The best of Baum's books not in the Oz series. 15 color plates and dozens of drawings by Frank Verbeck. xviii + 237pp.
21892-9 Paperbound $2.25

THE BAD CHILD'S BOOK OF BEASTS, MORE BEASTS FOR WORSE CHILDREN, A MORAL ALPHABET, Hilaire Belloc. Three complete humor classics in one volume. Be kind to the frog, and do not call him names . . . and 28 other whimsical animals. Familiar favorites and some not so well known. Illustrated by Basil Blackwell. 156pp.
(USO) 20749-8 Paperbound $1.50

EAST O' THE SUN AND WEST O' THE MOON, George W. Dasent. Considered the best of all translations of these Norwegian folk tales, this collection has been enjoyed by generations of children (and folklorists too). Includes True and Untrue, Why the Sea is Salt, East O' the Sun and West O' the Moon, Why the Bear is Stumpy-Tailed, Boots and the Troll, The Cock and the Hen, Rich Peter the Pedlar, and 52 more. The only edition with all 59 tales. 77 illustrations by Erik Werenskiold and Theodor Kittelsen. xv + 418pp. 22521-6 Paperbound $3.50

GOOPS AND HOW TO BE THEM, Gelett Burgess. Classic of tongue-in-cheek humor, masquerading as etiquette book. 87 verses, twice as many cartoons, show mischievous Goops as they demonstrate to children virtues of table manners, neatness, courtesy, etc. Favorite for generations. viii + 88pp. $6\frac{1}{2}$ x $9\frac{1}{4}$. 22233-0 Paperbound $1.25

ALICE'S ADVENTURES UNDER GROUND, Lewis Carroll. The first version, quite different from the final *Alice in Wonderland*, printed out by Carroll himself with his own illustrations. Complete facsimile of the "million dollar" manuscript Carroll gave to Alice Liddell in 1864. Introduction by Martin Gardner. viii + 96pp. Title and dedication pages in color. 21482-6 Paperbound $1.25

THE BROWNIES, THEIR BOOK, Palmer Cox. Small as mice, cunning as foxes, exuberant and full of mischief, the Brownies go to the zoo, toy shop, seashore, circus, etc., in 24 verse adventures and 266 illustrations. Long a favorite, since their first appearance in St. Nicholas Magazine. xi + 144pp. $6\frac{5}{8}$ x $9\frac{1}{4}$. 21265-3 Paperbound $1.75

SONGS OF CHILDHOOD, Walter De La Mare. Published (under the pseudonym Walter Ramal) when De La Mare was only 29, this charming collection has long been a favorite children's book. A facsimile of the first edition in paper, the 47 poems capture the simplicity of the nursery rhyme and the ballad, including such lyrics as I Met Eve, Tartary, The Silver Penny. vii + 106pp. (USO) 21972-0 Paperbound $1.25

THE COMPLETE NONSENSE OF EDWARD LEAR, Edward Lear. The finest 19th-century humorist-cartoonist in full: all nonsense limericks, zany alphabets, Owl and Pussycat, songs, nonsense botany, and more than 500 illustrations by Lear himself. Edited by Holbrook Jackson. xxix + 287pp. (USO) 20167-8 Paperbound $2.00

BILLY WHISKERS: THE AUTOBIOGRAPHY OF A GOAT, Frances Trego Montgomery. A favorite of children since the early 20th century, here are the escapades of that rambunctious, irresistible and mischievous goat—Billy Whiskers. Much in the spirit of *Peck's Bad Boy*, this is a book that children never tire of reading or hearing. All the original familiar illustrations by W H. Fry are included: 6 color plates, 18 black and white drawings. 159pp. 22345-0 Paperbound $2.00

MOTHER GOOSE MELODIES. Faithful republication of the fabulously rare Munroe and Francis "copyright 1833" Boston edition—the most important Mother Goose collection, usually referred to as the "original." Familiar rhymes plus many rare ones, with wonderful old woodcut illustrations. Edited by E. F. Bleiler. 128pp. $4\frac{1}{2}$ x $6\frac{3}{8}$. 22577-1 Paperbound $1.00

TWO LITTLE SAVAGES; BEING THE ADVENTURES OF TWO BOYS WHO LIVED AS INDIANS AND WHAT THEY LEARNED, Ernest Thompson Seton. Great classic of nature and boyhood provides a vast range of woodlore in most palatable form, a genuinely entertaining story. Two farm boys build a teepee in woods and live in it for a month, working out Indian solutions to living problems, star lore, birds and animals, plants, etc. 293 illustrations. vii + 286pp.
20985-7 Paperbound $2.50

PETER PIPER'S PRACTICAL PRINCIPLES OF PLAIN & PERFECT PRONUNCIATION. Alliterative jingles and tongue-twisters of surprising charm, that made their first appearance in America about 1830. Republished in full with the spirited woodcut illustrations from this earliest American edition. 32pp. $4\frac{1}{2}$ x $6\frac{3}{8}$.
22560-7 Paperbound $1.00

SCIENCE EXPERIMENTS AND AMUSEMENTS FOR CHILDREN, Charles Vivian. 73 easy experiments, requiring only materials found at home or easily available, such as candles, coins, steel wool, etc.; illustrate basic phenomena like vacuum, simple chemical reaction, etc. All safe. Modern, well-planned. Formerly *Science Games for Children*. 102 photos, numerous drawings. 96pp. $6\frac{1}{8}$ x $9\frac{1}{4}$.
21856-2 Paperbound $1.25

AN INTRODUCTION TO CHESS MOVES AND TACTICS SIMPLY EXPLAINED, Leonard Barden. Informal intermediate introduction, quite strong in explaining reasons for moves. Covers basic material, tactics, important openings, traps, positional play in middle game, end game. Attempts to isolate patterns and recurrent configurations. Formerly *Chess*. 58 figures. 102pp. (USO) 21210-6 Paperbound $1.25

LASKER'S MANUAL OF CHESS, Dr. Emanuel Lasker. Lasker was not only one of the five great World Champions, he was also one of the ablest expositors, theorists, and analysts. In many ways, his Manual, permeated with his philosophy of battle, filled with keen insights, is one of the greatest works ever written on chess. Filled with analyzed games by the great players. A single-volume library that will profit almost any chess player, beginner or master. 308 diagrams. xli x 349pp.
20640-8 Paperbound $2.75

THE MASTER BOOK OF MATHEMATICAL RECREATIONS, Fred Schuh. In opinion of many the finest work ever prepared on mathematical puzzles, stunts, recreations; exhaustively thorough explanations of mathematics involved, analysis of effects, citation of puzzles and games. Mathematics involved is elementary. Translated by F. Göbel. 194 figures. xxiv + 430pp.
22134-2 Paperbound $3.00

MATHEMATICS, MAGIC AND MYSTERY, Martin Gardner. Puzzle editor for Scientific American explains mathematics behind various mystifying tricks: card tricks, stage "mind reading," coin and match tricks, counting out games, geometric dissections, etc. Probability sets, theory of numbers clearly explained. Also provides more than 400 tricks, guaranteed to work, that you can do. 135 illustrations. xii + 176pp.
20335-2 Paperbound $1.50

MATHEMATICAL PUZZLES FOR BEGINNERS AND ENTHUSIASTS, Geoffrey Mott-Smith. 189 puzzles from easy to difficult—involving arithmetic, logic, algebra, properties of digits, probability, etc.—for enjoyment and mental stimulus. Explanation of mathematical principles behind the puzzles. 135 illustrations. viii + 248pp.
20198-8 Paperbound $1.75

PAPER FOLDING FOR BEGINNERS, William D. Murray and Francis J. Rigney. Easiest book on the market, clearest instructions on making interesting, beautiful origami. Sail boats, cups, roosters, frogs that move legs, bonbon boxes, standing birds, etc. 40 projects; more than 275 diagrams and photographs. 94pp.
20713-7 Paperbound $1.00

TRICKS AND GAMES ON THE POOL TABLE, Fred Herrmann. 79 tricks and games— some solitaires, some for two or more players, some competitive games—to entertain you between formal games. Mystifying shots and throws, unusual caroms, tricks involving such props as cork, coins, a hat, etc. Formerly *Fun on the Pool Table*. 77 figures. 95pp.
21814-7 Paperbound $1.00

HAND SHADOWS TO BE THROWN UPON THE WALL: A SERIES OF NOVEL AND AMUSING FIGURES FORMED BY THE HAND, Henry Bursill. Delightful picturebook from great-grandfather's day shows how to make 18 different hand shadows: a bird that flies, duck that quacks, dog that wags his tail, camel, goose, deer, boy, turtle, etc. Only book of its sort. vi + 33pp. 6½ x 9¼. 21779-5 Paperbound $1.00

WHITTLING AND WOODCARVING, E. J. Tangerman. 18th printing of best book on market. "If you can cut a potato you can carve" toys and puzzles, chains, chessmen, caricatures, masks, frames, woodcut blocks, surface patterns, much more. Information on tools, woods, techniques. Also goes into serious wood sculpture from Middle Ages to present, East and West. 464 photos, figures. x + 293pp.
20965-2 Paperbound $2.00

HISTORY OF PHILOSOPHY, Julián Marias. Possibly the clearest, most easily followed, best planned, most useful one-volume history of philosophy on the market; neither skimpy nor overfull. Full details on system of every major philosopher and dozens of less important thinkers from pre-Socratics up to Existentialism and later. Strong on many European figures usually omitted. Has gone through dozens of editions in Europe. 1966 edition, translated by Stanley Appelbaum and Clarence Strowbridge. xviii + 505pp.
21739-6 Paperbound $3.50

YOGA: A SCIENTIFIC EVALUATION, Kovoor T. Behanan. Scientific but non-technical study of physiological results of yoga exercises; done under auspices of Yale U. Relations to Indian thought, to psychoanalysis, etc. 16 photos. xxiii + 270pp.
20505-3 Paperbound $2.50

Prices subject to change without notice.
Available at your book dealer or write for free catalogue to Dept. GI, Dover Publications, Inc., 180 Varick St., N. Y., N. Y. 10014. Dover publishes more than 150 books each year on science, elementary and advanced mathematics, biology, music, art, literary history, social sciences and other areas.